SUCCESS
NEVER SMELL
SO SWEET

SUCCESS
NEVER SMELLED
SO SWEET

*How I Followed My Nose
and Found My Passion*

LISA PRICE
PRESIDENT OF CAROL'S DAUGHTER, INC.

and

HILARY BEARD

ONE WORLD

BALLANTINE BOOKS • NEW YORK

4

A One World Book
Published by The Random House Publishing Group

www.ballantinebooks.com/one

LIBRARY OF CONGRESS CATALOGING-IN-PUBLICATION DATA
Price, Lisa, 1962–
Success never smelled so sweet : how I followed my nose and found my passion /
by Lisa Price and Hilary Beard.
p. cm.
ISBN 1-4000-6109-1
1. Price, Lisa, 1962– 2. African American businesspeople—New York (State)—
New York—Biography. 3. Businesswomen—New York (State)—New York—
Biography. 4. Toilet preparations industry—United States.
5. Carol's Daughter, Inc. I. Beard, Hilary. II. Title.

HD9970.5.T654C337 2004
338.7'6467—dc22
[B]   2003069096

Text design by Mary A. Wirth

Manufactured in the United States of America
First Edition: April 2004

1   3   5   7   9   10   8   6   4   2

This book is dedicated to my mother,
Carol, and my father, Robert,
for giving me my foundation.

To my husband, Gordon,
for being with me in the present
as we make our past and future together.

To my children, Forrest and Ennis,
for showing me the importance of being in the moment.

And to Peggy and Charles Beard
for bringing Hilary to me
and to the world.

Prologue

Today I am a successful businesswoman. But when I was twenty-eight years old, I filed for personal bankruptcy. I had spent a number of years chasing dreams, living over my head and hoping that I would be able to pay for it later. Well . . . I did pay—just not in the way I had hoped. I reached a point where my credit-card balances were sky high. And I would later learn that with penalties and interest, I was also about $33,000 in debt to the Internal Revenue Service. I wasn't even thirty and I had already screwed up my life. I was certain that I had ruined it forever. How would I ever restore my credit? Who would marry me when I was in such a financial mess? Could I ever afford to have children? And how in the world would I ever pay back the IRS? I was working as a secretary, earning about $25,000 a year, and I only had a high school diploma. To say that I was between a rock and a hard place is an understatement. It's not as if I came from a rich family that could bail me out.

Over the next ten years, I focused on turning my life around—and did. Then, in June of 2002, I had the experience of a lifetime: I appeared on *The Oprah Winfrey Show.* By then, according to Oprah, I had become a work-at-home mom, entrepreneurial success story. I was the happily married mother of two young boys. In my early thirties, I had taken one hundred dollars and created a business out of my love of good scents and lifelong hobby of creating fragrances. I started selling "perfumes" at flea markets as a way of supplementing my income, always reinvesting the profit back into my business. As it turns out, people liked my products and my venture began to blossom. My hobby-turned-business grew slowly, without bank loans or credit cards—my finances were too bad to qualify for either. Yet before long I was able to quit my job and work for myself full time. That gave me the opportunity to craft more of my specialties, which by then had expanded to include natural hair, bath and body-care products with amazing aromas, and sell them out of my home. In time, my company, Carol's Daughter: Beauty by Nature, transformed itself into a successful boutique in the Fort Greene neighborhood of Brooklyn and on-line business (www.carolsdaughter.com). It attracted a large and devoted clientele that includes a number of celebrities, including Oprah herself, Halle Berry, Will and Jada Smith, Edie Falco of *The Sopranos,* and Chaka Khan. The company employs several members of my family and I make a decent and honest living. Plus I paid back every penny I owed to the IRS! In a short ten-year period, my life and spirit were transformed. God had made a way out of no way. I will eternally be grateful.

How did I get myself into such a tough situation—and, more important, how did I dig myself out? Like many people I overextended myself by trying to keep up with others. Back then, I suffered from "the disease to please." I was always looking outside myself for satisfaction, keeping other people happy and doing things to make them like me. In the process, I didn't honor myself. I made a hard bed and had to lie in it for a while.

But when we're open to it, life's difficulties can teach us lessons. In my case I learned to let go of my ego, strong will, and way of doing things and surrender to the desires of a Higher Power. I stopped trying to keep up with the Joneses and began to pay attention to myself—my inner Self. I learned to listen to the internal voice that spoke to me without fail, each and every day, whether or not I paid attention. You can say I learned to hear my God voice, the indwelling Holy Spirit, my first mind, intuition, gut instinct or whatever you want to call it. People use different language, but to me it's all the same thing: the power of our Creator speaking directly to us—I believe God speaks to everyone. And by learning to seek out and act on that Higher Wisdom instead of others' advice or societal norms, a whole new world of opportunities and possibilities opened up that I had never dreamed existed. As I lived my life, I started to notice magic taking place. Synchronous and serendipitous occurrences became normal. Time and time again I watched the laws of God trump those of man. All sorts of things people believe you can't do happened for me. Miracles took place all the time. Think about it: On paper I was bankrupt and I didn't qualify for credit. Theoretically, I shouldn't have been able to create a successful business. Nevertheless, I woke up every morning, walked into my kitchen, and created my products. I worked with my employees, sold my creations to customers, and paid Carol's Daughter's bills. In the meantime, my bank account recovered and I got back on my feet.

As this was happening I learned to trust my gifts and talents. In my case I literally followed my nose out of my difficulties and into a life I could never have imagined. It has been quite an experience. Although I've always loved good scents, who knew it could turn into a lifestyle, much less a way to support myself while bringing other people joy? Too often, we take our talents for granted. Or people—our parents, teachers, spouses, children, and employers—steer us away from the things we naturally love to do and into jobs and roles that are more "socially acceptable" or "financially secure." Some of us are able to pursue our real interests as hobbies; only a lucky few pursue them as full-time careers. As I run my company, teach classes, and speak to people, many tell me they long to do work that they love. Most tell me that financial fear keeps them stuck where they are. Not too long ago I felt trapped in a dead-end job like the seekers I describe. I want more women and men to experience the feeling of exhilaration and sense of satisfaction that living your passion brings.

Writing this book is my way of encouraging you to pursue the enriching life you dream of. So often, we see people presented as "success stories," as I was on *Oprah,* and assume that they are different—somehow better—than we are and have advantages we don't. But I want you to know that an ordinary person with no money and a lot of baggage can dramatically change her life in a reasonable amount of time. I pray that my story helps you understand what life may look like between wherever you are today and your vision for your tomorrow.

Throughout, I have interspersed photographs that I hope will help bring my family to life. I've also included healing rituals, recipes, exercises, and advice that correspond to my tale. The recipes are real. I kept them simple so you can make them at home. But before you do, please read the appendix in the back of the book. Many of the ingredients have aromatherapeutic properties—mood-altering abilities that correspond with their fragrances—and some have contraindications. For example, there are certain essential oils you shouldn't use if you're pregnant. You'll also find information about the natural oils and butters found in the recipes—the same ingredients that I use in the products Carol's Daughter makes. In addition, I've included some healing activities to help you restore and renew your spirit. They come from my knowledge of the rejuvenating powers of the ingredients, as well as many ancient healing practices to which I've been exposed.

I hope that my story helps you grow and brings you peace and joy.

Contents

SUCCESS
NEVER SMELLED
SO SWEET

CHAPTER 1

It Takes a Village

Here I am at eight months old, without a care in the world.

I am not sure of the exact beginnings—when and where I became enthralled with fragrance and flowers. Maybe I smelled the bouquets my
mother received when I was born. Perhaps it was her lotion or the shampoo she used in her hair. But the earliest memory I have of flowers making
a dramatic impression on my spirit is when I was five years old and participating in my aunt Judith's wedding. That's when I fell in love with the
rose—one of the most beautiful flowers God ever created. My memories of
that day are a little sketchy; however, my father claims to remember everything. To hear him tell the story, my love of that wonderful flower nearly
caused me to upstage Aunt Judith at her own wedding.

As Judith's favorite—and only—niece, I was chosen to be her flower girl. I didn't understand what that entailed; I had never been in a wedding before. But anything that involved flowers sounded like fun to me. On the morning of the ceremony, Grandma's house was the busiest I had ever seen it. There were people everywhere. I can't tell you how excited I was to see everybody dressed up in their finest clothing. I walked around the house wide-eyed, trying to take everything in, wearing a special dress my great-aunt Ismay had sewn for me. It was yellow and white and made of a fluffy fabric called chiffon. Every time I tried to look down at my white shoes, the dress seemed to float over and hide them. I loved my new dress but also felt awkward, because of its length—my other dresses hit me at my knees—and also because I could hear my grandmother's words: "Be careful not to get anything on your dress!"

Aunt Judith was my father's younger sister. Even on a normal day she was one of the most beautiful women I had ever seen, but on this day she had been transformed. Wearing the wedding dress Aunt Ismay had made her, I thought she looked like a princess. Aunt Ismay pulled at and patted her, trying to get every last detail in place. I couldn't imagine what else needed to be done. Aunt Judith looked perfect. Nothing could be more beautiful, I thought—that is, until I was handed a white wicker basket full of flowers that made time stop and my heart stand still.

After the basket was placed in my hands, I could barely hear the florist's instructions: "As you walk down the aisle, toss the petals onto the floor." All I could do was admire the brilliant shades of red and hot pink. They didn't come from carnations and mums, which Daddy often bought me. These petals belonged to *roses*! I was already very familiar with roses. Even at that age I was attracted to their incredibly sweet scent. Nana, my maternal grandmother, grew them in her yard. I was always sticking my nose into their bright peach blooms. Adults were constantly warning me to watch out for bumblebees—although for some reason they seemed not to get uptight when I smelled the blossoms Nana set in a vase on the kitchen table. But even though I loved the roses at Nana's house, I had never envisioned them as individual petals before. They were so delicate and divine. I cradled them like a secret treasure. I wanted to do a good job and make Judith proud. But I started to feel a conflict. *I can't throw all of these on the floor,* I thought. *Something this precious shouldn't be wasted. I have to do something to save them.*

As the music started playing and people motioned me to begin walking, I fashioned my own solution to the confusion I was feeling. I walked down the aisle taking slow and deliberate steps, just as I had been instructed to do. But rather than sprinkling handfuls of blooms across the white runner, I dropped a single petal with every step I took. When I arrived at the altar, there was a narrow line of brilliant color extending the length of the center aisle. It looked like Hansel and Gretel had deposited a trail of bright red bread crumbs. The entire church was in stitches. After my performance, says Daddy, Aunt Judith had a hard act to follow—even with the benefit of a wedding gown.

I recall feeling proud of myself. I had dropped the flowers just like they told me to, yet there were enough petals left over for me to keep. I sniffed them all day, and later had the good fortune to have one used as a tissue against my face. It was softer than I could ever have imagined. After the wedding I brought the blooms back home and saved them in a special place until Mommy made me throw them away. By then they were brown and moldy.

Aunt Judith was the sole daughter of my paternal grandparents, Hilda Ursula Hairston and Robert Powell Hairston, Sr., whom I called Grandma Hilda and Grandpa. Grandpa was the only one of my grandparents who was born in the United States. Grandma Hilda was born in Trinidad. Together, they had two children, both born in America. My daddy was the oldest.

My mother's parents, Marguerite Georgina King and Francis Michael Warwell, whom I knew as Nana and Gramps, were also native Trinidadians. They grew up and were married there. After they moved to the United States, Nana gave birth to seven children; my mother, Carol, was the youngest.

Both sets of grandparents and most of my aunts, uncles and cousins were scattered about New York—Daddy's people in Queens and Manhattan, and most of Mommy's in Brooklyn. All told, I had over twenty cousins, most of them about my age and almost all on Mommy's side of the family. The majority of us lived in the Bedford-Stuyvesant neighborhood for at least part of our lives, a part of town where the streets are lined with three- and four-story brownstones. Back then, Bed-Stuy, as it is now commonly called, had turned predominately black but was still sprinkled with older Italians, Jews and Irish, like Mrs. Tierney, who lived next door to Nana and Gramps on Van Buren Street. She would invite me to sit on her stoop with her and eat peach ice cream from a porcelain teacup.

Rose Potpourri from Fresh Roses or Rose Petals

Petals from a dozen roses, obtained from a reputable florist
Rose fragrance oil or rose absolute

1. Start with fresh roses or rose petals. This will help insure the heads of your roses will look full and robust once dried. Avoid the colors red, white, pale pink, and pale yellow, as they will turn brown or black as they dehydrate. For best results and bright colors when dry, stick with peach, orange, fuchsia, and bright yellow blooms.
2. You may enjoy your roses in a vase for a few days, but begin to dry them before the heads open fully or begin to droop.
3. Tie stems together with twine or a rubber band and hang upside down in a dry place away from direct sunlight. Leave for at least 2 weeks.
4. If you wish to preserve petals and not rose heads, simply scatter the petals onto a tray or cooking sheet and place in a dry area away from direct sunlight for at least two weeks. Then follow the steps below for both petals and rose heads.
5. Clip your rose heads from their stems and place in a jar.
6. Drizzle rose fragrance oil over the flowers—about 10–15 drops for each dozen heads. You may also use rose absolute, which is a pure rose oil and not a synthetic, but it is very costly (an ounce costs about ninety dollars). If you opt for rose absolute, you will only need 5–7 drops for each dozen heads. Seal your jar and place it in a cool, dark place for one week.
7. After one week open the container and drizzle rose fragrance again. Close jar and let it sit in the cool, dark place for two more weeks. This "curing" process results in a much longer lasting and more fragrant potpourri.
8. At this point, your potpourri is fully cured. You may place your roses in the container of your choice.
9. Freshen with fragrance oil when needed.

Nana and Gramps lived with Mommy's older sister, Ruby, and her husband, Stan. Aunt Ruby is also my godmother. Their home was the hub of activity for our entire extended family. That included my aunts, Sylvia and Joan, and uncles, Ronnie, Sonny and Hugh, and all their children and their children's children. We all moved in and out of that house. It was our daycare center, our playground, the place we ate many meals, but this wasn't considered an imposition. In an effort to protect their children from the hostility immigrants sometimes encountered, Nana and Gramps raised their children to count on each other. As a result, my aunts and uncles didn't socialize outside family and church circles. They repeated the pattern in my generation. My cousins and I played with and looked after each other. We felt like brothers and sisters. We just didn't live in the same house. It wasn't until I was an adult that it occurred to me that things could be another way.

In addition to believing in the importance of family, the adults in my world had a strong work ethic. Daddy was employed by an organization that found jobs for youths. Sometimes he would pick up an additional gig at night. Mommy and her sisters all worked for the phone company. They toiled away, saved their money and set about raising their families. But no matter what long hours or odd shifts my parents worked, my brother Philip and I were always cared for. Mommy kept our home neat, our clothes clean and a hot meal on the table. She coordinated childcare with her mother and sisters so well that to this day I can't tell you what shift my mother worked. The handoffs between my relatives were seamless.

Now that I am a mother myself, what's even more amazing to me is the way that my elders cared for me after Mommy gave birth to Philip. I was three at the time. Family lore has it that, shortly after giving birth, Mommy fell while stepping onto a bus. She was holding baby Phillip when it happened. This was the first of many times during my lifetime that Mommy's legs would fail her. What followed were innumerable doctor visits, hospital stays, and mysterious stumbles, until she was diagnosed with an illness called polymyositis. Polymyositis is a collagen vascular disease that, in my mother's case, affected her muscles. They became inflamed and, over time, very weak. There is no cure and the only known treatment were immunosuppressive medications, which came with their own "wonderful" side effects. Despite her illness and hospital stays, I have no real recollection of her absence. My memories of childhood with Mommy are only positive ones.

However, I do remember that I lived with my Aunt Sylvia and Uncle Robbie on and off between the ages of three and five. They loved me as though I were their own child. Through my eyes, my visits were special occasions. At that particular age I was stuck on birthday parties and wanted to have one every single night. Like an angel, Aunt Syl indulged me. Every dinnertime, she would put candles in Jell-O, or some other food that wasn't cake. Then she would dim the lights and we'd sing "Happy Birthday" to me. I felt so loved by everyone that I don't remember missing Mommy, or even wondering where she was. This kind of cooperation was typical of my mother's people. If somebody got sick or had to work late, there was this incredible communication about and coordination of whatever needed to happen. They cared for each other's children. They made and shared food. We stayed over at each other's homes. The care we received in my extended family amazes me to this day.

In addition to looking out for each other, my family believed in the value of education. From the time I was young the importance of being well-spoken and studying hard was stressed. My elders equated doing well at school with one's ability to move ahead in life, and my parents started educating me as early as I can remember. Mommy would line apples on top of the table to show me how to count. Later, she'd use them to teach me addition and subtraction.

When I was four, my family enrolled me in kindergarten at St. Cyprian's, an Episcopalian church on Bushwick Avenue that had established a school in the basement. Actually, it was a large, open space that had been partitioned into classrooms with blackboards and lockers. The space was very cold and dark—not like the bright and colorful places you'd send a four-year-old to today. All of the teachers were rigid, and all we did was work. They filled you with as much information as you could hold and then they pumped in some more. Recess was short. You couldn't laugh or yell or run too much. And God forbid you fell down and skinned your hands and knees. When I think of St. Cyprian's, I only remember sad faces. Today I call it Nazi kindergarten, because the educational process was so hostile and uninspired.

Of course, my family was thrilled with the education they thought I was receiving when I came home from class with dictation books filled with information I had transcribed. What they didn't know was that the teaching was so advanced that no four-year-old could possibly comprehend it. But when my family saw how well my handwriting developed, and heard me recite what I had written, they assumed I was comprehending it and was advanced for my age. I was ahead of my years, all right—but I wasn't learning what they thought I was. My experience at St. Cyprian's taught me to hate school, to work too hard and that it wasn't okay to work and have fun. In retrospect, I'm certain that my experiences at that school laid the foundation for my people-pleasing behavior. No matter how much effort I made, I could never do anything right in my teachers' eyes.

"Class, I want you to open your desks and take out a pencil, please."

My teacher, Mrs. Jones, a short and wide black woman with half glasses, stood in front of the class preparing to recite the day's lesson. I reached behind me and rooted through the book bag that was in the compartment on the back of my seat.

"George Washington was the father of our country," she read. "He was born on February 22, 1732, on a farm in Virginia and became our nation's first president. When George Washington was a little boy, he . . ."

Mrs. Jones droned on in the background, but I still couldn't find my pencil, so I turned around completely to dig more deeply in the book bag. Perhaps it was hidden in the crease at the bottom. Suddenly I felt something stinging my arm. "Ow!" I shouted, turning around, bolting up straight and grabbing my upper arm all at once. A welt rose up on my arm as quickly as tears welled in my eyes. Mrs. Jones peered at me over the top of her glasses with an angry look on her face and a piece of elastic swinging menacingly from her hand. She had just popped me with the "spaghetti," her euphemistic term for zapping me with an elastic cord that was a half inch thick and one foot long. It was the color of rusted metal.

"What is taking you so long?" she demanded.

"I, um, can't, um, find my pencil. It's at the, um, bottom of my bag," I pleaded, never removing my eye from the piece of elastic.

"Didn't I tell you to use a pencil case?"

"Yes, but . . ."

"If you had the pencil case, this wouldn't have happened. Now turn around and pay attention. Will someone please lend Lisa a pencil?"

A hand on the other side of the room shot up. Another student was trying to get on Mrs. Jones's good side, no doubt.

"Please pass the pencil to Lisa. Thank you. Now, as I was saying . . ." She continued with her lecture. After she finished talking about Washington we transcribed the contents of the chalkboard into our books. Then we moved on to Abraham Lincoln.

At some point that evening Daddy came into my room to give me a hug, as he always did. I said "Ow" when he hugged me, then remembered that I was trying to hide the welt on my arm because I thought I'd get into more trouble. Of course Daddy noticed. "What happened to you?"

"Mrs. Jones hit me with the spaghetti," I mumbled, tears pooling in my eyes.

"Spaghetti? Baby, what are you talking about?"

"I couldn't, um, find my pencil, so she, um, hit me with the spaghetti."

"What did the spaghetti look like?" Daddy asked, frowning as I described the long, thick piece of rust-colored elastic. The next day he drove me to school and confronted Mrs. Jones.

"When they misbehave, they get a lash," she explained unapologetically. "Those are the rules." Daddy usually stood up for me, but this day he didn't seem quite as strong. Maybe he gave her a private dressing down, or perhaps she intimidated him, too.

By the end of the school year, I was afraid to breathe hard in Mrs. Jones's classroom. No matter what I did, I couldn't make that woman happy. I memorized all sorts of useless things—I knew about the presidents and could recite the names of all fifty states. But no matter what I said or how enthusiastically I said it, Mrs. Jones seemed to have it in for me. I thought that perhaps I had done something wrong. So I tried even harder to read well, write neatly and keep my desk in order. *Maybe then she will like me,* I thought. But nothing I did ever was enough. After a while, I was almost too scared to ask any questions. My spirit was battered and bruised. But my reading, writing and recitation skills were so advanced for my age that my family didn't notice how anxious I had become. Grandma Hilda used to save my recitation books and brag about me to her friends. "Lisa is so smart," she would say. "She's going to be a doctor or lawyer."

That spring our class was to graduate into the first grade. Mrs. Jones gave us a handout to take home telling us how to dress at the ceremony. My hand shot up after receiving the paper, as I desperately tried to make a good impression.

"What now, Lisa?"

"My mommy bought me some fishnet tights. Can I wear them to graduation?"

Mrs. Jones breathed so deeply, she sucked all of the air out of the room. Then she exhaled so hard that the instructions she had just handed out practically blew off the top of my desk. When she paused it was so quiet that I could hear my classmates breathing. What had I done now?

"That's such a silly thing to think about wearing," she stated authoritatively. I felt foolish and ashamed for opening my mouth. "It's not even an appropriate question."

My whole extended family came to the graduation ceremony. The night of the program, Mommy dressed me up in my favorite pink dress, white gloves, and black patent leather Mary Janes. Needless to say, I didn't even think about wearing fishnet tights. Daddy primped and preened over me, while Mommy put some extra lotion on my elbows and knees so they wouldn't be ashy. My skin was always ashy. Everybody told me how pretty I looked.

Mommy, Daddy, Philip and I arrived at the school early so they could sit near the front of the auditorium. My grandparents and assorted cousins and aunts joined us. The students sat in rows on the stage. I was the best with recitations in my kindergarten class, my handwriting was excellent and spelling almost perfect. I was confident that I would get an award.

Graduation began with the Pledge of Allegiance. I was proud of myself, so I recited it loudly. Mrs. Jones flashed a frown in my direction. Another teacher stood up and talked about the year, and then they started handing out awards. I was eager for my name to be called. I prayed I didn't trip and fall.

"Tonya Adams . . ." A girl from my class stood and walked to the front of the podium, grinning. Everybody clapped. "Damon Carter . . ." Another kid from my class got an award, then another and another. "Michael Williams . . ." Then they moved on to another class.

Hey, what about me? I get good marks! I started to get an uneasy feeling, but tried to console myself with the thought that they might have saved my award for last. The longer the evening wore on, however, the more my spirits sank. At the end of the night my name hadn't been called and I sat in my seat stunned and dejected. I was one of the best students in my class. I didn't understand why I didn't get a certificate. Later I learned that I had missed being acknowledged by one-tenth of a grade point. For *kindergarten,* for goodness' sake! My family was furious, but Mrs. Jones stayed true to her nature and, apparently, wouldn't back down.

At the time I didn't know that my parents stood up for me behind the scenes. So, as I dragged off the stage and back toward my family, I came to the only conclusion that my young mind could imagine: *I must be stupid. No one will ever like me.* The awareness made my shoulders feel as heavy as lead. I wanted to run and hide my face. My head hung down to my knees.

Yet, as I walked over to my family, I heard a loud commotion. People were shouting. *What's happening?* I looked up and my entire clan was clapping and cheering for me. *Why are they happy and smiling?* I wondered. *I didn't win anything.* Still, everyone was beaming. I was shocked. *They still like me!* I ran into their loving arms.

That evening I learned how unequivocal my family's love was for me. It made me want to please them more. I resolved that there would be no other such ceremonies where my name would not be called to receive an award. I was determined to always make them proud—as proud as they made me that night.

CHAPTER 2

Home Is Where the Heart Is

After my parent's divorce, my father took my brother, Philip, and me on a trip to Montreal.

I graduated from St. Cyprian's at the end of the first grade. From there I went to P.S. 262, which is now known as El Hajj Malik Shabazz Elementary School near Malcolm X Boulevard and MacDonough Street. Things wouldn't get any better for me there. On the first day of school, the teacher, Mrs. Thomas, told us we would practice writing the letter *C*. Desperate to get off to a good start with her, I raised my hand.

"Do you want me to print it or write it in cursive?" I asked.

Mrs. Thomas stared at me for a long time before asking in a sarcastic tone of voice, "*You* can write it in *cursive?*"

"Yes," I said, beaming from ear to ear.

"Well, let me *see* you write it in *cursive.*"

I pulled out my pencil and wrote a perfect script *C.* "See!" I smiled, holding the paper up. Mrs. Thomas was shocked. "Oh! Well, I guess you can write it in cursive then."

My classmates, on the other hand, were not impressed at all. The fact that I had attended a school that had drilled me full of useless information set me up to be picked on, and my desperate desire to please the teacher only made matters worse. One day the class made flowers out of tissue paper and pipe cleaners. Mine was yellow with a bright red stem. It was so pretty I could almost smell it, and I couldn't wait to show it to Grampsie when he came to pick me up from school, as he did every day. I walked around holding my flower all morning. But while the teacher was out of the room, a girl who always bullied me snatched it out of my hand and scrunched it into a tiny wad.

"That's my flower! Why did you break it?" I shouted at her, trying to fluff it back up. She looked startled. It was the first time I had yelled at her; most of the time I just cried.

"I can tear up your flower and even beat you up if I want to."

"No you can't."

"Keep being so smart and I'ma kick your butt after school."

"No you won't!"

"Yes, I will."

"No you won't."

"Yes, I will."

"If you try to beat me up, my Grampsie will pick me up and lift me way over his head and you won't be able to touch me and he's going to get you in trouble."

"Oh, yeah. Watch me."

She stared at me for the rest of the day, mouthing across the room that she was going to beat my you-know-what. When we were dismissed at the end of the school day, I raced outside trying to reach the safety of Grampsie's arms before the girl could catch me. But when I made it onto the schoolyard, he wasn't waiting in his usual place. I stopped and looked around; he was nowhere to be found. My heart pounded out of my chest and I couldn't get any air. Gramps had never been late before. *Where is he?*

And what if he doesn't come? I eased my way over to the cyclone fence and pressed flat against it, certain I would see him strolling down the block. I waited and waited, but still no Grampsie. In the meantime I kept my eye out for that nasty girl from my class. Finally she saw me and screamed across the playground, "I'm gonna kick your butt!" She sprinted over the blacktop, her braids all akimbo, and a crowd formed around us.

"Where's your grandpa now, Goody Two-shoes!" she shouted. "You probably don't even have one. Whatcha gonna do now? Whatcha gonna do?"

"Leave me alone!" I whimpered, backing up, my mind furiously scrambling to figure out how to get out of my predicament.

"I'm gonna beat your butt," the girl said, pressing up against me. The smell of my own fear combined with her peanut butter breath and Ultra Sheen almost made me swoon. Suddenly she stepped back and shoved me—hard. The back of my body banged into the fence. If I could have squeezed through the wire mesh, believe me, I would have done it. Instead, I pressed against it as tightly as I could and tried to slowly slide away.

"Look out!" another girl shouted. "They're braiding you to the fence so she can beat you."

I reached back and felt somebody's fingers in my hair. Just as I jerked my head forward, somebody's grandmother broke up the crowd.

"What are you all doing?" she scolded. "You all should be ashamed of yourselves." Then I heard Grampsie call my name. His voice had never sounded sweeter. He came running down the block and I leapt into his strong arms, where I was enveloped by his familiar scent, which I now know to be a combination of peppermint, bay leaf, and spice.

"What's going on?" he asked the elderly woman.

"One of these children was trying to beat her up."

"Oh, are you okay?" I nodded, trembling with relief. Grampsie could fix anything—radios, toasters, televisions. I knew he could fix this, too. "Let's go home to Mommy and we'll have some juice and watch TV together. I promise you I'll never be late again." And he wasn't.

Most days, my trips home from school were far less eventful. Grampsie would meet me, we'd collect another one of my cousins, and we'd walk to the house he and Nana shared. I wasn't aware at the time that, due to my mother's illness, walking to pick me up from school was too much for her. So, Gramps assumed that responsibility. I never thought there was anything unusual about the arrangement. I loved spending time with Gramps. Whenever I entered his presence I would start looking for my treat, which would sometimes be the coconut patties he got from the crossing guard when she returned from her home in Barbados. Other times, my treat would be for him to swing me over mud puddles. If it rained, Grampsie would hold me by my hands and swing me high in the air over every mud puddle we encountered. *Wheeee!* Grampsie was six feet tall, and felt like a giant to me. When he swung me by my arms, I believed that I could fly.

Arriving home to Gramps and Nana's house was the highlight of my day. When Gramps walked into the house, his greeting was always "Maggie, I home," the reverse of his farewell: "Maggie, I go." The wonderful smells that warmed the air—the curry, the yeast from freshly baked bread, the coconut cake, or ginger and vanilla—intoxicated me, making me want to stumble toward the kitchen with my coat and boots still on. While Gramps unbuttoned me, I excitedly kicked off my galoshes. "Walk!" he'd warn as I made a beeline to the kitchen.

Nana always greeted me with a big hug that smelled like Pond's cold cream. She had the softest cheeks, creamy honey-brown skin, a Clara Bow mouth, and silver-gray hair that she pulled back in a bun. Compared to a day at school, her gentle voice and heartwarming smile felt like an oasis.

As I unwrapped myself from her arms, I quickly sized up her large kitchen. In a flash, I could tell what was going on, and if I was lucky I would be involved in what she would be doing next. The canisters labeled flour, sugar, coffee, and tea were neatly aligned along the counter. The measuring cup was out with two eggs sitting in it. A chair was sitting next to the chopping block. That was where she had me stand so that I could reach the table. We would be baking together today!

The next step of the ritual was for me to go wash up. Nana had a strict code of conduct for her kitchen. Rule number one was no dirty hands.

"Whatcha making?" I'd ask as I sidled up to the stove, my hands smelling like Dial soap. "It smells like curry."

"Don't get too close," she warned. "You'll burn yourself. It's curry chicken with chickpeas."

Nana lifted the lid off of the worn aluminum pot. Plumes of white steam swirled up, releasing an intense potpourri of fragrances. In my mind's eye I saw her chopping an onion and placing it in a skillet with a little bit of oil. I saw her sprinkling the ochre-colored curry powder into the skillet alongside the onions. I watched the fenugreek, coriander, turmeric, cumin and other spices dancing together as she sautéed the curry with the onions and oil to keep it from turning the dish bitter. The tip of the wooden spoon she used turned yellow as she stirred the golden curry. The chicken, chickpeas and other seasonings were added next, boiling them so that the liquid would reduce. The aroma trumpeted the secret of not just the recipe, but how well the ingredients held together. If I was lucky, she'd be testing the seasoning and I would get a little sip of the broth.

Nana opened a drawer and grabbed a large wooden spoon. My mouth watered with anticipation. She was going to check her spices. If I stayed still and was very quiet, I might be offered a sip of this elixir. She dipped out some chickpeas then fished for more curry sauce to get a good taste. She held the spoon over her free palm, blowing until it was cool enough to eat. She took a sip, then turned to me and said, "Open wide!" *Yes! I get to taste it.* My obedience had paid off. The warm curry, sweet and at the same time hot, filled my mouth, slid down my throat, and warmed my stomach. It was everything I imagined it would be.

"What are we baking?"

"Chile, how do you know I'm baking today?"

"I don't know, I just know."

"Well, I'm not—until tomorrow. Would you like to help me prepare the apples for turnovers for tomorrow?"

"Yippee!"

"Don't run!"

"I won't."

I walked across the faux brick floor until I got to the window overlooking the backyard. There were eight bright red apples perched like cardinals along

Nana's Kitchen Rules

1. Wash your hands.
2. Clean as you go.
3. Don't bring negativity into the kitchen.
4. No anger is allowed; it gets into the food.
5. No running or jumping when you're passing through the kitchen.
6. No loud talking in the kitchen.
7. Wrap your head in a scarf to keep hair out of the food.

the windowsill. Above them, three long twists of orange peel hung from a hook that had been screwed into the top of the window frame. Nana and Gramps had a special way of peeling oranges so that the skin came off all in one piece. Then Nana hung the peels from the hook to dry. With them she made hot tea for stomachaches. She taught me always to eat the pith; it, too, was good for your stomach. But in addition to making tea, Grampsie used those same orange skins to perform practical magic.

I picked up the apples and set them on top of the wooden table in the center of the room. She pulled up my chair and I kneeled on it, my elbows on the table.

"Are you comfort-*ah*-ble!" she asked. Nana had worked so hard to make her speech sound American that you could barely tell she had an accent. But her proper way of speaking and the broad sound of her *As* clearly revealed her West Indian origin. She used a paring knife to whisk the peel off of the apple, handing me the long red skin to nibble on. Then she sliced the fruit in eighths, cut the seeds away, dropped the pieces into a bowl, cut a lemon in half and handed a piece of it to me.

"Squeeze the lemon over the apples. They will turn brown if you leave them in the air too long. Lemon juice helps them keep their color." I squeezed, knowing that an hour from now my hand would still smell like that wonderful lemon. Next, Nana handed me a small sugar bowl and instructed me to sprinkle the sugar atop the apples, being careful not to allow it to fall onto the floor. While I did that she stuck a cinnamon stick in her spice mill. When I was finished she handed the cinnamon to me. I ground the aromatic bark onto the apples, its exotic fragrance warming my nostrils. When Nana wasn't looking, I stuck my pointing finger into the sugary cinnamon mixture that was now melting on the apples and let the amazing taste spread across my tongue.

"What is my grandbaby making today?" Grampsie's rich baritone love was the final spice we needed. Now the apples were ready to be put in the refrigerator overnight.

"Apples for turnovers, Gramps. Wanna taste?" I offered.

"Not until you bake them." He walked over to the window and pulled one of the orange peels down from the hook. His eyes sparkled and he spun the peel around his finger as he walked closer to me. "You ready?" he asked, as I gasped and waited. He spun the peel around his finger another couple of times. "What will it be—a surprise or a present?"

"A *present*!" I shouted, unable to contain myself.

"Shhhh . . . ," Nana gently reminded me as Gramps let the orange peel fly over his shoulder and fall to the floor. I scrambled over to where the peel fell and kneeled down to examine it.

"Did it land in the shape of an *S* or a *P*?" he asked.

"A *P*," I shouted, jumping up and down.

"Then a present it is!" he answered, reaching into his pocket and pulling out a peppermint.

CHAPTER 3

Finding My Voice

Graduation from St. Augustine's Junior High.
Although my grades were good, I felt like a failure and school felt like a job.

I f an orange peel could cause such glee, you can only imagine what
Christmas was like—especially in my house. Both of my parents loved
this holiday. Mommy, being the more practical one, would make sure that
Philip and I received as gifts the requisite number of pajamas, underwear,
and socks that every child needs. Daddy would be given the task of show-
ering us with all of the things we wanted. At the time, one of his jobs was
at Macy's, so his employee discount came in handy.

In the sixties in the Bushwick section of Brooklyn, where we lived, real live Christmas trees weren't in fashion; people purchased synthetic ones, instead, so the scent of pine wasn't in my home. But the fragrances of vanilla and cinnamon floated through the air from the cookies, cakes, rice pudding and different treats Mommy would prepare. She was very organized. She planned and got things done ahead of time, whereas Daddy would catch the Christmas spirit on Christmas Eve.

The spoiling he dished out every holiday season was very much a part of his character. Daddy would spend almost every cent he had on gifts, particularly for Philip and me. Philip and I would go to sleep on December 24 and, except for gifts for friends and extended family, the floor under the Christmas tree would be bare. But come morning, our presents would be piled high.

One Christmas, when I was still young enough to believe in Santa, I woke up around midnight looking for a tissue so I could blow my runny nose. Fortunately, Daddy heard the pitter-patter of my little feet before I walked in on the unwrapped toys and wrapping paper strewn across the living room floor.

"What are you doing up?" he asked, intercepting me in the hall.

"My nose is running. I need a Kleenex."

Daddy guided me into the bathroom, handed me a tissue, and escorted me back to my room. Then he reconsidered, returned to the bathroom, and handed me an entire roll of toilet paper. I climbed into my bed, toilet paper in hand. Daddy kissed me on my forehead and left, pulling my bedroom door shut. As I was snuggling down into the covers, I heard Santa Claus's voice.

"Ho, ho, ho! How are you, Mr. Hairston?"

"I'm fine, Santa."

"Are your children asleep?"

"I think so. My daughter just got up to get a Kleenex, but she's back in bed now."

I desperately wanted to see Santa in his big red suit, but I didn't want to spoil my presents or get a lump of coal in my stocking. So I shut my eyes as tightly as I could, pulled the blankets over my head and pretended I was sleeping. The next thing I knew, I was waking up. Santa had piled our presents as high as he usually did. Red and white candy canes were dangling from the colorfully lit tree, and our stockings were stuffed with candy canes, comic books, racing cars, jacks, and other small gifts.

In some ways my parents were the perfect couple. Both were the offspring of Trinidadian immigrants, they loved children, worked hard, believed in the American dream and knew the value of education. But Mommy had quite the opposite of my father's extravagant preferences. If Daddy loved standing on the mountain peak, Mommy was the bedrock of our family. She was a loving, sensible, hardworking woman who would eventually raise eight children. I know my mother wouldn't want me to make a distinction between her biological and adopted children, because to Mommy we were *all* her babies; however, I feel I must because it shows how big her heart was. In addition to Philip and me, she adopted six children during the course of my lifetime—all while facing serious health problems of her own. During my childhood, Mommy would periodically work at the phone company, but mostly she was a stay-at-home mom. She gave Philip and me those hard-to-put-your-finger-on values we all recognize as "good home-training."

Mommy taught us to be kind and respectful toward others. She taught us to be open-minded and humble. She taught us to never, ever tell a lie. (If there was one thing that Mommy abhorred, it was a liar, a trait I carry as well. If you told her a fib, she was through with you.) While the times I spent with Mommy may not have been at the opera or Radio City Music Hall, as they were with Daddy, they were nonetheless enjoyable; she knew how to make fun out of tasks that might otherwise have been drudgery—making my bed, cleaning my room, and straightening up my toy box, for instance. My mother taught me that if I took care with my belongings and put them back in an orderly manner, I would later experience the benefit of being able to find them in perfect condition, a discipline that would prove invaluable time and time again in my various career choices, and ultimately my business.

Consistent with his personality, my relationship with my father was a lot more dramatic. In many ways Daddy was my first beau and I was the apple of his eye. We were the perfect combination: He loved to show off his little girl and I loved it when he showered me with attention. Daddy was in love with the finer things in life and believed in exposing his children to them. Some of my favorite memories are when we would get all dressed up—he in snazzy suits and English Leather cologne and I in frilly dresses with matching hats, white gloves, and black patent leather Mary Janes—to go to lunch at Rockefeller Center, or the theater for Christmas to attend *The Nutcracker* or Radio City Music Hall to see the Rockettes. Together, we cut a handsome figure; I wanted so badly to be a little lady.

He shared his enjoyment of the arts at home, too, particularly his love of music. When I was an infant he pushed my crib up against the stereo speakers, so I would become accustomed to the sounds that filled our household. He would sing, although he couldn't sing. He would dance, although he couldn't dance. As I grew older he taught me to appreciate Miles and Coltrane and Charlie Parker and also to enjoy Barbra Streisand, Grover Washington, and Stevie Wonder. He even bought me a tape recorder so I could sing into the mike and record my own songs. When I was eleven I used to fantasize that I was Diana Ross in *Lady Sings the Blues.* I played the soundtrack over and over again and learned the snippets of dialogue it contained. It wasn't uncommon to find me in my room running my lines with Billy Holiday playing on the record player. Then I might burst into a blues song—"Lover man, oh, where can you be?" I secretly dreamed of a life on stage.

Daddy came by his love of the arts naturally. Grandma Hilda and her sisters Ivy and Ismay all knitted and enjoyed home crafts. Aunt Ismay loved sewing, crocheting, and crewel work. She could even reupholster her own furniture. One time she took me shopping in a fabric shop. The next time I came to her house, not only was the new tapestry on her furniture, there were coordinating drapes as well. She also taught me how to play Scrabble.

Aunt Judith was an artist as well. She studied drama in college and dreamed of being an actress, even if it was just in a community theater. But while she was able to get prime roles when she was in school, once she moved to Germany to be with her husband Hans, things changed. When she auditioned in a German theater, her German wasn't good enough for her to pull off the role. So there was a period of time when she spoke only German, to polish her language skills. And when she had perfected her German but couldn't get roles to play because she was black, she produced her own plays and cast herself in them. For over twenty years she managed a successful dinner theater in Frankfurt. One of the plays she produced even made it to Broadway.

Like Daddy, Judith also liked to give gifts. She never arrived empty-handed when she returned home to the States. For certain, she would bring a new bottle of perfume for Grandma. Grandma Hilda wore Coty Emeraude, Chantilly Lace and Madame Rochas for everyday wear. Judith's gifts, the colorful, cellophane-wrapped cartons containing more exotic perfumes from Europe, remained in her bureau drawer unopened. But when Grandma wasn't looking, I would sneak in to her bedroom and try to smell them through the wrappers.

"I'm saving these for a special occasion," Grandma would declare.

But while I was around, that special occasion never came, leaving me to fantasize about what they smelled like. My vivid imagination created aromas I experienced in my mind. As I approached my teens the mysteries behind the cellophane were finally revealed to me, as I walked through the fragrance section of any department store and could smell the very perfumes that Grandma kept hidden in the recesses of her drawer. How she kept them locked up for so long was beyond me. I was taken, captured and in love.

Of course, I couldn't afford department store fragrances, but Mommy and Daddy would buy me little-girl scents. And when I was a preteen and got an allowance, I headed to the drugstore where I bought perfumes like Heaven Scent, Love's Baby Soft and some kind of green apple bath set that smelled so tart that I just had to have the bath oil, the lotion, the powder and the cologne. Fragrances were my friends. They made me feel pretty and made bad times seem not so bad. Like when I was ten and my parents' marriage ended.

Mommy and Daddy did a great job at parenting Philip and me, but for whatever reason weren't able to remain husband and wife to each other. Because of how honorably they handled things, when my parents split the separation wasn't traumatic. It was clear to us both that our father would continue to be a part of our lives; we just wouldn't live in the same house anymore. Afterward, in some ways we were even closer to Daddy. In retrospect I suppose the strain of a marriage that was ending may have caused him to not be home as much, although it didn't disrupt our relationships with him at the time. When they separated, he remained in our house; my mother didn't want to because it was owned by Daddy's family. We moved into an apartment in Aunt Syl and Uncle Robbie's building. Suddenly Philip and I had to share a bedroom. But even though our lifestyle had changed, our time with Daddy was planned, deliberate and always fun.

When Daddy was a boy, one of the things he looked forward to every week was Saturday afternoon at the movies, when thirty-five cents helped him escape into another world. He passed that enjoyment on to Philip and me by taking us to the cinema on our weekends together. Afterward, we would all return to a home-cooked dinner Mommy had made. In front of us kids, Mommy and Daddy handled their relationship as though nothing had happened between them. He continued to come over several nights a week, help us with our homework and put us to bed. Then he would return to his house for the night. But we stayed with Mommy, so the bulk of the responsibility fell on her shoulders.

Despite the divorce, Philip and I did not have the luxury of the "I'm going to get bad grades now because my parents aren't together" syndrome. Academic excellence was still expected. When I was eleven, I attended St. Augustine's Prep, where the staff pushed us hard, hoping the school would regain its reputation following a financial scandal. One of its strategies was to send its graduates to the best high schools in the city. Technically, I should have been in the seventh grade; however, most of my classes were at the eighth-grade level. I also took ninth-grade algebra and French.

But even though I was academically advanced, learning didn't feel anywhere near as good as my grades looked on paper. I found school very confusing. On the positive side, I would get praised and rewarded every time I did well on tests or recited my lessons from memory. Daddy and Grandma Hilda were always showing off my report cards, and I was held up as the "golden child" to my extended family. And there were other good moments, like when my fifth- and sixth-grade teacher Mrs. Jackman praised me, which she did often. Among many other compliments, she told me that I was a wonderful saleswoman. She could give me a tray of sweets from a bake sale and trust that I could sell them.

"Lisa," she'd say, "go sell this stuff. You'll come back with the money and an empty tray."

But for the most part, school was not enjoyable. It felt like a job. The environment was strict and emphasized discipline. And while I strived to get high marks to make the adults around me happy, doing so alienated me from my peers. Inside, I just knew I was a failure. No matter how hard I studied, it was never good enough; I always had to work harder, go higher, get a better score. My brain was crammed so full of facts I had to memorize, I thought I couldn't remember one more thing. To me, being smart felt like a façade and it was sure to tumble down at the most embarrassing moment.

In retrospect, I understand I had mastered the ability to memorize, but I wasn't really learning. I was trained to spit back the things people told me to say without processing them through my own mind and experience. In a subtle way, this taught me that my thoughts didn't matter. I was learning everything except who I was, what I liked, and what was important to me. Over time, the price I would pay for doing so was steep. I would grow to dislike aspects of myself.

If that wasn't hard enough, I was being prepared to go to high school at as young an age as possible. As I neared the end of the eighth grade at the tender age of eleven, momentum was building to send me to Bronx High School of Science, one of the best academic high schools in the city. St. Augustine's was pushing for me to go to Bronx Science to boost its own reputation. My father wanted me to attend because tuition for a private high school would have been difficult if not darn near impossible to pay. But he also had reservations about sending me to what only a few years earlier had been a school for boys. Mommy also wanted me to go to Bronx Science. I was totally against it because of the commute.

"I can't spend two and a half hours on the train each way," I begged. On top of the fact that I hated science, the thought of spending all that time in the subway made me want to scream.

There were a couple of other options. The one that was most interesting to me was High School of Music and Art. I thought I could audition as a visual artist because I had done some painting. Unfortunately, my repertoire consisted of some kind of nondescript flowers in a vase. Upon reviewing the application, I realized that I needed to have a portfolio, which consisted of several media—oil, watercolor, charcoal, etc. When I heard the word charcoal I envisioned charcoal briquettes, so it became clear that wasn't the route I should take. Thank goodness a teacher at St. Augustine's had noticed I could sing.

From time to time at St. Augustine's we would have an assembly. Many times these gatherings opened with the national anthem. I didn't know it at the time, but the national anthem is a particularly tough song to sing. It spans several octaves and has very high notes at the end, when many singers' vocal cords are exhausted. Even the most accomplished professionals rehearse diligently before performing it, so they don't embarrass themselves with a voice cracking on "And the rocket's red glare . . ." in the middle or "O'er the land of the free . . ." at the end.

Unlike almost everyone in the auditorium, I could sing "The Star Spangled Banner" and hit all the high notes without my voice cracking. At the time I didn't really realize I was doing something special. Yes, I knew that from time to time someone would look at me when I sang, as though they were asking, "Who's that?" Sensing their admiration, I would sing a little louder. But no one had ever told me I had a beautiful singing voice, so I didn't really understand that I had been given the gift of song.

"I think I can teach you to sing a tune well enough to get into Music & Art," one of my teachers offered. She had attended Music & Art years before and apparently the test hadn't changed much.

I was ecstatic! I began to think of going to Music & Art as my escape route—my way of getting off of this miserable academic merry-go-round and into something I might even enjoy. Three weeks before auditions, my first voice lessons began.

"The test consists of three parts," the teacher informed me. "You'll sing a song, then they'll play something on the piano and you'll have to play it back. There's a rhythm test where they tap something out and you'll be asked to repeat it."

For three weeks, we worked together each day during lunch. At night, I practiced what I had learned that day. The more I practiced the more worried my mother looked to me. To this day, I don't know if she felt that I didn't have enough talent or if she felt that my audition song didn't suit me. I just remember this look of concern when I practiced that never left her face.

"Oh, that's nice," she would say, wearing that look. Mommy would never discourage me. But she did keep reminding me of my other options.

"Well, you know, there's still Bronx Science. Music & Art isn't the only school out there."

All their lives, she and Daddy aspired and prayed that they could send their children to college. The way Daddy saw it, in a big city like New York, my ability to go to college hinged on getting into a competitive high school. Mommy always taught me to be whatever I wanted to be, but teaching an eleven-year-old girl who had never even sung in a choir how to ace a vocal audition seemed like a long shot, even to her.

The song that gave her pause was a Negro spiritual "Let Us Break Bread Together," which was very staid and solemn, not pretty at all. It is the kind of hymn you'd find the oldest member of the senior choir warbling at church. And that was exactly how I was instructed to sing it. No wonder Mommy looked worried.

> Let us break bread together on our knees
> Let us break bread together on our knees
> As we fall on our knees with our face to the rising sun
> Oh Lord, have mercy on us please . . .

In retrospect, it was all very ridiculous. I stood there singing with my nonexistent chest puffed out and sounding like I was an old lady, though I was only eleven years old. But there was a method to the madness. The teacher had chosen this particular song because at the Music & Art audition, the panel was notorious for cutting you off before you could finish. This spiritual climbed to the high notes very quickly, so by the time they stopped you, you would already have demonstrated your range.

On the day of the audition, Daddy drove me to the school. The parents had to wait in the auditorium, so I obtained my room assignment and took the elevator up to the third floor alone. As I looked for my audition room, I heard people singing. I realized that if I got in, these beautiful sounds would be a part of my school day, every day—not just the fleeting exposure to music during the weekly mass that was held at St. Augustine's.

"I *have* to go here," I thought as I waited to be called for my audition.

Two women judges evaluated me. One sat at a desk and the other at the piano. At first, I had butterflies.

"We are going to start with scales. The pianist will play a melody on the piano and you are to sing it back using 'la.' "

As I started singing, whatever nervousness I had left me; I knew I was fully prepared. We repeated the exercise five or six times.

Then I was instructed to turn my back to the judges. One tapped out a rhythm with a drumstick and I tapped it back. Each time, I repeated it perfectly.

By the time I had to sing, I felt confident, because I hadn't made a mistake. I sang my selection a cappella. They told me where to stand—my back to the pianist, my profile to the other judge. I looked out the window onto a park, which made me feel peaceful. As I began the second verse, I heard the words, "Thank you. That's enough. You may go now."

At the end of the audition, I knew I was in. I was elated, absolutely ecstatic! In that one simple act of auditioning, I had discovered something that I could do—and do well.

I am a singer, I thought to myself, and practiced saying it out loud. "I am a singer. I am a singer," I repeated as I walked through the halls.

Unfortunately, I'm not sure that my parents shared my excitement. Three weeks later, I stumbled across my acceptance letter buried in Mommy's dresser drawer.

Identifying your Gifts and Talents

There are a number of talents within us as children that we somehow learn to suppress or forget. For example, young people love to dance and sing and paint. It doesn't matter if they know how to do any of these things well, they just do them because they feel good.

Once we begin to receive criticism of our "talents" we often stop engaging them. Some children have the gift of leadership. But we may label them "bossy" when they are children. Other kids may possess great analytical abilities, but may get teased for being "nerds." When I look back at my life, I realize that the seeds for the skills I have drawn upon as an adult were planted in my childhood: my natural love of good scents, being in the kitchen with Mommy and Nana, my ability to be well organized, watching my aunts and uncles carrying on their various duties to move the family unit along. These same scenarios play themselves out now in the day-to-day operations of my company.

I believe it is helpful to sit down and think about as much of your childhood as you can remember and write down the things you most enjoyed doing. When I did this, I remembered what my fifth-grade teacher, Mrs. Jackman, said after I had taken a tray of baked goods around to other classrooms during a bake sale and sold everything on the tray. She told me I would grow up to be a businesswoman because I could sell. I had long since forgotten her prediction, but remembering it gave me more confidence in my selling skills. Surprisingly, even though I am in the retail business, I never thought of myself as a good salesperson. The memory of my fifth-grade bake sale reminded me that this talent was always a part of me.

When you were a child, did you love to paint? Did you enjoy playing with dolls? Did you enjoy being outside and running around the yard? If so, you may have natural abilities to be an artist or interior designer; a mother or an educator; a dancer or track star. Look at your life, taking note of the activities you loved to do most, things that other people noticed about you, tasks that you thought were easy but that other people struggled to accomplish. These may provide you with clues about your natural talents. The world is awaiting your gifts.

CHAPTER 4

My Nose Knows

At Music and Arts High School I could feel myself coming alive as I grew to love listening to the sound of my voice. My goal was to one day avenge Diana Ross's stolen Oscar for her portrayal of Billie Holiday in Lady Sings the Blues.

I stood under the hot, bright lights of the Shrine Auditorium in Los Angeles, making my acceptance speech for my first Academy Award.

"I'm accepting this award on behalf of Diana Ross for her performance in *Lady Sings the Blues,* who was robbed of her award by Miss Liza Minelli for her performance in *Cabaret,* which in my opinion paled in comparison to Miss Ross's portrayal of the tortured, heroin-addicted blues singer, Billie Holiday."

"Lisa," I heard my mother's voice coo.

"Mommy, why are you calling me now? I'm accepting my Oscar."

"Lisa, it's time to get up. What time is your first class?"

Mommy knew I was a heavy sleeper. She would wake me up by making me think, to answer her questions.

"Eight-thirty."

On any other school day, I would have pulled the covers over my head and she practically would have had to drag me out of bed. Today she didn't have to tell me twice. I snapped out of the Shrine Auditorium and back into my life. It was the first day of school, my first step toward making Diana proud.

The smell of the fresh cantaloupe that Mommy was cutting in the kitchen in the next room made me dress faster. It smelled sweet and fresh, the last hint of summer.

"You don't want to be late," Mommy continued. "You have a long train ride ahead of you."

I gobbled down my breakfast and grabbed my book bag. Mommy gave me extra carfare and a dime for a phone call. She also reviewed the trip with me to make sure I knew all of the stops and train changes I would have to make. Thinking back on it, I can't imagine how nervous she must have been to send her twelve-year-old out at six forty-five A.M. to take a bus to the subway for what would be a one-and-a-half-hour train ride from Flatbush, Brooklyn up to Harlem. But all I got that morning was the smile on her face and a warning not to be late for school.

The subway ride that morning seemed to take forever. It wasn't the same as the practice run I had done with Daddy, which wasn't during rush hour. Fortunately for me, I got on the train early enough to get a seat, but as the trip progressed the train quickly filled with people on their way to work. At the stops, I closely observed the people that boarded the train. I noticed how the riders changed along my route, from brown-skinned to white and back to brown again.

When I got off the train, a whole bunch of kids got off with me. Being surrounded by so many kids who were probably going to Music & Art was comforting. Together, we headed up out of the subway and into St. Nicholas Park. As I stood at the bottom of the massive staircase that winds through the park, I felt like a different person. There was something liberating about being in an entirely different part of the city. This was

Manhattan, home of Carnegie Hall, Radio City, Broadway—all the places Daddy took me when I was little and we dressed up and went out on the town.

"Amazing, isn't it?" he had said, as we stood dressed in our finest on Broadway late one Saturday night.

I looked for what he was talking about, but didn't answer him out loud.

"People come here from all over the world to live their dreams, baby," he continued. Together, we breathed in the red, white, yellow and blue flashing lights, the shiny black limousines and the fancy, perfumed people who emerged from them. Daddy raised his hands toward the sky, "There's no city like it in the world!"

Now that I was alone in Manhattan, the pulse of the city had quickened; even something about the air was more vibrant. I felt safe as we ascended the long, steep staircase. Listening to the kids talk to each other, I realized I was entering an environment where many of the students actually loved school. A bunch of teenagers was already hanging out in the park—some sitting on the three-foot-high walls that lined the staircase landings; others perched on pedestals of white marble statues; still others gathered in cross-legged circles beneath the large leafy trees, while squirrels and birds chattered overhead. That was surprising to me. *Why would anybody come to school early?*

People were laughing, joking and greeting each other with warm hugs and kisses, and sharing their experiences over the summer.

"Hey, man, you look like you spent the summer at the shore. . . ."

"I went to Oberlin music camp for the summer. . . ."

"I just hung out here and smoked dope. . . ."

The excitement in the air was almost overwhelming. *Something is really different here.* The first thing I noticed was the way people looked. Unlike the uninspired uniforms we wore at St. Augustine's, these kids had on bell-bottom jeans, tie-dyed shirts in rainbow colors, headbands, peasant blouses, funky Earth and platform shoes. Some of the girls had fresh flowers in their hair like they had walked straight out of Woodstock. Sounds of the Beatles, Stevie Wonder and Phoebe Snow drifted through the air, along with a strange scent I would later learn was marijuana. Once classes started, it was common to see kids in the park painting on easels, singing a cappella on the staircase landings or sitting in the grass playing the flute. Walking through St. Nicholas Park this and every subsequent morning felt like my own daily journey through the Garden of Eden. It didn't matter that it took an hour and a half to get there each day.

Of course, some of the things I saw were quite an eyeful for me. I was only twelve, after all. As the only twelve-year-old in the entire school (or so I thought), I spent a lot of time figuring out the rules and observing what teenagers do. Needless to say, I had to make some social adjustments. Because I was so young, during my freshman and sophomore years I wasn't very active socially. But the kids were very nice to me and some even treated me like I was their little sister. Fortunately, by the time I was a junior there were other fourteen-year-olds in school. I didn't feel as out of place, even though they were only freshmen.

At Music & Art I could feel myself coming alive. There were student-painted murals all over the walls, singing reverberated through the hallways and musicians were even practicing in the stairwells. I got to take choir and voice lessons several times a week. Before long, I grew to love the sound of my voice as it arced through the air carrying high notes I could never hit before. When my emotions poured out of my heart and I transformed them into sounds, I felt a power I had never experienced. The layers of shyness and self-consciousness slowly began to recede. I realized that there was something I could do well and that felt good. I was so young and innocent, I felt like anything was possible.

Of course, attending an arts high school didn't exempt me from taking academic courses. Music & Art had a reputation as being one of New York's best public schools, and, as always, my father expected excellence.

"You're only twelve now. You'll be sixteen when you graduate from high school—fifteen if we do the accelerated program—which means you could be as young as nineteen when you graduate from college!" To my dad, this seemed ideal. To me, it meant that I would always be the youngest kid in the whole school, even in college.

"Dad, please. I don't know if that's what I want to do," I sighed.

"You'll still be young enough to audition for all the roles you'd like. And if for some reason that career doesn't pan out, your degree will still be in your desk drawer."

By now, the conditioning—to push ahead academically at all costs—had taken root in my consciousness. So, when I was assigned to French and algebra courses I had already taken at St. Augustine's, I protested until I was placed in higher-level classes.

"I did all of this in junior high," I insisted, and took a test to prove it. But when the results came back, there was still a question for some reason; possibly my age or race.

"Does this prove anything?" I asked my counselor one afternoon. I turned to the back of the first-year algebra text and to her embarrassment, solved all the problems printed there.

"Well, we have procedures . . . ," she stuttered.

"You don't understand," I exclaimed. "I had to do twenty years worth of Regent's exams to graduate from St. Augustine's. I've done this work already."

I was finally placed in the right classes—geometry and French II. By then, I was already two weeks behind and it took a while to get caught up. I got a sixty-five on my first math exam.

"You're going to have to work hard to get your grades back up," he said.

"But, Daddy, I started class later than everyone else."

"I know, but a 65 will bring down your average."

I knew he was right, but I didn't want to hear it.

"Well, we have to figure out what we're going to do. This isn't going to help when it's time to apply to college. Maybe there's some tutoring available."

Tutoring? What are you talking about? I've never gotten lower than a ninety during my entire academic life! I didn't need such things.

But I knew better than to mouth off much more than I already had, so I resorted to rolling my eyes and heaving a hefty sigh. I got a tutor for geometry, and on my midterm exam I got a ninety-five. Then, just for good measure I *became* a tutor.

In addition to finding my voice and conquering geometry during my early teenage years, I was experiencing an awakening of another kind—my nose seemed to be coming alive! All my life I had been attracted to yummy-smelling things. But as I began to come into my own, my love of good smells became more intense, and I had a number of memorable encounters with fragrant scents.

The first time an aroma knocked my socks off, it caught me by surprise. Early in my freshman year, as I walked down the hall, a tiny, delicate-looking girl with a bright orange Angela Davis afro came striding around the corner. Her hair formed a halo of dancing fire around her café au lait face. Her clothes were light and airy and seemed to float around her. I tried

my best not to gawk at this sunburst of a woman, but I had never seen anyone like her in my whole entire life. She caught me pretending not to stare
and smiled at me as she floated by. Busted, there was no reason to act like
I wasn't looking, so I turned and watched her drift away.

The girl was several steps beyond me when, suddenly, I was enveloped
in a wonderful wind stream of fragrances that breezed along behind her. It
was like all the people in the hallway stood still. Swirls of strawberry, coconut and frankincense wrapped around me and lifted me off my feet. It
felt like I was the only one there. When the aroma dissipated and I returned to earth, I was startled to find that I was standing in the middle of
the hall being jostled by students.

Who was that? I wondered of the red-haired girl. *I want to be like her!*

Later, I pointed the redhead out in the cafeteria to one of my older ac-
quaintances. "Oh, that's Flame Brathwaite," said the girl. "She's a senior."

"Music or art?"

"Music. She's a singer."

Several weeks later I summoned the courage to approach Flame while
she was standing in the cafeteria line. This time I was enveloped by her gardenia and jasmine blend.

"Excuse me. Flame?" I asked nervously. "My name's Lisa and I'm a
freshman. I don't mean to bother you, but you always smell so unbelievable. I was just wondering if you'd tell me what you are wearing."

"Oh, you're not bothering me. I just buy a lot of different oils and mix
them together."

"Oils?"

"Perfume oils—like coconut, strawberry, frankincense. I wear a lot of
different things at one time."

"Wow!" I stammered. "You just smell so amazing. And I think it's the
coolest thing."

"Thanks," she said, turning back to the cafeteria line.

Wow, I thought. *She is so sweet and she answered all my questions.*

I wanted to mix oils, dress like Flame and have my own look that was
uniquely mine. Well, I wasn't a size four and I didn't have red hair. But
maybe I could find these "oils." *Why didn't I ask her where she got them?* I'm
sure Flame never thought of our encounter again, but I was changed forever.

In another amazing experience with fragrance, when I was thirteen I
was asked to be a vacation companion to a five-year-old girl named Eve.

My job was to keep Eve entertained during her travels to South Jersey and Saratoga Springs, New York. All of my expenses would be covered. And at the end of my five-week job, I would be paid a hundred dollars, which was a lot to me. I traveled with her uncle and his girlfriend, who I thought was gorgeous. She was a flight attendant, which I thought was so cool. She could have been a black Charlie's Angel—and she always smelled fantastic.

One afternoon while at the amusement park, the girlfriend spilled her perfume in her purse. The wonderful aroma she exuded got all over everything she owned. She reeked of it.

"Tony's going to kill me," she said. "White Shoulders costs like a hundred dollars an ounce."

Later that day, she gave me a twenty dollar bill so I could go on some rides. But as soon as she put it in my hands, the intoxicating scent of White Shoulders that had spilled on the money made me go weak in the knees. Rather than hop on the ferris wheel, I found an empty park bench and held that bill to my nose, inhaling as deeply as I could. If I could have sniffed all of the fragrance out of it I would have. Instead, I tucked it into my pants pocket. I didn't spend it until the heady blend of honeysuckle and jasmine had dissipated. It would take a year for me to find it in Macy's fragrance department.

"White Shoulders," I sighed. "One day I'll be able to afford a bottle of my own."

There would be many more experiences like this during my youth— occasions when I was overcome by a particularly wonderful smell and it seemed as though time stood still. Years would pass before I realized these experiences that I remember so well, this natural attraction, was a way my spirit spoke to me.

Of course, one of the reasons females wear fragrances is to attract men's attention. And even though no one I knew was interested in me, as I entered puberty my hormones came alive. But that raised a whole new set of social issues. In addition to being younger than everyone else, I was bigger than many of them. Sometime between the ages of nine and thirteen, I had started to gain weight. I was shopping in the chubby section of the department store. To make matters worse, I was starting to have unpleasant encounters with people who disapproved of my size and didn't have a constructive way to talk about it.

I was about ten when another kid called me fat for the first time. That was when I realized that I was bigger than everyone else. When I was eleven I flew to Germany to visit my Aunt Judith for the summer.

"We're going to put you on a diet," she announced on the day I arrived.

"But I'm hungry," I pleaded.

"You're at my house now and there are different rules. You're not going to eat like back at home."

So Aunt Judith fed me grapefruit for breakfast every morning and watercress sandwiches for lunch. I wasn't allowed to eat snacks between meals, much less treats like the sweets I got from Nana and Grampsie. Needless to say, I stayed hungry.

That summer Aunt Judith's family and I traveled to a commune located in a large castle in southwestern France near the Pyrenees mountains. I had never heard of a commune before. It was filled with a whole lot of white people running around naked. And they served both meals with meat and ones with only fruits and vegetables. Aunt Judith told me I couldn't have meat, but I could eat anything I wanted off the vegetarian menu, which in her mind equaled "diet." I was very happy. Finally my stomach felt full.

Also when I was eleven, some kid on the playground noticed the stretch marks that had developed on my upper arms.

"EEEEEW!" he screamed at the top of his lungs, causing all the other kids to freeze in their tracks and look in his direction.

"What?" I asked, conscious that he was gawking at me.

"What's wrong with your arms?"

I grabbed my arms and studied them. My face felt as flushed and hot as I did.

"What are you talking about?"

"You have worms on your arms. Look!" he shouted. "You're nasty!"

The squiggly marks on my triceps that hadn't mattered a few moments ago suddenly became the source of tremendous shame. I ran home crying and put on a long-sleeved shirt. After that, I didn't wear short sleeves for years.

There were many other incidents like these—times when adults I didn't know would remark that I was bigger than my mother, or tell me what I should or shouldn't eat.

Between experiences like these and being younger than my classmates, I didn't feel ready for dating. Plus, who would want to ask me out when I had so many things wrong with me? But I listened intently to the older girls whenever they talked about boys—which was always. I knew they kissed and touched in different ways, and there were things they did in the dark. I didn't understand what they were talking about, but I knew I wanted a boyfriend one day.

I realized I wasn't cute like the other girls and I couldn't wear the same stylish clothing. *No one will ever want me because of how I look,* I thought. *But in the dark, you can't see the other person.* I decided the only way I could attract a boy was if I was very different. So in an attempt to flip my misfit status, I made a declaration to myself: I will wear clothes that float in the air like Flame Brathwaite's. Bells will ring when I walk. And I will always smell fantastic and have the very softest skin.

Who could have known that this declaration I made to myself in a moment of pain had the power to create my future?

My high school years flew by in the blink of an eye. During the summer between my sophomore and junior year, Daddy remarried. Some people at the wedding made biting comments about my weight. Afterward I went on a crash diet. I was so mad about being slighted that I didn't have a problem staying on it. My anger fortified my resolve to stick to the strict seven-day plan, which I repeated three times. Plus, I was determined to show Daddy what I had accomplished when he returned from his honeymoon.

That summer Gramps traveled to Trinidad. While there he fell gravely ill. Aunt Sylvia and Aunt Ruby had to fly down to bring him home. Upon returning to the States, he was sent straight to the hospital, where he was confined to bed. Nana, his children and grandchildren all tended to him.

Even though Gramps was not around to cast his magic that summer, I got to spend a lot of time with Nana, who was full of her own secrets and mysteries. One of them concerned my favorite confection—butter cake. Whenever I wanted to make one, Nana would pretend she didn't have the ingredients, though we both knew otherwise. This became a ritual we shared. I would come into the kitchen and scope out all the ingredients beforehand. Once I was sure that we had everything, I'd ask her if we could make a cake.

"No, I don't think we can do that today; I don't have enough eggs," she'd reply, as she continued with her current activity.

"Yes we do," I'd answer. "We need six eggs, right?"

"Yes, child."

"There are ten eggs in the refrigerator."

"Oh, but we don't have enough butter," she would answer. When I was younger, Nana tricked me with that response; she was often low on butter in the kitchen refrigerator. But as I grew older, I learned to check the freezer, which was always overflowing with everything.

"No, Nana," I'd respond. "I saw butter in the freezer."

"Are you sure?" she'd ask, with a twinkle in her eye. "Last time I checked, I thought we were out."

"Yes, Nana, I'm sure," I'd say, smiling. To this day I am uncertain about the exact reasons behind this little game. But it always happened before we baked that particular cake.

In the summer it was hard to get Nana to use the oven because it was so hot. But if you could convince her the night before, she would make the cake early the following morning. That way, the oven would be off before the high heat of the day.

We would set the butter out overnight on a plate to soften. When it was ready, we would cream it with the sugar, finding just the right balance between sweetness and grittiness. Then Nana would supervise as I cracked the eggs.

"Break them in separate bowls in case there's blood in the yolk. That way, you don't spoil the whole batter," she would say.

Carefully, one by one, the eggs were added to the butter and sugar mixture, changing its pale yellow color to a sunny hue; and after the eggs, the vanilla; and after the vanilla, the flour and milk, alternately. While Nana finished mixing the batter, I would grease a Bundt pan with Crisco and dust it lightly with Gold Medal flour. She would use a saucer to fold the batter into the pan. Then she would intentionally drop the pan on the table to break all the bubbles.

As the cake baked, the scents of vanilla, butter, and sugar would fill the kitchen. You could taste it even before it came out of the oven. I would imagine its perfection with a cup of tea; something else Nana made particularly well.

Even though I had spent the summer in Nana's kitchen, by the time September rolled around, I had lost twenty-one pounds. When junior year started I was able to wear jeans and other stylish clothes, rather than the shapeless, polyester clothes from the chubby shop. *Now that I look like the other kids, maybe I will even get a boyfriend,* I thought.

Unfortunately, my struggles with teachers continued. I used to feel humiliated in creative writing class on a regular basis. Not that the instructor meant it; I can't say with certainty that she was trying to pick on me. It may have just been the first time in a long time a teacher wasn't enamored of me. Or that I had encountered someone who was brutally honest, as she was about my work. I was certainly challenged academically, and I didn't know how to handle it. She constantly discussed topics I really didn't understand. I can't tell you how many times she read a paragraph out loud, explaining some idea that the other students seemed to comprehend, while I was left wondering where she got that. She also talked a lot about what was expected in college. I felt very intimidated, because all the smart, intense, white violinist types nodded their heads and seemed to understand what she was saying. I didn't. Remember, I was two years younger than most of my peers. I was also paying for the fact that as a child I had been taught to memorize things; I still hadn't learned to think for myself.

One day, our homework assignment was to write about being afraid. I chose to pen a story about being kidnapped. Well, apparently I didn't have all my facts straight and the teacher thought it was imperative that my mistakes be brought to the attention of the whole class.

"You wrote this story based on a movie, didn't you?" she inquired in front of everyone.

"Yes. . . ." I was getting the feeling this wasn't going to be a pleasant exchange. But I hadn't copied the storyline. I didn't understand what the problem was.

"One thing that good writers do is get their facts straight. You should have called a police station to find out how a kidnapping would really have happened instead of getting it from TV."

"I thought what I wrote is what happens. . . ."

"Well, your story isn't acceptable because that's not what takes place in real life."

I would have asked her what made her an expert on kidnappings, but I didn't have the courage.

"I'm sorry. I didn't mean—"

"When I was a child," she said, glaring directly at me, "I wanted to write a story about someone being locked in a closet. Do you know how I gathered my facts?"

"Nooo . . ."

Nana's Butter Cake

1 lb. of butter (Nana always preferred Land O Lakes)
2 cups of sugar
6–8 eggs, whole
1 tbsp. of vanilla
3 cups of flour (Nana's favorite: Gold Medal)
3 tbsp. baking powder
1 cup of milk

1. Soften butter. Nana always kept extra butter in the freezer, so she would place it on a plate and set it out on the kitchen counter overnight. If the butter is coming out of the refrigerator it may take about 2 hours to soften at room temperature. Note—do not melt the butter in the microwave!!

2. Grease and flour your cake pan. Nana's choice: Crisco shortening. Start with clean hands so that you can use your fingers to get the vegetable shortening into all of the corners of the pan. After you've done that, lightly sprinkle flour on top of the shortening. Do this over the sink, tapping the pan in your hand as you turn it. Turn pan upside down. The excess flour will fall into the sink and you will have an even distribution, with no caking.

3. Preheat your oven. You will be baking on the center tray at 350 degrees.

4. Mix ingredients. Of course, when Nana developed this recipe, she did everything by hand—no cake mixer. By the time she taught me, she would use a hand mixer as well as her wooden spoon. I have since made this in a freestanding mixer and it comes out fine, but keep the wooden spoon handy for ambience. The first thing to go into the mixing bowl is the butter. Add sugar and cream them together. When it's finished it resembles fluffy icing.

5. Add eggs. The number of eggs depends on their size. If you have extra large or jumbo eggs, use 6. If you have anything smaller, use 8. The eggs should be cracked one at a time in a separate bowl, and then added individually to the mixing bowl with the creamed butter and sugar. This way, if you have a bad egg it won't contaminate the others. Blend together until the mixture looks wet, but doesn't separate.

6. Add vanilla to the mixing bowl and blend for a few seconds.

7. Sift flour and baking powder together.

8. Measure out one cup of milk.

9. Add some of your flour and baking powder mix, add milk, then turn on your mixer. Alternately add the flour mixture and the milk a little at a time until it's all mixed into a thick, creamy cake batter.
10. Remove the bowl from the mixer. Nana always used a saucer to fold the cake mix into the pan. I suspect this had something to do with her arthritis and not wanting to drop the bowl full of batter. Whatever the reason, this method works great.
11. After you have folded the batter into the cake pan, hold your pan about a half inch above the table and let it drop. Repeat this a couple of times, to break any air bubbles.
12. Place in the oven for 60 minutes, and adhere to Nana's kitchen rules: No banging, no running and no jumping while it's in the oven. After 60 minutes, test it by inserting a tester stick into the center of the cake. If your tester stick comes up dry, and the cake is golden brown and your whole house smells sweet and warm, then it's done. If it isn't, you may just need another 10–15 minutes.

Suffice it to say, with a pound of butter and at least 6 eggs, this is not a low-cal, low-fat, or low-anything dessert. Eat with caution. Smile.

"I locked myself in a closet!"
Geez!

Early that semester Mommy told Philip and me that we would be moving into a new apartment at the end of October. We were thrilled because we would be living across the street from Mommy's brother, Uncle Ron, his wife, Aunt Norma, and their four children. We would inhabit two floors of a four-story brownstone and Philip and I would have our own bedrooms. The morning of the move, Philip and I were in our room packing when Mommy walked in with a somber look on her face.

"Grampsie died early this morning," she said.

"Are you all right?" Philip asked. I was thinking the same thing but was afraid of her answer.

"Well, of course I'm sad," she said, "but he was suffering and now I know he is at peace. I can't be too sad about that." With that my mother smiled at us and added, "Hurry up with your packing. Your uncles will be here with the truck soon."

Gramps had been sick for a long time. The family seemed to be prepared for the event. I don't remember a lot of crying. Several members of our extended family arrived to help with the move, as scheduled. The men loaded the boxes on and off the truck and the women helped my mother organize, clean the bathrooms, put fresh linen on the beds, and prepare food for us to eat.

But the next morning, Halloween, everything fell apart. We received a devastating phone call—Nana had collapsed in the shower. My mom, aunt and uncle, cousins, Philip, and I ran the five blocks down Lewis Avenue to her house on Van Buren.

When we arrived the scene was bedlam. Nana was lying in the bed with her eyes closed. Uncle Stan was yelling at a 911 operator to get someone quickly. Aunt Sylvia sobbed, "I want my mother, I want my mother, I want my mother," as Aunt Norma cradled her. *What is happening to my family?* I thought.

Several of my cousins and I were sent out to the store to buy food for the people coming over to pay their respects to Gramps. As we walked up and down DeKalb Avenue looking for stores that were open on Sunday, we convinced ourselves that all would be fine; that by the time we made it back to the house, they would tell us that Nana was okay.

When we returned home, everybody was quiet.

I asked Uncle Sonny, "How's Nana?" My uncle turned from me.

I asked again, "How's Nana?"

"Sit down," we were told. Our parents surrounded my cousins and me as we sat at the kitchen table. Someone's hands were on my shoulders. They weren't Mommy's. I could see her across the room holding Annette. I was getting frustrated because I wasn't getting an answer.

"How is Nana?"

"Nana didn't make it," Mommy answered. Upon hearing the news of our beloved Nana, my cousin started to wail. "No, no, no," and collapsed. I couldn't stop sobbing. My Nana was gone.

Once again, my mother was composed as she delivered such difficult words to those she loved. It wasn't until later that night, when she and Philip and I lay in her bed, that she began to cry and scream.

"I'm an orphan! You're all I have."

Philip and I held her until she fell asleep. But when she was in front of the family, she was the epitome of strength.

What followed was a week of being at Nana's house—viewings, the wake, the funeral and the endless parade of family members and friends. When the commotion died down and we all returned to our routines, I did everything I could to bond with Nana and Gramps. I ate extra oranges and tried to keep the skins in one piece when I peeled them. I hung the peels from the window in Mommy's kitchen. When I went to Nana's house, where Aunt Ruby and Uncle Stan continued to live, I sat in Nana's chair, stared at their pictures on the wall and sniffed her Chanel No. 5.

One day, I decided to make the butter cake. Maybe it could help to lift the intense sadness I was feeling. I asked Mommy if it was okay, and checked the fridge to make sure we had everything I needed—eggs, butter, flour and sugar, milk, vanilla and baking powder. They were all there.

I set the butter out on the stove to soften, just as Nana had shown me. Then I started weighing out the other ingredients as I remembered them. But things didn't turn out the way I planned. The first time I made the cake it came out flat and dense. The second time I made the cake it collapsed in the middle. The third time I tilted the pan when I was putting it in the oven. Batter spilled all over the oven door and dripped down the front of the stove. I slumped onto the kitchen floor, buried my face in my hands and cried and cried while the batter burned. How could I have forgotten? Mommy heard me bawling and came in to see what was wrong.

"I messed up the cake again. I can't get it right."

"Yes you can," she told me. "Just pray to Nana and ask her to help you. She will, you know."

I did what Mommy told me to do, but I did not have the courage to fail, yet again. I needed to wait and build up my confidence. My cousin Sharon and I baked chocolate chip cookies, oatmeal cookies and banana bread, all successfully. When she brought me a recipe for lemon butter cake that she saw in a magazine, it helped me remember Nana's mixture.

Later, it dawned on Mommy and me that Nana's measurements were based on her teacup, which was about 50 percent larger than a standard eight ounce cup. Now that I had been reminded of the recipe and understood the problem with the measurements, I tried baking again. Nana's butter cake came out just right and I was comforted by the warm smells of butter and vanilla. For that brief moment I felt that I had connected with my grandmother. She was in the kitchen with me, just like before.

Mourning the loss of both of my grandparents was a little too deep to share with the average high school junior. So now, even more so than before, my cousins were my friends. That is, until I met an art major named Lori. Before long, she and I became bosom buddies. She pulled me out of my depression and helped me reenter the world. That winter we ripped and roared back and forth between her townhouse near Central Park West and my home in Brooklyn. I had never met anyone like Lori before. She introduced me to the world of expensive tastes. One of her favorite places was Bloomingdale's. She was the first person I knew who paid fifty dollars for a pair of jeans—granted, they were Fioruccis, but fifty dollars was a fortune back in the mid seventies. Lori fit right in with my cousins, and we were as close as sisters. We braided each other's hair and put beads in it. We listened to music and talked on the phone. We laid out our clothes for the whole week and read *Right On!* magazine.

I finally had a friend in high school that was my age. It didn't matter that she was a freshman and I was a junior. We were fourteen. Hanging out with Lori I started feeling more confident.

"It's hot!" she said to me one unusually warm day in May. Then she gave me a quizzical look, her almond-shaped eyes squinting and her head tilting to the side like a curious puppy.

"Oh my God! I have never seen your arms! Why are you wearing a long-sleeved shirt? It's too hot."

"I'm okay. It's not that bad." I lied. I was sweltering. "Plus, I'm kind of shy. And I have these marks on my arms."

Lori grabbed my sleeves and pulled them up. She stared at my upper arms, then looked me straight in the eyes.

"That's nothing," she announced in a definitive voice.

That Christmas she bought me a burgundy chiffon blouse with cap sleeves. I wore it for New Year's Eve. I was cured.

Lori also cured me of my fear of singing in public. I loved my voice classes, and the skills I had developed over the past two years earned me a spot in the Solo Voice class. This meant I was first in line to audition for solos in our semiannual productions. That is, if I could get past the giant butterflies in my stomach that fluttered their way into my throat and made my otherwise dulcet tones quiver. Lori's remedy: singing on demand for her friends—in her house, in school, standing outside, anywhere. At first it was awful, but eventually I looked forward to it.

In the spring of 1977, the choir was to perform the *Carmina Burana.* My command performances for Lori gave me the courage to audition. I did not get the part I wanted. Because of my age and youthful appearance, my teacher picked me for another role—that of the virgin. Appropriately, I sang about being alone and dreaming of having a boyfriend.

The summer between my junior and senior year, Lori and I both worked—she in Bridgehampton, Long Island, and I in Manhattan. We got together on weekends, when I would go to the Hamptons and we would lie out and sun our bodies. Lori would take me to Sag Harbor, where all the boys were brown and beautiful. We became so close that Lori sat at the family table in April of my senior year, when Mommy married her second husband, Ken. Being fourteen and now the same age as many of the other students added to the fun of senior year. My classes were more enjoyable, too; they were more musical and creative than academic. I was able to take musical comedy and theater, solo voice and senior chorus. For the spring semiannual performance that year, Verdi's *Requiem,* I set my sights on and actually obtained the solo I wanted. It was a difficult piece that rose to an F above high C, accompanied only by the chorus. That meant that if I went off key, I would lead the choir out of tune, which would be disastrous. I practiced night and day. Fortunately, my hard work paid off. I received standing ovations from the chorus and orchestra during both my audition and the final rehearsal before the performance.

On the big night, my family took up almost two rows of the auditorium, hoping with bated breath that I'd hit the high F successfully. I did. My father was so proud. Had video cameras been as commonplace back then as they are now, there would be people sitting in his living room today in Jackson, Mississippi, listening to my performances. He was already known for bragging that I was studying Puccini and Verdi, but if he had caught it on tape, he would have gone over the top.

On the not-so-positive side, despite my obvious vocal talent, Daddy was hell-bent on me becoming a lawyer. To appease him, I applied, took the test for and was accepted into City College of New York's Urban Legal Studies program. It was an accelerated curriculum that culminated in a bachelor's degree and juris doctorate in six years, instead of the normal seven. This meant that had I completed the program successfully, I would have been a lawyer at the tender age of twenty-two. Can you imagine?

In my mind this would have been my backup plan, had no other university of merit accepted me. Fortunately, seventeen, including Judith's alma mater, the State University of New York at New Paltz, asked me to be a part of their graduating classes of 1982. Victory! I narrowed my choices down to a university in New Mexico and the University of Miami in Coral Gables, Florida, solely based on the fact that both were located in warm climates. When I found out that my buddy Dawnn was planning to attend the University of Miami, that cinched it. I was nervous about leaving home, but this made it better. Plus, Dawnn had been skipped forward in junior high, like me, so we were very close in age. We made plans to room together. She would major in drama and minor in voice. I would major in voice and minor in drama. It was all so perfect. That is, until Daddy intervened and put a kibosh on the whole thing.

"Why didn't you say that before I applied?" I cried.

"I'm sorry, baby. I know you're disappointed. I guess I just hadn't thought it through, but your mother and I feel you're too young to leave home."

Too young to leave home! Are you out of your mind!? Why did we go to the college fairs? Why did I read all of those brochures? Why did I fill out all of those applications? I wanted to scream these words out loud at my parents, but I knew better. We did not do that in my family. Instead I fumed. One negative thought after another filled my head as I listened to my dad lay out "The Plan." It was best for me to stay in New York, live at home, and attend City College.

"*City College!*" I wailed. "The law thing?" I had nothing personal against CCNY, but it wasn't Miami and it wasn't music.

Daddy apologized profusely, but no number of apologies could improve the situation. He went on to point out the value of having a law degree as my "safety net." "Just think," he said, "you will be twenty-two when you're done. You can take a break, go on all the auditions you want and if the music thing doesn't work out, you have that degree in your desk drawer."

"A law degree! I don't want to be a *lawyer*, Daddy. I want to be a *singer!*"

"You can, Lisa. You can do both."

There would be no University of Miami. That was the final word.

I knew that Daddy wanted only the best for me, but I was bitterly disappointed. The fantasies that I had about singing professionally began to become foggy and fade. I would not avenge Diana Ross's stolen Oscar after all.

Yet a part of me was secretly relieved by my father's decision. I really didn't want to leave my family and friends behind. And since it wasn't in my nature to disobey or figure out how to go to Miami on my own, I tried to persuade myself that becoming a lawyer was a good choice and that I could become a singer later. There was only one problem: my spirit wasn't convinced.

My girlfriend, Dawnn Lewis, graduating class of 1982, University of Miami at Coral Gables, went on to become an accomplished actress, singer, composer and star of the popular television sitcom "A Different World." Greg Louganis, of the same class, made his country proud by winning Olympic gold medals. Lisa Hairston attended CCNY's Urban Legal Studies program and flunked out in less than a year.

CHAPTER 5

Good Morning,
Heartache

*During this period in my life I studied Ausar Auset, a pan-African religion
that focuses its attention on the practice of Khamitians, another name
for the ancient Egyptians. I also changed my name to Khoret Amen Tera,
which came to me during meditation. My family wasn't pleased.*

The words embarrassment and shame don't even begin to describe
what it was like to fail for the first time—and in such a big way. I went
from being Miss Perfect, the one everybody in the family talked about, to
being the one they were ashamed to mention. I had started college out on
a good foot, but by the second semester I was forced to withdraw from several
classes to avoid receiving Fs. I became very depressed. The only class I
looked forward to showing up for was African dance, which I took during

my sophomore year. Described in the school's curriculum as a lecture course, it turned out to be a master dance class. I learned that despite my size, I could move, and move well. I was flexible, I was graceful—all the things fat girls aren't supposed to be. The class had a unique smell that I loved, the smell of bodies gyrating and muscles stretching and moving. In that course I was also introduced to many aspects of African culture that fascinated me—head wraps, fabrics, colors, oils—and I met many wonderful people who are still in my life today.

I stretched the boundaries of my world even further with new clothing, new scents, new friends and a new lifestyle. But even though I was seventeen and a sophomore in college, I still had not had a boyfriend. Several one-sided romances and one brief encounter in a closet at a Christmas party, where I learned that, yes, I can tongue kiss, had gone nowhere. I was eager to fall in love.

On a subway train on my way home from Lori's one Sunday afternoon, I met a man who liked me. With my new, bohemian, slightly Afrocentric look, a more toned body and a dancer's flair, I was no longer the shy little girl I used to be. So when I noticed this fine brother with green eyes trying to catch my attention from across the car, I didn't look away; I looked back. I later found out that he noticed the colorful beads that covered one braid in my hair as I was standing on the subway platform. My style of differentiating myself from everyone else had worked. Our glances turned into a couple of smiles. Eventually he stood up, came over and held onto the strap above me. The scent of frankincense hovered above me like an aromatic umbrella.

"I don't mean to be too forward and I know how this sounds, but do I know you from somewhere?"

"I don't know," I answered, "but I was kind of thinking the same thing."

"My name's Manuel," he said, smiling.

"I'm Lisa."

"Nice to meet you." We were quiet for a moment. "I'm trying to think where I know you from."

"I don't know," I answered. "I take this train a lot. . . ."

"Really? You live in the city?"

"No, Brooklyn. I was visiting my girlfriend, Lori."

"What part of Brooklyn?"

"Bedford-Stuyvesant."

"Oh, okay." It was quiet for a moment. I wondered what he was thinking about.

"Where do you live?" I asked, happy that I had found a way to move the conversation forward.

"Uptown—155 Street."

"Oh. Are you in college?"

"I was, but I'm not right now. How about you?"

"I go to City College."

"Really? My old high school is right around the corner from there."

"That's my old high school! You went to Music & Art?"

"*That's* where I know you from. I knew I knew your face. What year were you?"

"'78?"

"Oh, okay, I graduated in '76. I was a couple of years ahead of you." My heart sank. He would probably think I was too young for him. "So when I was a senior, you would have been a . . ."

"Sophomore."

"Yeah, sophomore, right. . . ." He frowned like he was thinking of something. "I wonder if we had classes together. Did you take any painting classes?"

"No. I was a voice major."

"Oh, a singer! Wow! So am I standing near the next Chaka Kahn?"

I just smiled. I hoped I wasn't staring at his eyes too much. His gaze fixated me, and he had a very warm smile.

"Ohmygoodness! This is my stop. I gotta get off," he said.

"Oh . . ." My heart skipped a beat. He was going to leave and we would never get together.

"Give me your number and I'll call you," he said as he inched toward the door.

"I don't have a pen or paper."

"Just tell me," he begged, now standing between the open subway doors. "Hurry up!"

Much to my surprise I blurted out my phone number.

He repeated it, stepping onto the platform.

"Yes. That's it," I shouted, as the doors closed.

He repeated it through the window of the train. I nodded to let him know he had gotten it right. As the train pulled off, I watched him mouthing the numbers and wondered if I'd ever see him again. His scent lingered in the air around me. Later he called and regaled me with stories of running through the streets of Manhattan repeating my phone number like a mantra until he found pen and paper. We had so many things in common. He was a dancer—an African dancer! We shared stories about dance classes we had taken. Needless to say, I was captivated.

Our first date—my first ever!—took place one week later. We went ice skating at the outdoor rink in Central Park. The rink was filled with couples, it was cold and sparkling white Christmas lights were up. Manuel and I could barely skate, so we held each other's hands. He put his arm around me. His cheek rubbed against mine. I noticed he smelled good—clean, just out of the shower. I felt like we were a real boyfriend and girlfriend. We kissed. I was just smitten.

In spite of my head-over-heels fascination with my green-eyed demigod, my mother was not impressed. Mommy didn't like his overalls. She thought they were something to paint or lay Sheetrock in, not for taking her only daughter out on her first date. I tried to tell her that they were the style, but she wasn't having it.

Manuel was Panamanian. I liked the fact that his family was from a foreign country, just as mine was. He was also a vegetarian. One day he asked me if I was interested. I became vegetarian, too. Manuel also practiced Yoruba, a West African religion. Of course, my traditional Episcopalian family thought his beliefs were witchcraft.

Daddy's opinions of Manuel were formed by what Mommy told him over the phone. By now he had moved to Washington, D.C., to attend Antioch law school. He became a long-distance peacemaker between Mommy and me. I was surprised by how much Mommy didn't like Manuel. She thought he was a bad influence. Her perspective was confirmed when I told her that I didn't want to go back to school for the following semester. She assumed it was his idea.

"As long as you're under my roof, you are going to college."

I didn't want to hurt her. But I was too afraid of becoming depressed again to risk taking those awful classes.

"If you feel that way," Manuel offered, "why don't you live with me?"

"You live with your mother," I replied.

"You have a job. I have a job. Maybe we could get a place," was his response. *Could it be that simple?*

I was scared of the idea of living with a man, but felt like he was coming to my rescue. I couldn't go back to hating my classes pretending to be happy. Before long, Mommy and I fought, and I moved out. We didn't speak for five weeks. It was the longest I had gone without being in touch with my family and the only time we experienced that much conflict.

One day she called and asked me to come over.

"I feel horribly and miss you terribly," she admitted. "And you're too young to be living with a man. Please come home. We can work out the school thing."

"I love you and I miss you, too, Mommy," I replied. "But I'm not a little girl anymore. I'm already living with a man. I know it's only been about a month, but I can't leave him."

Mommy and I repaired our relationship, but agreed to disagree about Manuel. I continued to live with him. She, in the meantime, opened her home to the first of many children she would adopt. Little Aerol entered our lives in early 1981. Many of my most joy-filled moments were spent helping to care for him.

Unfortunately, I didn't experience such bliss when I spent time with Manuel. It's hard for me to think of happy occasions with him other than our earliest encounters. There were so many things that were wrong from the start. But because of my inexperience, I didn't know they were problematic. I thought we were in love and working our differences out. I didn't understand that love doesn't chip away at your spirit. I don't think it's an understatement to say that we were doomed from the start.

Together we became vegans, traveled to Senegal and danced. Manuel continued painting and studying African dance. While learning more about being vegan, he stumbled upon a group of Afrocentric black Americans in Harlem who studied ancient Egyptian (they called it Khamitian) culture and taught such practices as vegetarianism, fasting, chanting, and meditation. We began taking classes. Eventually, the courses and the place where they were held, "The Space," became known as The Ausar Auset Society. Ausar Auset is a pan-African religion that focuses its attention on the practice of the Khamitians. Khamit is the original name for the land of Egypt. It means land of the black man. Today, some of the ideas taught in Ausar Auset are considered very enlightened. But back then, most people didn't know much about them. All my family knew was that what I was studying wasn't Christian; therefore, it must be the work of the devil. Today, of course, many scholars recognize that many spiritual practices of ancient Egypt were incorporated into modern Christianity. Some even say that Jesus studied in Egypt during the years he was absent from the Bible.

Meditating, chanting, and deep breathing were practices I really came to enjoy. I also liked learning that we all have a direct line of communication to God. I was comforted to discover that God speaks to each of us in different ways—through meditation, dreams, visions; you don't need an intermediary. But the founders stressed that you had to learn how to quiet and still your mind and body so that Spirit could talk to you.

When I first started meditating, I kept a journal of what I experienced. At first I had a hard time stilling my mind. I would obsess about my problems or think of things I had forgotten to do. After a while I began to hear a woman's voice in my head and would stop to write down what she said. Over the years I recorded messages, sketches, patterns for clothing, ways to wear my hair, jewelry designs—all sorts of information. Sometimes an older female, who I believed to be an ancestor, would come to me in spirit form.

Once, when I meditated, the voice said a name to me: "*Khoret Amen Tera. All that is, was, and ever shall be stems from Amen [God], is Amen and is becoming Amen. Tera—the light energies of Ra, which powers the sun and the Son. Those who walk with Amen and Ra shall be self-realized. This is who you are.*" With that, I changed my name. My family wasn't pleased.

Manuel and I were married when I was twenty. It seemed like the logical thing to do. I was young, inexperienced, and thought no one else would ever want me—no one had desired me before and I didn't see how that would change. He was my first boyfriend, the first man I dated, the first person I had sex with, and we were living together. The way I looked at it, not marrying him somehow invalidated all that we had. I loved him, I knew he loved me, and I thought that was enough.

The ceremony consisted of a group wedding with twenty-one other couples, the first of many such weddings I would witness in Ausar Auset. Most of my family did not attend, and even my mother could not endure the five-hour ritual. Despite all the chanting and dancing and prayer that joined us in matrimony, I was never truly happy and couldn't figure out what wasn't right, what was missing. There were times when this man I once found tremendously loving could be just as tremendously insensitive, cruel and demeaning. He was constantly unhappy, he was constantly angry, and I couldn't understand why.

No matter how hard I tried to please Manuel, I could do nothing right. If the apartment was too hot, of course it was my fault. The toast was always burnt. The lights were too bright. Clothes I had just taken out of the dryer were still a little damp. He was always criticizing me and chipping away at my spirit. Eventually he started calling me names. Unfortunately, at the time I didn't equate this with abuse.

It wasn't until we started to hang out with Sule and Vanessa, another young married couple in our circle, that I saw all that was missing in my marriage. Manuel and Sule often danced at the same events. Sule was a very talented dancer, and handsome. Vanessa had a very fair complexion, a thick mane of black hair and a smile that actually made her eyes twinkle. They seemed nice and they were young. Everyone in Ausar Auset was so much older than we were. I longed to have friends, but I was too shy to approach them. She and I would wave or smile at each other from across the room.

One day I invited them to a surprise party I was throwing for Manuel's birthday. There, Vanessa and I talked about everything. To my surprise I found out that Vanessa was funny as hell.

Why haven't we ever talked before? I wondered.

After that, we started getting together regularly. Manuel and I would dine at their house and they would come to ours. As we talked, Sule's fascination with Ausar Auset grew. Before long, they began to attend classes. I learned a lot from hanging around them. Sule and Vanessa laughed and joked, and were attentive to each other. Manuel was always acting sullen. They were affectionate. We weren't. They went to the movies together. Manuel and I never went out. Sule was able to tend to himself. I was always jumping up to get something for Manuel.

One day we all went to the beach together. I rubbed suntan oil on Manuel's back, shoulders and the backs of his legs. As he lay basking in the sun, I proceeded, quite awkwardly, to apply suntan oil to my own body. Manuel did not move—hell, he hadn't even said "Thank you." I flapped my arms about, slapping as much oil as I could on my shoulders, oblivious to how ridiculous the situation was. This was just how my life was and unfortunately, I accepted it. Later, I found out that Sule wanted to put the oil on for me, but felt it inappropriate. He and Vanessa were also curious to see how long Manuel would lay there, ignoring me. It was all afternoon.

Khoret's Magic Lotion

This recipe is from the days before I knew how to make lotions and creams on the stove. It is a result of my own concocting as well as a trade secret another sister shared with me. I wore it on my wedding day and later used it to transform my mood when I wasn't feeling so wonderful. It leaves your skin feeling and smelling edible, sexy, and delish!

3.5 oz. *of your favorite unscented cream or lotion*
1 tsp. *cherry fragrance oil*
¼ oz. *Shalimar-type fragrance oil*

1. Into an empty 4 oz. bottle, pour in slightly less than 3 oz. of an unscented lotion. You may also use a jar, and unscented cream instead of lotion.
2. To this, add 1 tablespoon of cherry and 1 oz. of Shalimar-type fragrance oil.
3. If you are using lotion, shake your mixture thoroughly. If you are using cream, stir gently to incorporate oils.
4. This is an all-over body perfume; a fragrance, not a moisturizer. So first moisturize your body after your bath or shower. Then rub this on all over, except on your face. (I don't recommend that fragrance oils ever be put on your face.) After you've applied your magic lotion, be still for a few moments and inhale your own loveliness.

Eventually Manuel stopped hanging out with us as much. He would break our dates, but I continued to spend time with Vanessa and Sule. They laughed. They were fun. I enjoyed their company. I watched them play with one another while preparing a meal. They threw food. They played good music. They sang to each other. There was light at their house. I had been living in darkness for so long, I forgot what the light felt like. *Dear God, what have I done with my life?* Rather than be honest with myself and answer that question, I chose to soak it all up, to gather all the light and joy that I could from these two precious people. They became my salvation.

Manuel's temper and mouth not only affected our marriage, but also got us kicked out of our apartment. Fortunately, Mommy came to the rescue and we moved into her newly vacant fourth-floor apartment. I felt safer, but things continued to deteriorate, to the point that he wouldn't come home after working his graveyard shift at a nursing home. He said he wanted to hang out in the Village. I didn't care. I was relieved; I wouldn't have to see him or be subjected to his daily laundry list of complaints about me or our home.

One night Manuel and I argued and he called me a fat pig. That was the straw that broke the camel's back. I couldn't take it anymore. I called Vanessa and Sule's house bawling my eyes out. Once I calmed down, Vanessa said, "I don't know if this is the most sensitive thing to say, but all I can say is thank God! I thought you liked your situation."

"You see it, too?" I thought I had hidden things pretty well. Now that I knew my cover was blown, I poured my heart out to them.

"You need to find out what he's running away from, Khoret," Sule advised.

"Don't let him get away with saying mean things to make you cry. That's his escape. Stand up to him." Vanessa was right. So what if he called me a fat pig? He had called me worse and I was still here to talk about it.

Manuel couldn't handle our confrontations once I stopped running away and crying. His verbal abuse didn't deter my resolve to make him talk to me. One day he flipped out and ran toward me across our living room with his arms extended, screaming. I thought he was going to choke me. I grabbed my keys and ran down two flights of stairs.

"What are you going to do, Khoret—tell them I tried to hurt you? I was going to hug you." I barely heard his words as I rushed out of my home. Once in the street I kept running for blocks. I'd taken a lot of shit from him, but I'd be damned if becoming a battered wife was going to be my next experience.

I went straight to Vanessa and Sule, to where it was safe, to where there was peace. They told me it would all work out and set me up in the living room for the night. I slept soundly. The next morning I did not want to arise from my perfect slumber but I was pulled back to the physical realm by a voice, and the smells of cinnamon, vanilla, and peaches.

"Khoret Amen Tera, wake up," the voice called.

It was Sule. I smiled. I was safe. "Okay. I'm up," I answered as I stretched.

I could tell from the scent in the air that Sule was making oat groats, my favorite breakfast. It was never just oats; he always added peaches or mangoes or apples, and they always tasted delicious. I looked at the clock and saw how late it was. Vanessa was already gone and I knew Sule had to get to work soon. I washed up, brushed my teeth and got dressed. I went back to where I had been sleeping to fold up my bedding. As I was putting away the sheets, Sule and I passed each other in the hall.

What was that? There was an energy between us. To this day, I can't describe it exactly, but it caused both of us to jump. I looked at him and was instantly terrified. I left the house quickly. There would be no oats today.

What was that feeling? Am I falling in love with a married man? I wondered. *I can't do that. I'm already married. Vanessa is like a sister to me. This is insane.* I wanted to banish the thoughts from my head, but they would not go away. I had to admit I was falling in love. Polygamy was an acceptable practice in Ausar Auset. Several of my friends had made the nontraditional choice to enter into a polygamous relationship, and they seemed happy. I argued with myself—one part of me acknowledging how unhappy I was and that perhaps a polygamous marriage to Sule and Vanessa could solve all of my problems; the other part rejecting that option. I can't walk out of one life and into another just because I am unhappy.

Later that day Sule called me from work.

"Khoret, we have to talk about what happened this morning."

"Nothing happened, Sule. There is nothing to talk about."

I was embarrassed. In fact, part of me is still embarrassed about it. Sule, being the stubborn man he was, made me talk. He made me give voice to the torment I had experienced that day. I had fallen in love with one of my best friends and he was in love with me. It just so happened that he was someone else's husband and that "someone else" was also dear to me—not to mention the fact he worshiped the ground she walked on. He and I talked about our feelings and the craziness of it all. It took a couple of days for us to discuss it with Vanessa. I was terrified that first she'd kill me and then never be my friend again. The latter scared me more than anything.

Vanessa, being the wise woman she is, did not flip out. She simply made it clear that she was not interested in polygamy at this time and did not know that she ever would be. But she didn't want to expel me from their lives. She needed to know that we would respect her, and we did. The three of us continued to be friends.

During the next month, Manuel and I sought counseling. Before long, he stopped going. Now that I had been attracted to another man, I no longer felt compelled to make things work with him. I reached the conclusion that our marriage wasn't going to last. I told Mommy that I was going to ask him to leave. She promised the apartment to my cousin Karen.

"You have to move out," I told him.

"Well, what about you?"

"I'm not going with you."

Manuel broke down and started crying and apologizing. He was confused about our relationship and didn't know what to do. He said no one had ever loved him the way I loved him.

"Please don't make me leave, Khoret," he begged. "I'll do anything you want."

I felt the need to rescue him. Falling in love with Sule made me feel guilty, and perhaps I believed that sticking with Manuel was my penance. I decided to let him stay. As I held him, his tears wet my skin and I thought, *Maybe we will love again.*

With our apartment now spoken for, we would have to move into a bedroom in Mommy's house, which Manuel didn't like. We didn't have money to move someplace else, though. Plus, the way things were going, I wasn't leaving the safety of Mommy's home.

The final straw came on the day my mother found chicken blood and feathers all over our bedroom. Without my knowledge, Manuel had called his Yoruba godfather to "purify" the room. Manuel was supposed to have left Yoruba behind a long, long time ago, and here he was disrespecting my mother's home. I was humiliated and furious.

"Lisa, he has to go," Mommy announced. She wanted him gone as quickly as possible. Later, my aunts swooped in and doused the place with holy water.

"I can't live with you like this," I told him. "But I'm not going anyplace with you either. We have to separate."

"What are you trying to say, Khoret?"

"Our marriage is over."

Manuel took off his wedding band, and rifled it at me. Then he stormed out of the house. The next day he left a suicide note at Vanessa's job before overdosing on No-Doz. Some friends found him wandering around Prospect Park a few hours later. He stayed in the hospital for a couple of days. I think he then went to stay with his mother—all I knew was he wasn't staying with me.

When he called again to get his stuff, Mommy advised, "He's not stable, so let him take what he needs."

"But Mommy, these wedding presents were given to both of us."

"These are just things, Lisa," she stated firmly. "Let's just get him in and out of here so you can get on with your life."

"But Mommy this isn't fair. I bought this," I retorted as I held up my new citrus juicer.

"Lisa, he is acting crazy. You will get new things. Let him take what he wants and let him go!" There was no arguing with Carol when she spoke in that tone.

When Manuel came by to pick things up he was very petty.

"This is mine," he said as he dropped a stapler into a box.

"This is mine," he announced, picking up a pencil.

"This is mine," he repeated, picking up a ninety-nine cent cactus.

The entire situation was very stressful. Boy, was it a relief when the whole thing was over. I didn't cry for a couple of weeks, but when I did I really cried. The sadness just bubbled up from somewhere deep down in my gut. Although I had the wherewithal to get out of my marriage, a lot of damage was done in that one year's time. I had allowed myself to be mentally and verbally abused. I didn't understand how important it is to protect your spirit at all costs. At the time, I believed the bad things he had been saying about me. It would take years for me to undo the damage, and also realize the importance of guarding your soul.

But Manuel, it turns out, wasn't crazy—just confused. Years later he would admit to me that after our marriage he realized that he was bisexual.

Oat Groats

You will find oat groats or steel-cut oats at health food stores or large supermarkets in the health foods aisle. These oats differ from the rolled oats you get in the grocery store; an oat groat is the whole oat grain before it's rolled into the oat flake used to make oatmeal. Because they haven't been processed, oat groats contain more fiber.

1. Bring 4 cups of water to a boil. Before it boils add 1 pat of soy margarine (butter is fine if you don't do soy).
2. Once boiling, add 1 cup of steel-cut oats. Lower flame. Cover, and stir often.
3. Once your mixture has thickened and all the water has boiled off, remove from heat.
4. Add 1 teaspoon of vanilla, 2 dashes of cinnamon and a sliced, fresh peach (pit removed).
5. Stir, add honey to taste and serve.

He apologized for all that had happened between us. Sule, Vanessa and I remained very much in love, as a nonsexual threesome, for about two years. They would always be one of the most important loves of my life. In my mind, they saved my life. Losing my husband at such a young age and in such a confusing way could have damaged me forever. Their love cushioned the blow, and gave me many good memories to outweigh the bad ones from my marriage. Then one day, they pushed me out into the world to experience life on my own. They knew what I didn't—that I no longer needed them as a security blanket to protect me from life's ups and downs. Thankfully, we're still friends today. But at that moment, without them standing beside me, I was nervous about my future and uncertain about what life had to offer. It was the first time that it was just me. I was on my own.

Man-Mourning Ritual #1; or How to Wash That Man Right Out of Your Locs

First things first: This is not about male-bashing. We will not be listing all of the reasons you feel men are dogs. This is about *you,* and identifying what attributes inside of you drew you to this person.

WHAT YOU'LL NEED:

1 sage smudge stick (it's for burning, not cooking); or 1 white candle
1 pink candle
Patchouli or sandalwood soap, body wash or essential oil
Almond oil

1. Start by burning sage, which has cleansing properties. Please be careful. If you are not familiar with the practice of burning sage, use a white candle, again exercising caution when dealing with an open flame.
2. As you inhale the sage or stare into your white candle identify why you were drawn to this person. Sometimes we attract exactly what we need to bring something out in ourselves that forces us to grow. When we resist evolving, our spirit often says, "Next!" The Universe works its wisdom and circumstances arise that cause the person to leave us. Our lesson must be brought to us another way, but we may not want to accept it. Instead we say, "He's a dog. Why did he leave?"
3. Put out your sage or white candle and light a pink candle. Or simply close your eyes and imagine a pink light. Send the person love, not animosity. You cannot grow, pray or ask God to help you if you hold hate in your heart. Your heart must be light as a feather. Send him pink light and love so that he can grow from where he is now. Now it's time to focus on you. Send the light to yourself. See yourself bathed in a beautiful pink light. Feel love for yourself. Remind yourself that if you can't love you, how can anyone else? And if you don't, who will?
4. Wash your body with sandalwood and patchouli. You may be able to find soap or body wash already scented with these oils. If not, buy the essential oils from a health food store and drop them onto a bar of soap before you wash. As you cleanse your body, allow yourself to move on. Let go of the past. Literally wash him, or her, off of your skin and out of your hair. Let the negativity flow off of you and down the drain.

5. Once your body is clean, pour a jasmine bath over your head and down your whole body (see recipe below).
6. Meditate as you air dry. This is a ritual you may need to do a few times. Observe your emotions each time you do it. You may need to meditate on being able to forgive or move on or send love. As you pray, ask to see more clearly and choose better in the future. Ask for the lesson you are to learn from this experience to be revealed.
7. Massage your body with almond oil (see recipe below).
8. Blow out your pink candle.

Jasmine Bath

14 drops of jasmine fragrance oil; or 7 drops of jasmine absolute
28 oz. of spring water; or 14 oz. of jasmine tea and 14 oz. of spring water

1. Blend oil and water together, shake, and it's ready to be used in the recipe above.

Almond Massage Oil

2 oz. of sweet almond oil
8 drops of bitter almond essential oil

1. Pour into a bottle, shake, and it's ready to use in the recipe above.

CHAPTER 6

Searching for My Self

I called myself Topaz when I was in the musical group Fedora.
I had spent all my life playing by the rules and doing what other people told me.
For once, it was going to be all about me.

Being on my own had its pros and cons. Mostly cons. But as the saying goes: That which does not kill you makes you stronger. Like many single people, I had to learn how to go out to dinner alone, go for a walk in the park alone and go to the movies alone. It wasn't easy. It wasn't fun, either.

One Sunday I found myself at a theater in Greenwich Village watching *Purple Rain*. I had listened to Prince in the late seventies but hadn't heard any of his music since "I Wanna Be Your Lover." Watching the movie, I experienced the antithesis of everything in my Ausar Auset lifestyle. I meditated. I wore specific colors on certain days to correspond to spiritual energies. I was a vegan—the list of things I didn't eat was longer than the list of things I could. I didn't go to parties. I didn't do drugs. Now I was watching a movie that was oozing sex and rock and roll. It was a really big reminder of things that were missing in my life. I was in my early twenties, after all.

I was so enthralled by *Purple Rain* that I stayed for a second showing. Afterward, I purchased all of Prince's music I had missed between 1978 and 1985, and have been a Prince fan ever since. Well, not a real fan. I never rimmed my eyes with black eyeliner or wore poet shirts with ruffled fronts or donned lace gloves with the fingers cut out. But I was definitely hooked on his music.

In the late seventies and early eighties, Prince was a bit of a rocker type. No one listened to that kind of music in the religious circles I was in. But after Manuel and I split, I began to push the envelope. When he and I had been together, I didn't buy my clothes; I sewed them to keep him happy and stick to the "budget." In Ausar Auset, women wearing pants was frowned upon, so I didn't wear them. But after Manuel and I ended, I started to become less rigid and less Afrocentric.

The worlds of American popular culture and Ausar Auset were as different as night and day and incompatible as oil and water. Most people in the society believed that the American system of values was undermining the well-being of black people, their families and communities, even the planet. The "wild, wild West" was what they called Western culture. In their minds an Eastern way of life—the East, in their worldview, includes Africa—was superior.

I agreed with them to some extent. I knew that many aspects of American life were unhealthy and destructive. This was the 1980s. Large numbers of people were snorting cocaine when they went clubbing, which is the environment I would have been in. Who knows what I would have been exposed to. Remember, people didn't consider coke dangerous back then, they thought it was "recreational"; folks were just starting to have problems with it. Some people were using crack, although quietly at first. And AIDS was spreading. There was definitely a stability and sense of peace that came with my lifestyle. But I was growing tired of the discipline and sacrifice. I started feeling like I was back in Nazi kindergarten.

At first I didn't want to admit how deep this conflict was, because I was close to so many people in the community and believed in many of the teachings. I also felt like I had messed up again because the huge life-change I thought was so right for me was turning out to be so wrong. Rather than walk away from Ausar Auset, I dabbled in both worlds, trying to figure out the balance between "Eastern" and "Western" cultures, but deep down inside I knew that one day I would have to choose.

Despite my spiritual and lifestyle dilemma, my working life was going fine. Just before my marriage ended, I began a temporary work assignment with the United Nations. I was hired as a messenger and eventually brought on full-time. Being at the United Nations was like entering a world within a world. People work and visit from all over the globe, creating great diversity not only in language and physical appearance, but also in style of dress.

For the first time in my adult life, I wasn't always being stared at. Having an Afrocentric look wasn't as common back then as it is now. Many people disapproved of my braids, beads and, when I chose to don it, my ethnic style of dress. And if they didn't disapprove they gawked. But at the United Nations people dressed in apparel from around the world. I was no longer a freak of nature. For the first time in my life I completely fit in, from the braids on the top of my head to the sandals on my feet. My self-confidence was boosted. I was in a place that accepted me for me—"wild, wild West" me and "Eastern" me.

While working at the U.N., I made friends with people from all over the globe. We laughed, enjoyed ethnic food and learned how to pronounce each other's names. I learned Spanish while I worked there. My colleagues taught me Portuguese as well as Togalog, a Philippine dialect. I learned that family customs and responsibilities varied widely from culture to culture. I was particularly impressed by the resourcefulness of women around the world, which inspires me to this day. For instance, the East Indian women I met turned their checks over to their husbands, who controlled family finances. However, they would sell crafts to make their own money and maintain their independence. And people used loans they took out from the U.N. credit union, which did not appear on their credit report, to supplement traditional banks loans. They used the money to start businesses—restaurants, travel agencies, catering companies—while they were still employed full-time. Working entrepreneurs were all around me.

It was while working at the U.N. that I learned how to shop on credit. Now that I was making good money—$15,000 plus overtime was a lot compared to what my peers were making, especially since I didn't have a college degree—I indulged my shopping jones at Bloomingdale's. After depriving myself for three years to satisfy Manuel, every time I walked into the store I was overcome with the desire to spend. Combined with credit cards that kept coming in the mail, that was like putting gasoline to a flaming match. I was too inexperienced to understand the implications of running up a lot of bills.

My shopping trips to Bloomingdale's helped me to push my East-West boundaries even further, and the East was losing. I took out my braids and blow-dried my hair straight. I wore pants more often and I bought designer perfumes. In Ausar Auset fragrance was another way of bringing the energy of the gods close to you. I was supposed to wear a scent that corresponded to the energy of the day. But when I purchased perfumes, I didn't always know the exact blend of fragrances and I didn't care. I trusted my instincts. If it felt right to me, I wore it.

Before long, the battle between the two worlds started playing itself out in my mind. Rather than hearing the voice of my ancestor during meditation, Prince would talk to me. He would also show up in my dreams. Fortunately, my spiritual studies in Ausar Auset had taught me to listen to my intuition and dreams no matter how unusual they were. I knew that ideas in your subconscious could be represented by symbols and images. For example, your spirit may choose to send you a message through some kind of image it knows you'll pay attention to.

My subconscious chose Prince to be one of my messengers. My higher self knew that the more earthbound part of me would listen to whatever he had to tell me. One day after I started dating again, I got dumped by a guy who went back to his old girlfriend. I was at work crying when I put the new Prince cassette into my Walkman. The next thing I knew I was singing along: You need another lover like you need a hole in yo' head. It was as if it had been written just for me. It became my theme song as well as my mantra.

Prince also made appearances to deliver meaningful insights about my life. Once, I experienced a waking dream where Prince walked into my bedroom.

"Why are you in Ausar Auset?" he asked.

"I don't know," I answered. "I love the people and I've learned so much."

"Yeah, Khoret," he said. "But it's about time for you to leave."

"I can't. Who would I be without it? And how could I leave all my friends?"

"What do you mean, 'Who would you be'? You'd be yourself. Who else do you need?"

"What about my friends?"

"Friends are very important, Lisa, but this is a box. There's so much more to life than you've experienced here."

"Yeah, I know, but . . ."

"You think this is magic," he said, pointing to the altar I had created on my mantle. "There is so much more than this. You were meant to do more. You have to go out and live your life."

Another time I dreamed that I was at dance rehearsal at Ausar Auset. Prince was criticizing what we were doing. The next day I saw his new music video for the first time. He was wearing the exact same clothes he had been wearing in my dream. This happened on several different occasions. I knew that I was divining something.

Early in the summer of 1986, I participated in a wedding at Ausar Auset. While I was watching the ceremony, I felt my chest and throat began to tighten. All of a sudden I couldn't breathe. The words "get out, get out" echoed in my head, just like in the movie *Amityville Horror.* I tried to ignore it, but breathing became more difficult and the voices got louder and louder. I took this as a sign that I should leave. I got up abruptly in the middle of the service and ran outside to get some air. Out on the street I could breathe again. I started walking and didn't turn back. Later on there were times when I returned to Ausar Auset, but it never was the same. I was no longer in it or of it.

During that time I started hanging out with my cousin Sharon and a college friend of hers, Delliah. Delliah—Dee, we called her—was very beautiful and was studying to be an actress. One of Sharon's talents was that she had confidence for days. She was also a very big thinker. Sharon believed that Prince should see Dee so that he could cast her in one of his movies. A group of us decided to see him in concert that August. While Dee and the rest of us were watching the show, Sharon worked her magic to get us backstage. She wasn't successful, but she did manage to get us invited to a private after-party. There Dee met Prince, but it was she and Jerome Benton of the group Morris Day and the Time who hit if off. He invited her to Minneapolis to celebrate his birthday. Who knows if he was joking, but she took him seriously. Several of us tagged along for the ride.

True to her big-thinking ways, Sharon thought that as long as we were going to be in the company of famous musicians we should be prepared with some music. On the day I walked out of Ausar Auset, Sharon asked me to come over to give Dee a voice lesson. But once Sharon heard us singing together, she got an even better idea: The song that I was to teach Dee, we would sing together.

Sharon had heard in music circles that producers were looking for female singers. Exposé was burning up the charts and En Vogue hadn't been discovered yet, so the girl-group category was wide open. Taylor, a friend of Dee's from Brooklyn, was invited to join us, and the three of us started rehearsing. I was the only one with formal voice training and had the strongest voice, so I helped coach the others. Dee could carry a tune all right, plus she had an exotic appearance—blonde hair and hazel eyes— that was popular at the time. Taylor wasn't much of a singer, but she could dance and she had that eighties look—lots of makeup and big hair—but in a good way. Together, we figured we had what it took.

Ausar Auset behind me, I decided to take the chance. I had spent all my life playing by the rules and doing what other people told me. I was sick of being practical and doing what I was "supposed" to. For once, it was going to be all about me. I was going to Minneapolis no matter what it took. So I joined a group that was basically a lie and charged up an airline ticket I couldn't afford. Obviously, this wasn't a wise choice.

A couple of weeks later we all flew to Minneapolis. Upon our arrival Jerome took us to his brother's studio. Little did we know his brother was Terry Lewis—as in the producers Jimmy Jam and Terry Lewis! Panic began to set in. *What if they ask us to audition?* It was bad enough that we had lied and said we were a group, but we had barely rehearsed.

We did everything we could to try to keep from singing. We literally had put our coats on before Terry Lewis sat back, put his feet on the desk and said, "Why don't you sing a little something for us before you leave?"

We crooned "Good Morning, Heartache," as best we could. We each took a verse, but except for the last lines—Good morning, heartache/Sit down—we never sang in unison. They were very kind to us; it was obvious we had never practiced harmonizing before. We were clearly not the group we had represented ourselves to be.

"Y'all need some work because you don't blend," Terry said when we finished. Then he looked me right in the eye: "But *you* have a voice. *You* can sing!"

Needless to say I was on cloud nine, although I had to play it off in front of the group. Also my ecstasy was tempered because I was embarrassed by our miserable performance. As we walked out of the studio on that freezing cold night, Delliah, Taylor and I resolved to come back and knock them on their butts. Terry was right, we needed some work.

Still, there was light at the end of the tunnel—a big light! When we returned to Brooklyn, we were on a mission. We were going to be the latest and greatest black girl-group sensation. But when word got back to Taylor's mother, Esther, that Terry Lewis had said I could sing, it became a bone of contention that she kept picking at. It didn't matter much at first, since Sharon was our manager. But eventually Esther convinced the other group members that she had certain connections and resources that made her better for that job. Sharon remained our manager in title only and Esther became our agent and called all of the shots.

As the idea of making it in the music industry gelled in my mind, I made a vow that I wouldn't allow my dreams of being a vocalist to escape me again. I felt like I had been given a second chance. I decided to do everything in my power to make my singing career happen. I would work during the day, and network, get gigs and be in the studio at night, I promised myself.

Fortunately, my job as a messenger was easy, attendance policies at the U.N. were liberal, and you could even get extra days off. All you had to do was say your back was hurting. Everybody did it and even though I knew it was wrong to lie, I justified it because it was such a common practice. I started going to clubs, concerts and music industry functions at night, networking with everyone I could. Anytime I stayed up too late, I'd call out in the morning. I did the same anytime I had a daytime performance or had to travel with the group. Since I was still living at home, Mommy would witness how much I was missing work. She wasn't very happy about all the lies I was telling. Even though she supported the idea of me singing as long as I had a steady paycheck, she thought I needed to slow my roll.

"Don't you think this music business is getting a little out of hand?" she asked me one morning.

"No," I lied. "Everything is fine. I have to do this. I have to try."

"But you are not acting like yourself. Why are you wearing makeup? It's ten-thirty in the morning."

"I know, but I am trying to get better at applying it. I always have to ask Delliah to do my makeup."

"Lisa, you don't need it. Your skin is fine."

"Mommy, you just don't understand."
"No, I don't, and I don't want to."

One time and against her better judgment, my mother forged an absence note from the doctor's office she worked in to keep me in good standing at the U.N. That gave me the bright idea of making copies of the letterhead she wrote the note on. Unbeknownst to her I started forging doctor's notes whenever I thought I needed them. I know it sounds horrible, but on some levels it was no big deal; work was slow—I often spent time reading or crocheting—and nobody really cared as long as the mail got delivered. *You gotta do what you gotta do to get ahead,* I told myself.

Over the next year we rehearsed regularly. With Esther's assistance we trademarked a name for ourselves—Fedora. We ordered head shots, had a letterhead made up, set up a corporation, a press kit—the whole nine yards. We also honed our image. We decided we should be sexy but classy, but that started to be a problem. Even though Esther told me how much she liked my hair and what a pretty face I had, she never missed an opportunity to say how much better I would look if I were thinner. Her hints were subtle but effective. I tried to fit in and lose weight, but it was difficult. I would never be a size six like Dee and Taylor. I am naturally large-boned.

I stayed on a diet but I wasn't always successful. Esther just thought I was lazy and didn't have any willpower. My weight wasn't the only thing she harped on. She was very smart and knew how to identify and exploit your weaknesses quickly. I had already changed my hair; I was wearing it long and straight. But Esther thought it would be better if we all got weaves. She had a way about her that would make you feel it was all your fault if you didn't do something and the group failed.

She also made me look like an idiot on more than one occasion. For instance, if we were going to a concert I might call Esther to talk about our attire.

"How are we dressing tonight?" I would ask.

"Oh, casual. Nothing fancy. I think Taylor is going to wear jeans."

"So if I wear my blue WilliWear pantsuit, a pink T-shirt and flats, that will be all right?"

"Oh, that should be fine."

I would arrive to find Dee and Taylor dressed up in ultrafeminine wear—cinched up, cleavage, tons of makeup, and big hair. I looked like their lesbian bodyguard.

"I thought you guys were wearing jeans."

"Jeans? Who said that?"

Later I learned that when I arrived Esther trashed me to them behind my back. "You're not going to believe what she has on," I was told she said. "She looks horrible."

The more Esther took swipes at me and made me feel small, the more steps I took to change who I was. I was accustomed to things being wrong with me. I was a square peg trying to squeeze myself into a round hole. I tried to conform to an industry that didn't value people who look like me. Once I relented to taking out my braids, getting my hair relaxed and getting hair weaves, I became detached from the part of myself that at one time I really liked.

In one attempt to fit in, I decided to change my name. For years I was known as Topaz in the music industry. In my imagination Topaz was slimmer, prettier, sexier and more fashionable than either Lisa or Khoret Amen Tera. But in spite of the diets, hair weaves and name changes, nothing I did could make me the right size. Nor could it make Esther like me. I wasn't aware of it at the time, but she continued to screw me over. In December of 1986, I hit my head on a car door and got a concussion. We had been invited to a party at Eddie Murphy's house for New Year's. Well, I thought "we" had been invited. Later I discovered that she only RSVPed for Dee and Taylor.

"Well, I wouldn't be able to go with this concussion anyway." I tried not to sound hurt, but I was devastated. "Tell them I said to have fun."

"I sure will, sweetie," she purred. "You get better now."

While I was in Fedora I started playing things fast and loose. The balances on my charge cards soared higher and higher. I charged perfume, costumes, relaxers and hair weaves, furniture and stereo equipment. At some point I ran my bills up so high that I couldn't keep up with them. I was forced to obtain a debt consolidation loan so I could make my payments. Of course that just flagged me as creditworthy—or naive or foolish—in some financial institution's computer. Next thing I knew, I was getting more credit cards. So I ran them up again.

I knew that this didn't feel right; it wasn't how Mommy had raised me. But I had tasted life as an average person, going back and forth to a regimented job every day and watching TV at night. It was horrible compared to my fantasy of being a singer. I didn't want to live like that again. *This is my one and only chance to live my dreams,* I told myself. *I have to go for it.* I knew I was wrong to keep spending money; I just didn't know another way to get what I wanted. My credit situation was closing in on me and I knew it.

I also started going out more, handling Fedora business during the day and calling out from work relatively frequently. My first bosses at the U.N. weren't sticklers for attendance. Most of the time they left you alone as long as everyone got their mail and didn't complain. But in December of 1986, they hired a new supervisor from the U.S. Postal Service and he was whipping things into shape. He wanted to eliminate some of the layers of supervisors, so he really ran a tight ship. The first thing he did was make us wear uniforms. That way everyone knew who we were and what we were supposed to be doing, which made it difficult to say hi to my friends around the building. He also doubled the number of mail runs we had to make each day.

One morning when I arrived at work, I was sent straight to the office of the medical director of the entire United Nations. I didn't know the medical director, but I did know that the U.N. has a medical department. You could get X-rayed there or even see an ob/gyn.

"Lisa, please have a seat," he told me when I walked into the room.

"Okay," I answered nervously. I wasn't sure why I was there.

"How's your back?" he asked, looking over the top of his black half glasses.

"It's okaaay . . .," I answered. I was starting to feel like this was a trap.

"Funny, Dr. Goines said he didn't remember you having back problems. . . ."

"Huh?"

"I mean that I called Dr. Goines. It is Dr. Goines who excused you from work, isn't it?"

"Yeeess . . . I don't understand what you mean."

Shit!

"Well, he didn't know what I was talking about either. He said he didn't write these notes excusing you from work. What do you have to say about that?"

There was nothing I could say. I was very ashamed; I had lied and now

I was busted. It was as simple as that. Thankfully, he allowed me to resign instead of firing me. With U.N. policy, that meant that my record would be clean. All they would say about me was that I had resigned.

I walked to the lobby and collapsed in a phone booth. I was mortified. I cried and cried. I called Esther. I didn't yet understand that she was not to be trusted. She told me not to worry and that I would have the last laugh when we were a success. I called Dr. Goines to apologize. I was so embarrassed. He had been one of our family's doctors for years.

"I wish you had told me, Lisa. I could have covered for you, but I didn't know. . . ."

I couldn't believe he was being so nice. *My God! What have I done?*

"I'm so sorry. I was desperate and did something stupid. I'm so ashamed of myself!"

"Oh, don't worry about it. It's just that I was caught off guard when they called," he continued. "I didn't know what to say."

"You shouldn't have had to say anything that wasn't true," I said. "Will you do me a favor and please let me explain it to Mommy? She's not going to be very happy and I'd rather that she hear it from me."

"Of course," he said. "I won't say anything about it. I'm just so sorry that you lost your job."

To this day, he has never said another word to me about it.

When I got off the phone with Dr. Goines, I mustered up the courage to go back to the Medical Director's office. I knew he wasn't going to give me my job back, but I needed him to know how sorry I was and that I had truly loved it at the U.N. I had only myself to blame. This was my responsibility. I had lost the only job I'd ever loved. And now all I wanted to do was turn back the clock so I could fix things. He was very gracious. He wished me luck with my music, and I felt a little better. If, financially, things weren't bad enough before, now I was in deep doo-doo.

It took a couple of weeks, but I got another temping assignment. This time I wasn't making anywhere near as much money as I had been at the U.N. Money was too tight to mention. My phone bill and my rent to Mommy were the only things that got paid—barely.

I was still struggling to make Fedora work. But I had started to feel convinced that Esther had it in for me. I couldn't quite put my finger on it, but I always felt bad energy when I was around her. I really, really wanted a record deal, and to become a star, so I ignored my gut instinct that something was wrong and tried to stay focused on making it.

One day I went to the hair salon to get a touch-up. At that time I had my hair permed, and I had stopped wearing the weave. I had new growth and wanted my hair trimmed so the style would be more controlled. Unfortunately, the hairdresser didn't understand exactly what I had in mind, so she cut off a lot more hair than I wanted. Now I had a hairstyle I didn't feel like I could do anything with, and styling my hair wasn't something I was good at. With all the pressures that had been building up, I felt like this was the last straw. I came back to my room and really started stressing out.

Oh my God, what am I going to do? There's no way anyone will want me in the group with my hair looking like this. I'm not going to look good enough and I'll screw things up for everyone.

Looking back, I think I suffered a nervous breakdown that day. I picked up scissors and cut off even more hair. I cried and cursed myself in the mirror.

"You're ugly. You're a fat pig," I repeated to myself in the mirror over and over again. It didn't take long before I messed my hair up even more. Now there was really nothing I could do with it and everyone would see what I had done.

Rather than enduring more emotional abuse from Esther I decided not to go to rehearsal that night. I just couldn't take all the pressure anymore. Instead of going to practice, I wanted to sit in my room in the dark. I didn't answer the phone.

When the other girls stopped by a couple of hours later to pick me up for rehearsal, I didn't answer the door.

"Topaz, come to the door."

I didn't respond.

"What's going on?"

Silence.

"What's wrong, Topaz? Open up the door and let us in."

I still refused to answer.

"Topaz!" they continued to yell from the street. "We can see the light from your TV. Open up the door."

I shut off the TV.

"Very funny."

Nothing.

"Fine, Topaz, if that's how you want to be, we're leaving."

I heard Dee say, "No, I'm going up there."

And Taylor, who was angry with me, said, "No, let's go. If she wants to stay up there, let her."

With that, they left. Finally.

I just couldn't face them. I felt lost, like things were coming unraveled. I didn't know who I was or what I was doing with my life anymore. I prayed, but I wasn't sure to whom I was praying. I wasn't really Christian anymore and I wasn't practicing the ways of the "East" either. So I asked for help from the sky. *Help me. I don't know what to do.*

I sat in the dark watching TV all night. In the morning I felt a little better. I made an appointment at another beauty parlor to see if they could help fix the mess. Thank goodness for that hairdresser. When I walked out of the salon, my hair actually didn't look too bad. It was very short, but it had a great shape. All of the relaxer had been cut out and I was left with my curls. The style grew on me. I liked it. It made me look at my face and be okay with me.

Relaxing Lavender, Oatmeal & Rose Bath Tea

6 tbsp. lavender herb
4 tbsp. chamomile
5 tbsp. rose petals
3 tbsp. marigolds
3 tbsp. oatmeal

1. Blend the herbs in a bowl. I like to use my hands.
2. If desired, drizzle essential and/or fragrance oils of your choice over the herbs and flowers and mix with your hands.
3. Spoon into ready-to-use muslin bags or store in a jar.
4. Toss the muslin bag into your bath or attach it to your showerhead. You may opt to float in a field of flowers, but I warn you—you could clog your drain and cleaning is not easy or fun.
5. You can blend any herbs you like. In researching the various properties of herbs you may decide to try a different blend, but the directions will remain the same.
6. You can accent your bath by adding sea salt, powdered milk, honey or a complementing bath oil.

That afternoon, I decided to go to our voice lesson and face the music, so to speak. Dee and Taylor refused to speak to me the whole time. I knew they hated my hair. Our vocal coach, Maria, loved it. Maria sensed all of the tension between us and spoke with me privately. She told me that I was the only singer in the group. "Without you, there is no group. Do you understand that? You are its talent." Maria reminded me of my strengths, and for once I did not feel the need to defend my sister group members. I had hurt myself so badly my spirit needed some encouragement, so I let Maria continue. "Don't ever let anyone tell you that you can't do this. Out of all of them, you can stand alone and make it."

During this summer of my discontent, Delliah's niece was in town and hanging out with us. One day Dee was driving me home and told me we needed to talk. Apparently her niece had noticed Esther telling Dee one thing and me another. She brought it to Delliah's attention. Dee and I started to compare notes.

"Topaz, do you remember that time when Eddie Murphy invited us to that party on New Year's Eve?" she asked.

"Yeah . . ."

"Why didn't you come?"

"I was flat on my back with a splitting headache from my concussion. Didn't Esther tell you?"

"A concussion? I knew you had hit your head, but I didn't know you were that bad."

"The doctors were so worried about me, Philip had to stay up and talk to me all night so I wouldn't fall asleep and die!" I shared. "Why did Esther tell you I wasn't there?"

"She said you didn't feel like coming."

"That I didn't feel like coming!" I was shocked.

"Yeah, Topaz. She was really mad because you were shirking your responsibilities."

"Shirking my responsibilities?!"

"That's what she said."

"Aw, hell no. That's a lie! I can't believe she said that."

"Oh, man, Topaz. I'm so embarrassed; I believed her. And I was kind of mad at you."

"No, Dee! I would have killed to be there. But you know what? She told me I hadn't been invited. She said the invitation was for just the two of you."

"What? That is a lie from the pit of hell! Oh my God."

"I felt bad that I was hurt and didn't know how to bring it up with you guys." We were both quiet for a while. This was all so amazing.

"Topaz?"

"Yeah?"

"Can I ask you something else?"

"Yeah."

"What happened that day you cut your hair off? Were you going to kill yourself?"

"*No!* I was upset and depressed, but I never once thought about hurting myself. What makes you ask me that?"

Dee hung her head and sighed. "When you wouldn't come to rehearsal that night, Esther told us you were depressed and suicidal, and to prepare ourselves because you were going to kill yourself."

"She said *what?*"

"She said that you had all these problems and issues and were too fragile to be in this business. Then she said you were going to kill yourself."

"Man, Dee, how could she say that?"

"But you know what was deep, girl? When she was telling us all this stuff, I felt like your spirit walked into the room, because all of a sudden Esther whirled around like someone was standing there and then she stopped talking. It was deep, girl."

Dee and I sat in the car for hours that night exchanging stories, feeling stupid and naive, and apologizing to each other. We realized that Esther had been playing us against each other the whole time she was managing us. It also dawned on us that when we agreed to make Esther our manager, we had helped her sabotage Sharon without even knowing it. We were all getting played. Dee and I both agreed that we still cared deeply for Taylor, but vowed to keep her mother at a distance.

It was embarrassing to admit to myself that perhaps my desire to succeed and become famous had blinded me to what was happening—not that it would ever have occurred to me to suspect Esther of the dastardly things she was doing. But Sharon, Dee, and I were good, good friends. There was no way that someone we didn't know should have been able to drive a wedge between us. We shouldn't have needed a person from outside the group to point this out to us. But Esther had kept the three of us in a box—our own little world. We couldn't see how many things were wrong until we started interacting with other people and they started pointing them out to us. It felt kind of spooky that someone was able to get so close to me that I would believe her, rather than questioning the negative things she was saying about my friends. Perhaps I overlooked these characteristics because I felt like I was close to achieving my dreams. Thank goodness for Dee's niece. We never would have figured things out if it hadn't been for her.

Now that we were hip to Esther's nasty little games, the next couple of months proved interesting, to say the least. Riding in the car on the way to appear on the "Joe Franklin Show," a late-night TV talk show that featured local talent, we stumbled onto the fact she had rewritten our bios. They each used to be about the same length, but now Taylor's was much longer than either Dee's or mine. Dee discovered that work she had done in college was now included under Taylor's name. I realized that even though I was twenty-five, and Dee and Taylor were twenty-two, they were listed as being twenty and twenty-one, while my bio now said that I was twenty-six!

Two days before our performance at Sweetwater's, a cabaret club near Lincoln Center, I informed Dee that I couldn't take it anymore. I had to quit. Sweetwater's would be my last show. Everyone was feeling good about things that night. Our performance was solid, and our backup band, One Blu Shu, was fantastic. On top of that, a few days before the show, Roger, the bass player, had started to flirt with me. But I had vowed that I was going to quit, and I kept my promise. I phoned Esther a few days later to tell her. That's when she showed her true colors.

"I always knew you were trouble. You will never amount to anything in life. You don't have the guts. You're *nothing*, you stupid girl," she hollered at the top of her lungs. "Do you hear me, you're *nothing*!"

"Well if I'm nothing, you should be happy to be rid of me."

"I never should have trusted you or let you be in the group in the first place."

"Let *me* be in the group? Let *me* be in the group? If I remember correctly, we were forming a group before you even arrived on the scene."

"You'll never amount to *anything*! You're *street*!"

I had too much good home-training to stoop down to her level. In her defense, she had spent a lot of time and money on us. I was causing it all to fall apart and for that I was sorry. But there was no other choice.

"Good-bye, good luck, and thank you," I said, then hung up the phone.

I felt relieved to be out of Fedora, but for a long time I felt like I had just wasted two years of my life. And I felt responsible that I had allowed somebody like that into my world. *What is it about me?* I wondered. *Am I a bad judge of character? What made me give another person that kind of power over me?* It didn't help that I had lost a great job and destroyed my finances and my reputation at the U.N. in the process.

At least I have a good friend out of it, I thought, reflecting on my relationship with Delliah. I also stayed in touch with Bert, the leader of One Blue Shu, and later would do studio work and sing background vocals for them. I hadn't give up on my aspirations to sing. Fedora couldn't take that away from me. No one could.

$\mathcal{F}acing\ the\ \mathcal{M}usic$

The expression on my face pretty much says it all.
Here I am sitting miserably in a room surrounded by things that I cannot afford.

The sound of the telephone ringing beside my head woke me up from my nap. It was August of 1987, five months after I had been fired from my job at the U.N. Since then, I had worked a bunch of temporary assignments, but none of them paid as well or were as cool as the U.N. And temp assignments were just that—temporary—which left me searching for new jobs before too long. After my most recent assignment ended, I applied for a bunch of gigs and had even asked for help from a friend with connections at an employment agency. Someone had to be hiring, and I didn't want to stay away from home for too long because I didn't want to miss the call.

"Hello?" I answered with enthusiasm.

"Hi, I'm looking for Lisa Hairston," responded a cheerful, female voice.

"Who's calling?"

"Is she available?"

Shoot! This person sounded more like a bill collector than an employer. But I had to be careful; I didn't want to let on that I had credit problems to someone who might want to hire me.

"May I ask who's calling, please?"

"Are you Lisa?" That gave it away.

"Who wants to know?"

"I'm Mrs. Haynes calling with some important information for her. You're Lisa, right?"

"No, Lisa's not here."

"Oh, I thought you might be Lisa."

"Well, you thought wrong."

I hung up, but two minutes later the phone rang again. With my employment situation as it was, I didn't dare not answer.

"Hello?"

"Lisa?" *Dang, they're persistent!* "I told you she's not here." Click.

I was depressed, so I rolled back over and went to sleep. A couple of hours later I woke up again to call some more temp agencies. But when I picked up the phone I didn't get a dial tone. I jiggled the hang-up button a couple of times and checked to make sure the plug was in the outlet. Then I remembered getting a disconnection notice earlier in the week.

"Oh, no!" I moaned, flopping down onto my couch. *Don't I have enough going wrong?* The last thing I needed was another problem.

My eyes got hot with tears and embarrassing scenes flashed across my mind: I'd have to ask my mother if it was okay for people to call me on her phone, and my friends would find out that I couldn't pay my bills.

As I wallowed in self-pity, I heard my cousin Michael's footsteps as he trotted downstairs and down the hall in the direction of my bedroom. Michael was my cousin Karen's son and, ever since Manuel and I split, they had been living in the upstairs apartment.

"Hey, Lee," he said, sticking his head in my room.

I tried my best to blink back my tears and smile at him, but I couldn't get it together in time. Of course, he noticed.

"You all right?" he asked. I didn't answer—I would have, but I couldn't. I was really close to all of my cousins and we were all about the same age, except Michael, who was eight years younger than me and felt like a little brother. Michael looked up to me and since we lived in the same house, he spent a lot of afternoons hanging out in my room. Deep down inside, knowing that my room was his chill-out spot made me feel grown-up and cool. Now I was in tears because I didn't have sixty-six dollars. Real cool, huh?

"What's wrong?" Michael insisted.

I was ashamed to tell him the truth even though he was bound to find out. As close as everybody was, there weren't many secrets in our house.

"My phone got cut off because I don't have sixty-six dollars to pay my bill," I admitted.

"Oh." There was so much concern in his face for someone so young. He was always a child ahead of his years, and right now I felt as if he had a few years on me.

The floodgates burst and I started to cry. "Nothing's going right," I sobbed. "I can't believe I've been so stupid."

Michael sat still and listened as I told him how much financial pressure I was under. Then he gave me a hug, told me he'd be back in a minute and headed upstairs. As I watched him leave I dried my eyes and looked around my room—my beautiful room—at all the things I had bought on credit: a queen-size platform bed covered in a paisley Egyptian-cotton comforter in shades of lavender, blue, and celery; an oatmeal-colored designer sofa from Bloomingdale's; an expensive stereo system whose interest charges were still being paid now, two years after I bought it; a TV and VCR from the local rental center. I looked at how empty the top of my dresser had become. One or two perfume bottles now stood where once there had been a veritable smorgasbord of designer fragrances—all courtesy of my Bloomie's card. I thought about the tickets I had charged to fly to Minneapolis, costumes I had purchased to perform in and concert tickets I had bought hoping to get backstage to network my way into a recording contract. Buying things I could not afford left me feeling empty in a room full of material possessions.

A few moments later Michael reappeared.

"Got something for you," he said, upbeat and smiling.

"What is it?"

He dug his hand deep into his pants pocket, pulled out a big wad of money and held it in front of my nose. For a brief second I thought I caught a whiff of freedom.

"What's that?" I asked, trying not to sound too excited.

"Your sixty-six dollars."

"Where'd you get it from?"

"I had it in my room."

Oh, great! Michael was trying to make me feel better, but now I felt even smaller. My sixteen-year-old cousin had more money in his piggy bank than I had in my bank account. And it wasn't like he was handing it to me in quarters and ones!

"Michael, I don't want your money," I lied.

"Just take it so you can get your phone turned on."

If the circumstances had been different, I would have insisted, but I knew that this was not the time to be proud. I needed money desperately, even if it came from someone I used to baby-sit.

"Okay, Michael. Thank you *so* much." I almost hugged the life out of him.

"You don't even have to pay me back!"

Good thing, I thought. *I can't.*

On that day, accepting money from my teenaged cousin, I thought I had hit rock bottom. I couldn't imagine that things would go from bad to worse.

A couple of months before I quit Fedora, I started having a relationship with a brother named Dennis. Dennis made music videos and came around the group from time to time. I can't remember what attracted me to him because it didn't take long for my feelings to fizzle. I imagine that had something to do with the fact that he didn't want to be seen with me in public. Yes, that's right. He thought it was bad for his image to be seen with someone who was overweight.

If I had been feeling better about myself, I would have sent him packing. But I already felt bad about my size, so I accepted that slap in the face just like I had taken everyone else's criticism of my weight. He would come over to visit me and we would watch my cable TV. I would cook and sometimes I would wash and twist his hair. But he never even did so much as bring over a container of orange juice. What a fool I was to let someone do this to me. I was getting tired of the relationship but I still hung in there until he did not show up for a performance—a performance he promised me he would tape. No call. No show.

So, when Roger, One Blu Shu's bass player, started flirting with me, I flirted back. I thought I'd make Dennis a little jealous. It wasn't the smartest thing to do—especially since Dennis wasn't around to see it. I did it anyhow.

Following my last show with Fedora, Roger and I started to hang out as friends. After a while I figured it would be better to be with him than someone who didn't want to be seen with me. We became more romantic and confided in each other. One day he told me he had a health problem and was on some medication that made him sterile. One thing led to another and eventually I slept with him. I think we had sex all of two times, and the second time barely happened. Certain things about his personality had started to make me uncomfortable. I quickly regretted becoming involved with him.

One afternoon while I was taking a shower, I heard the phone ringing in my bedroom. I ran down the hall to pick it up. Out of breath, I answered.

"Hello?"

"Who the hell is there with you?" a voice on the other end demanded.

"What? Who is this?"

"Who's there with you?"

"Roger? What are you talking about?"

"Why are you huffing and puffing? Who are you with?"

"I don't know what you're talking about."

"You're out of breath and it took you a long time to answer the phone."

"And you think that's because I have a man in here?"

"What the hell am I supposed to think?"

"You know what? You're an idiot," I shouted. "You have never been here to my home and you have no idea where rooms are located and where my phone is in relation to those rooms. I ran from the bathroom to get to the phone in time, stupid. This is ridiculous and I will not be interrogated in my home by a fool while I'm in a towel, freezing. Good-bye!"

With that I hung up the phone.

"Crazy-ass motherfucker," I mumbled to myself. I returned to the bathroom as the phone rang again. It continued for at least five minutes. I didn't want to talk to him again; however, the Universe had something different in mind.

On the morning of Christmas Eve, I went out to do some last-minute holiday shopping. On my way home, I stopped at the drugstore to pick up a pregnancy test kit. My period was going on two weeks late. My period was never this late. When I got home I stood in the bathroom watching the pregnancy test strip turn blue.

Shit!

"I think you need to have a talk with your doctor," I told Roger over the phone. "Evidently your medication isn't working."

"What are you trying to say?"

"What do you think I'm trying to say? I'm pregnant."

"Oh, that's just fucking great," he replied. "That just makes my muthafuckin' day. As a matter of fact it makes my muthafuckin' year. So, what do you want from me now?"

What do I want him to do now? Die, I thought, but that seemed too kind.

"I am not calling you to ask you for anything," I told him. "I am simply informing you that the medicine that supposedly has the side effect of making you sterile and which makes you feel comfortable going around having sex with women with no thought to birth control is not foolproof. You needed to know this so that you may discuss it with your physician. I will handle my business. Merry Christmas."

I was vulnerable, alone, and feeling stupid. But it was also Christmas Eve and Mommy's turn to host the family dinner. She needed my help. I had allowed Fedora to become so all-consuming that I hadn't been as involved with my family as I usually was. Philip had moved to Mississippi to go to college near my father, and was now home for the holidays. Christian, a three-week-old brown butterball who was the latest addition to our home, was keeping Mommy up at night. He missed nary a feeding. I had a wonderful family. I did not want to think about Roger or my pregnancy now. It was Christmas and I wanted to be happy, even if it was a lie.

Out of the corner of my eye I noticed a movement in the doorway of my bedroom. It was my brother Aerol, who was now six years old.

Oh my God. Did he hear me?

"Hi," he said.

"Hi, sweetie."

I was embarrassed. I loved Aerol to death, but hadn't been spending much time with him either. It was hard to believe that six years had gone by since Mommy and her husband, Ken, had adopted this angel. I couldn't believe how tall he was. He seemed to have shot up overnight.

"Is there something wrong? I thought I heard you crying," he queried, still standing in the doorway.

"There's nothing wrong. Come here, Habib," I said. We jokingly called him that or sometimes Pedro. With his brown complexion and jet-black, wavy hair, his look was somewhere between African-American, East Indian and Latino. He gave me a big hug. Aerol loved to hang out in my room as much as Michael did. He had already told me that it was going to be his when I moved. He had claimed my bed, my television, and everything, except he couldn't get the details quite straight—he called my Fisher stereo a "Fisher-Price."

Aerol sat with me for a few moments. I smelled his hair.

"Did Mommy just wash your hair? It smells good."

"Yeah, last night, but I got soap in my eyes. It hurt."

"Oh, poor baby."

I kissed his nose and tickled him. He smiled at me and laughed and squirmed to get away.

"Get on downstairs. Mom's going to have dinner ready soon, right?"

"Oh, yeah. I was supposed to tell you that. Are you going to eat?"

"Tell Mom I'll be down soon."

"Okay."

And with that he bounced on down to supper.

Over the holidays I immersed myself in my family and reflected on my life. Everything was going wrong. I was beyond broke. Now I had gotten myself into this situation. I hurt so bad. I replayed my earlier conversations with Roger over and over in my mind. *Why in the world did he tell me he's sterile,* I wondered. *We were at the kitchen table when he told me. It's not like we were about to have sex. What did he get out of that?* The raging hormones of pregnancy did not help my emotional state. The need to be held had my mind playing out scenarios that were based in fantasy and desperation. I needed to decide what to do.

"Maybe Roger and I can work things out," one part of me considered.

"Yeah, right," the other side replied. "He lied and he's acting crazier and crazier."

"But I should at least try; she needs her father in her life." (I was convinced my child was a girl.)

"Try! He's not giving you much to work with."

"Well, maybe Roger and I don't have to be together. Maybe we can live apart, but have some kind of relationship for her sake."

"He'll be in and out of her life. Can't you see that?"

"Maybe having a new baby will make him get his act together. . . ."

"Yeah, but even if he eventually does, what kind of example can you set for your daughter when you're so messed up yourself? What do you have to offer her? And how are you going to turn your *own* life around?"

I racked my brain searching for an answer, but I didn't have a response to that question.

I wanted to talk to my mother, but didn't want to burden her. I just couldn't imagine myself sitting down in front of her saying, "Guess what? I screwed up again." The only time she had met Roger I could tell she wasn't feeling him. She said there was something about his appearance that reminded her of a roach. From then on, that's how she referred to him.

I realized that I would have to figure things out for myself. In the coming weeks I thought about the state of my life. I was living in Mommy's home. Her husband, Ken, was constantly yelling at me. Even though I was paying rent and doing household chores, in his eyes I couldn't do anything right. If I didn't do my chores on his unspoken timetable, he would start berating me. I didn't want my daughter to see her mother treated like that.

By January I still hadn't decided what I was going to do. I didn't want to have an abortion. I would never tell another woman how to handle an unplanned pregnancy, but terminating mine didn't feel right to me. So I started asking Mommy if I could care for Christian at night. I thought it would give me an idea of what it was like to wake up and feed a baby several times a night. It also made me consider how I would care for my own child. I would have to go back to work. That meant I would have to impose on Mommy to care for my baby. She already had physical challenges with her own health, and now she had two small children of her own, Aerol and Christian.

The more I tried to figure out how I could make a decent life for my baby, the more I realized I didn't know how. It was bad enough that I was pregnant by a jerk, but I felt I had nothing to offer a child. I was a mess. I couldn't see the tunnel, let alone the light at the end of it.

After weeks of indecision I realized that this was something I couldn't solve by myself. It was time to have a talk with a higher power. I was a little out of practice. I had allowed my life to get so busy I hadn't really meditated regularly since I left Ausar Auset. Unfortunately, when I bolted away from that part of my life, I discarded many really valuable practices. With all the confusion swirling through my head, I knew it was time to return to them. I needed to slow down and listen to my inner wisdom. So I put on some quiet music, lit my jasmine incense, burned a white candle for clarity, and sat patiently on my bed.

In the beginning my mind raced with memories, judgments, angry conversations, things I would have/could have/should have done. But after a while, my thoughts calmed down and for the first time in a long time, I heard my inner voice. It sounded as clear and beautiful as a church bell ringing on a crisp winter day.

How can you be a mother now? Look at your life.

After hearing those words, the confusion lifted. Several days later I made an appointment at the clinic. But I didn't really want to have an abortion, so I kept listening for word that I should change my mind.

Word never came.

What did come was more clarity. And what I discovered about myself wasn't always pretty. I was angry with myself for putting myself in the position where I was pregnant by someone I didn't love.

What was the point of sleeping with him? I demanded of myself. I worked to hold myself to a higher standard. In my attempt to make one idiot jealous, I slept with another idiot, and in the end only succeeded in making a fool out of myself.

The more I examined what I had done, the more the truth hurt. But I was determined to learn the lesson because I didn't want to be in this much pain ever again. I prayed for forgiveness. I wrote in my journal for hours at a time, peeling back the layers of my life and trying to figure out what had gone wrong. All my life, I had allowed other people's opinions of me to dictate how I felt about myself. I had changed my look, changed my friends, changed my name twice, and changed my body—all trying to please other people. No matter what I did, it never seemed to be enough. And I still hadn't made myself happy.

The more I thought back on the situation, the more I realized how much my own actions had hurt me. Yes, I was pregnant because Roger lied to me, but I was also pregnant because I hadn't respected myself.

After I started being brutally honest with myself, I was also able to see how not honoring my values had gotten me fired from the U.N. How not having more self-respect kept me in Fedora, enduring abuse for longer than I should have. I realized that I had to take more responsibility for my actions and stop blaming other people for my mistakes. It was agonizing, but eventually, telling the truth made me feel a lot more peaceful. Even though my heart ached, I knew I was headed in the right direction.

During those dark days of self-examination, I desperately needed to pamper myself. I continued to wear and mix fragrances. Even though my life was miserable, I kept myself surrounded by really good smells. I nurtured myself with fragrant baths. One of my favorites mixed comforting lavender with jasmine and sandalwood. I would turn off the lights, light white candles, and place them around the edge of the tub. As I bathed, I prayed for serenity, and to let go of negativity. When I stepped out of the tub, I massaged the fragrant oils into my skin. The least I could do was care for myself in the days before my abortion.

In February of 1988 Dee went with me to terminate my pregnancy. I loved her for that. It was against her beliefs, but the thought of me going through the procedure alone was too much for her to bear. When we arrived, we sat in the lobby together. The place smelled like a hospital—cold and antiseptic, with a hint of death. It made me feel sick to my stomach.

Professional wrestling was on the TV. Across the aisle from us, a couple in their thirties was crying together. To my right was a woman with her eleven-year-old daughter. The mother just kept talking to nobody: "What do you think I'm gonna do? Do you think I'm going to let her keep it? There's no way; she's eleven years old!"

Eventually someone called a list of names. Mine was among them. We were led down the hall together, then escorted into separate rooms. A counselor was waiting to speak with me.

"Is this your first abortion?"

"Yes."

"Have you been pregnant before?"

"No."

"Have you ever had any children?"

"No." *Didn't I just tell her that I hadn't been pregnant?*

"When was your last period?"

I told her.

"Is it regular?"

"Yes."

Then she talked to me about my decision to have an abortion.

After our conversation I was led to another area, where I was instructed to change my clothes and put on a hospital gown. Once dressed, I was shown to a different lobby. Wrestling was also on this TV. I tried not to listen.

To my left a woman was casually chatting, "Oh, yeah, this is my fourth one."

Say what!

Another woman was getting married in two months. She seemed totally relaxed. "Yeah, you know, we're having this big wedding and my mother would totally freak out if I started to show before the ceremony."

What am I doing? I wondered. *I don't belong here. This is not a place I'm ever supposed to see again.*

Another list of names was called. I heard mine. I stood up. There was an indignity to the way they herded us about, barely dressed, in hospital gowns. I wondered how many women or girls had gone before me wearing this same smock. We had to undergo pelvic exams to confirm that we were pregnant. A doctor and nurse were already in the room that awaited me.

"We have to do an internal exam to make sure that your dates are correct," the nurse informed me. "If we can't verify the dates, they have to do a sonogram."

"I know exactly when I got pregnant," I told her. "It was the Friday after Thanksgiving. I haven't had sex since."

"Yeah, you know, but we don't," she responded.

I climbed onto the exam table and put my feet in the stirrups.

"When was your last period?" she asked.

I answered.

"Have you ever been pregnant before?"

"No."

"Is this your first abortion?"

"Yes."

"Have you ever had any children?"

"No." *What, can she not read what the counselor wrote in my chart?*

The whole time I was in the room the doctor never looked me in the eyes. I guess I was just another body in the assembly line that Saturday afternoon. When the nurse finished asking me questions, he walked over between my legs. Then without saying as much as hello or good morning, he shoved what seemed like his whole hand and forearm into my vagina, so violently I saw stars.

"*Ow!*" I cried out. He didn't respond or soften his touch.

"She's too fat," he said as he yanked his arm out. "I need a sonogram for dating."

"No, please don't," I begged. "I know exactly when this happened and exactly what time." I did not want to undergo any procedure that would make the fetus real to me. I didn't want to have to acknowledge my baby. "Please don't make me do this!"

"Calm her down, will you," the doctor told the nurse, as though I wasn't even in the room to hear him.

"I'm sorry. I don't have a choice," she said to me. "The doctor needs it. He has to prove you're as far along as you say you are."

Could it get any worse?

I was sent out to another lobby to wait again.

When I was called in for my sonogram, I was asked the exact same set of questions about my pregnancy. Now, I suppose that women are not always honest and many don't know exactly when they conceived. But I knew when I got pregnant and that it hadn't happened before. Being interrogated over and over felt insensitive and offensive. *What, do they think that I'm lying?* I wanted to tell them that the only lie was the one I told to myself—that it was okay to have sex with Roger in the first place. It was a mistake I would never forget.

I made another major error as the sonogram was being performed. I looked at the monitor as the ultrasound transducer was passed across my abdomen. I saw and heard a heart beating.

It's real! I sobbed. *Why did they have to make it real?*

After that exam was over I was led to a different area for the final wait. Wrestling was playing on the TV there, too. To this day professional wrestling makes me sick in the pit of my stomach.

Finally, someone called my name and I was escorted to undergo the procedure. Afterward, as I came out of anesthesia, the first thing I heard was the woman who was getting married in two months screaming at the top of her lungs, "I killed my baby! I killed my baby! Why did you let me kill my baby?"

Needless to say, this wasn't a good thing to be listening to as I was coming to my senses. The first-trimester nausea I had experienced earlier had been replaced by a hollow ache in my belly. My baby was gone. I wanted to go home. I wanted my Mommy.

I waited until spring before telling my mother what I had done, though. Mommy was silent as I spoke. Her face registered no visible emotion; she didn't seem upset or angry or relieved.

"Mommy, I am so sorry to disappoint you again," I confessed. "I'm sorry I didn't tell you before, but you had so much on your plate and I needed to solve it without running to you for an answer. Plus, I know how much you disliked Roger. I just couldn't look you in the eye and tell you I had been that dumb."

My mother waited until I was finished. Then she looked at me, folded her hands and leaned forward onto the kitchen table. I held my breath as she spoke.

"So, the father was the Roach?" she asked.

"Yes, Mommy, the Roach," I replied, holding back a chuckle.

"I may have had a grandbaby that looked like a roach?"

"Mommy . . ."

"I know, I know," she said. "I'm just teasing. It's okay. I think you made the right choice and I still love you."

And with that we moved on. Mommy was very sorry for me, but, as usual, supported me a hundred percent.

During the months that followed, I kept taking more responsibility for myself and my situation. While it would have been easy to pass the buck and blame Roger and his lies for what happened to me, at the end of the day, Lisa was the one who had to have an abortion. Lisa had to terminate a life. Lisa, who, ever since she could remember, dreamed of being a mother. I had gotten myself into a situation that was wrong for me, and I had only myself to blame. I knew that I needed to hold myself accountable for my actions and make better choices in the future.

Sometimes my mind was in a battle with itself. It was all I could do to focus on getting from second to second and moment to moment, putting one foot in front of the other. I spent more time with my family. Christian's dimpled face grinning at me lightened my sorrow. Sean, a new arrival Mommy took in shortly after Christian, was two months old and as sweet as a lamb. Helping to take care of the two babies and Aerol made me feel better. The process was slow and painful, but gradually I started to heal.

Self-Forgiveness Ritual

In order to forgive yourself, you have to know what you did wrong. If you pigged out on Oreos when you were supposed to be dieting, then you need to pardon yourself for breaking a promise to eat healthy foods. What you're not supposed to do is say, "Well, if my boss hadn't pissed me off today, I wouldn't be so stressed out and I wouldn't have eaten the Oreos." Wrong! Your boss has nothing to do with it. Gorging yourself was how you handled what your boss did to you. You can't heal him or her and if you need your job, you can't quit right away. So identify the mistake for which you need to be forgiven.

1. Say your mistake out loud.
2. Vow to yourself that you will not do this to your spirit again.
3. Ask God to forgive you and help you to do better in the future.
4. Before you get into the shower, make a white flower bath by mixing the following together in a bowl: 1 cup of milk, the petals from 7 white flowers (pom-poms or carnations are fine), ½ cup of Florida Water (this can be purchased in Latino grocery stores or religious stores), and 4 cups of spring water.
5. As you shower, tell yourself over and over that you are sorry.
6. Once you are clean, turn off the shower and pour your white flower bath over your body from the neck down.
7. While still wet, massage your body with coconut oil, preferably virgin coconut oil.
8. Dress in white bed clothes or wrap yourself in a white sheet. If your skin feels oily from the coconut oil, don't put on your best bed clothes or you will stain them.
9. Pray as you drift off to sleep.

$\mathcal{L}ove\,\mathcal{M}e\,\mathcal{B}y\,\mathcal{N}ame$

When I first met Gordon I asked myself if he was "the one."
All the while I knew the answer, although I wasn't ready to admit it.

In the months following my abortion, I felt lost and confused. I had disconnected myself from the people and practices familiar within Ausar Auset, and nothing I had learned in the "wild, wild West" could help me center and balance myself. While I was still a member of the society, I had been able to use spiritual tools such as chanting and meditation to help me divine the answers I needed to important situations. But aside from discerning what to do about my abortion, it had been months since I had been able to figure anything out. My poor choices left me having a hard time trusting my intuitive abilities. When I needed spiritual help, I wasn't clear about where to turn.

Often on my lunch break I would walk by a place where a woman read tarot cards. One day the woman said, "Stop crying over the baby." It stopped me in my tracks.

In July of that year, I ran into my girlfriend Erica, who now goes by Alake and runs a popular natural hair salon in Brooklyn bearing her chosen name. I knew Erica from my days in Ausar Auset. We were good friends, but our relationship wasn't consistent. We would bond, fall out of touch with each other for a couple of months and then bond again. During one of our marathon, catch-me-up-on-the-last-three-months-of-your-life conversations, I shared my spiritual dilemma with her.

"Oh, my goodness. I have the *best* person to give you a reading," Erica told me. "It's only forty dollars, you'll be there for hours and you'll be amazed by what he'll tell you."

I was relieved to have a referral from someone I could trust and who shared my spiritual background. So I made an appointment with a spiritual advisor who went by the name of Mr. K.

As I walked down the hallway of his Bronx apartment building, I was greeted with the familiar scents of my spiritual past: Florida water, cigar smoke and sage. I knocked on the door. A woman answered.

"Good afternoon," she said.

"Hi. I'm here for an appointment with Mr. K. Erica sent me."

"Come in."

She asked me to remove my shoes and gestured toward a chair in the middle of a crowded living room.

"Take a seat. He'll be right with you."

Although the apartment was very congested, the vibe felt calm and peaceful. There were newspapers, books and African artifacts and statues everywhere. By the front door was a shrine to the Yoruba deity Elegba, who governs the crossroads of our lives, and a plate of food I assumed was set out for the ancestors. With the exception of the smell of hamburgers cooking in the kitchen (you would never smell meat at Ausar Auset; we were all vegans), it was what I would have expected.

Mr. K. entered from a hallway, smelling of soap and shower steam. He was wearing traditional West African dress—a grand buba over a dashiki and tshukatos, the authentic version of what many people know as M.C. Hammer pants.

"Forgive me for being late. I've just gotten in from work and needed to freshen up."

I tried not to stare at his Mohawk haircut. It didn't fit my image of a Yoruba priest. I would later learn that one of the ways he would earn a living was as a Mr. T. impersonator. Had I known that in advance I might not have made the appointment.

He read a prayer to the orishas, the Yoruba word for deities representing the spiritual energies of God. He also consulted an oracle. Then the reading began, and any doubts I may have had regarding my choice to consult Mr. K. quickly vanished as he began to tell me about my life. Without any prompting from me, he told me things that only I could know.

"There is a couple in your life with whom you were deeply in love," he said, staring intently into my eyes. "They're not as much a part of your physical life as they had been, but they still think about you and love you very much."

I gripped the sides of my chair tightly to keep my face from showing how startled I was.

"There's a very dark person who lives in your home," he said to me next. "You need to get away from him. You need to move out. A way will come and it will come soon."

This really surprised me because I hadn't shared my desire to move out of Mommy's house with anyone. A week prior, I punched my fist through a wall after arguing with my stepfather. I was sick of the demeaning way he interacted with me, but he was the man of the house and he was not going to change. *How does Mr. K. know this?*

"You really don't like your job," he announced, "but it's very good for you. Things will get better and you will like it more soon."

The more that Mr. K. read my life, the more I trusted what he said. There was no way for him to know these things. I went from doubting Thomas to true believer in less than fifteen minutes.

"There's a man in your life that you're interested in," he continued. "But, believe me, this is not the man for you. You're too wrapped up in this person. You think it's going somewhere, but this is just for fun."

After talking for what seemed like an hour, he stopped and looked at me.

"What is it that you want to know?" he asked.

Without thinking I said, "How will I recognize the man for me?"

"You're going to know him when you meet him. When you look at him, the first thought will be 'That's the man I'm going to marry.' Then you're not going to trust yourself because why would you feel that way the first time you look at someone?"

I just looked at him.

"You will know it's him the minute you look at him," he repeated. "But you'll dismiss the thought. And then you'll watch it play out right in front of your eyes because you won't trust that first thought."

As incredulous as it sounded, I had no choice but to believe him. Everything he had said up to this point was true. Why would this be a lie?

As I was about to ask, "When will I meet him?" But Mr. K. anticipated my question and said, "Before you meet him you will date a lot of different men."

This gave me pause. Mr. K. sensed it.

"Enjoy yourself and don't worry about it," he continued. "You have to date a lot of different people so you will know your husband when you see him."

It made sense to me. Up until that point, my relationships were so few and far between that anybody was appealing, since it was better than being alone. However, it was difficult for me to grasp the concept that I would be dating a number of men, because it had never happened before. *Where will all of these men come from?* I thought.

"Why do you doubt yourself?" he said, reading my mind. "You are Oshun's child."

Once again, he was right. This corresponded exactly to what I had learned about my spiritual energies when I was in Ausar Auset.

"Oshun is the goddess of love, the player of love games. Attracting love should not frighten you."

How does he do that? I thought as he picked up my thoughts again. But attracting love did frighten me. My "attractions" up to this point had been disastrous.

"There is something I want to give you," he said, before disappearing into another room. When he returned he was carrying a black case. He pulled out a tall, narrow clear glass container that looked like a hot-sauce bottle. I watched him as he added items from the case to this bottle, one by one: corn kernels, copper dust, a cinnamon stick, honey, Florida water. These were the only ingredients I could identify, but there were others. As he began to sing what I assumed to be a song to Oshun, he added various fragrances to the bottle. I tried to smell them as they were being poured but the scents were mingling with one another in the air, creating a union undecipherable from its parts. It smelled like perfection!

"Take this with you," he said, handing me the vial of liquid.

"It smells wonderful. What is it?"

"An attraction oil," he answered. "I want you to wear it every day. It will let brothers know that you're interested in love. Apply it liberally after you shower. Splash it on and rub your body down from head to toe. Don't be stingy with it. If you shower at night, reapply it in the morning before you go out. Then stand back and let the men come to you. Just work your Oshun and deal with it."

I held the bottle to my nose, inhaling my special elixir. My own "hot sauce." I was looking forward to using it. It had been a while since I had had money to spend on perfume. I wanted to savor the potion and make it last. But I would follow instructions and apply it liberally.

After I left that first consultation, my head was spinning. As I traveled home I reflected on things that had happened in my life. Mr. K. was right; my job had been getting better. In April, New York Health and Hospitals Corporation (HHC), the organization that had hired me as a temp, had brought me on full-time. Even though the job was boring, the steady paycheck was helping me catch up on some of my bills.

But shortly after I had started full-time, a new person joined the company. Her name was Marie Gibson—Mrs. Gibson to her subordinates. Mrs. Gibson was from Grenada, about ten years my senior, married and had a son. She had brown skin and a mischievous smile that always left us wondering what she knew that we didn't. It didn't take long before the woman started getting on my nerves. Not only did she want me at work Monday through Friday, she wanted me to come in on Saturdays as well. I was desperately trying to play by the rules and do the nine-to-five thing, but I still had stardust in my eyes. Well, in my case it was black eyeliner; I was still chasing that Minneapolis dream. If I hung out late at a party that I thought would help me musicwise, it had been my practice to call out from work the next day. A practice Mrs. Gibson was hell-bent on stopping.

"I'm sick, Mrs. Gibson, and I can't come in," I'd tell her in my best "I'm dying" voice.

"Really, what's wrong? What kind of sickness do you have?"

"I have a splitting headache and my throat is very sore."

"Do you have chills?"

"No."

Why the hell did she ask me that?

"Good, no sign of fever. Well, drink some lemon tea for your throat.

Attract Love Massage Oil

Remember, I didn't see what Mr. K. put in the bottle he gave me. This recipe combines my memory of the oils I could identify and my own knowledge and experience about what fragrances attract people.

1. Mix the following into a beautiful bottle, measuring 4 oz.:
   * *1 dried rose head—preferably a yellow one*
   * *1 stick of cinnamon*
   * *1 dried vanilla bean*
   * *2 seashells, preferably cowrie shells*
   * *a tiny sprinkling of copper mica*
   * *3⅞ oz. of a base oil. Choose from or use a combination of soy, sweet almond, corn, or sesame.*
   * *⅛ oz. wheat germ oil*
   * *5 drops each of the following scents: rose, sandalwood, mango, gardenia and vanilla*
2. Dip your finger in honey and rub it around the rim of the bottle. Close the bottle tightly.
3. Shake the bottle for 25 seconds.
4. Open it and inhale the aroma. Hold your breath as you say your prayer to yourself, for example: "Bring to me the love my spirit needs."
5. Exhale your wish with your breath into the bottle.
6. Seal it and let it sit for about 5 hours.
7. It is now ready to be used lavishly. Good luck!

And do some deep breathing exercises. That will get rid of your headache. I'll expect to see you in an hour."

Damn! Why wasn't I quicker with that chills thing? What does she care if I don't come in?

I would then be compelled to shower, get dressed, and head into the office. This went on for months. After a couple of other attempts to stay home or leave work early, I gave up. Mrs. Gibson was always a step or two ahead of me. If I was out late and came home at six A.M., I learned to drink coffee, shower, drink coffee, go into the office and, you guessed it, drink coffee.

"You really need to stop all that hanging out, Lisa. You're getting too old for that, and what about your job, here?"

"What about it?"

"You want to keep it, don't you?"

"Of course. I do what I'm supposed to."

"Well, sometimes you need to do more than just what's required to get by. Take care of first things first. How are you going to be a singer if you don't have a regular income? Have you earned any money singing yet? It seems to me that someone like you really needs a steady job."

Oh, that's it, I thought. *I may have to cut this bitch.*

"It seems to me," she continued, oblivious to my disgust, "what makes a singer is if you can sing. That doesn't mean you have to be a star or perform in shows or anything. Singers just sing."

I didn't like what she was saying, but hadn't thought of it like that before. When I sang in school it wasn't about stardom, it was about the craft. Somewhere between Music & Art and Lake Minnehaha, I had lost sight of that. This kind of dialogue continued between us for much of the year— she, my uninvited mentor, and I, her unimpressed, but slightly intrigued pupil. Over the next several months, Mrs. Gibson and I grew close. I realized that the discipline she fought to instill in me was exactly what I needed. It took time, but I had to admit that her pushing was good for me.

Later that year many wonderful things began to happen. Mommy took in another child—a two-year-old boy, named Phillip. Since I already had a brother named Philip, this one was called "Little Phillip." On top of that, the predictions Mr. K. had made continued to reveal themselves to me. Things got better and better at work. I moved to the Upper West Side, out from under my stepfather's thumb, into an apartment I shared with two guys. My "hot sauce" also worked and I began to date in earnest. Over the next eight months I would go out with more men than I had in my entire life. But in my wildest dreams I never could have imagined what would happen on a Friday night at Nell's.

Nell's, a popular nightspot in Manhattan on Fourteenth Street between Seventh and Eighth Avenues, was also a favorite hangout for Prince. In my travels in the music business I had often been in the company of Prince, but unlike Delliah, I had never spoken to him.

One night, the deejay was especially good. I danced for five and a half hours straight. Truth be told, I needed to dance because it had been nine months since I'd had sex and, while I enjoyed dating, the no-sex thing was getting to be a bit much. When I finally came off the dance floor, Dee came over to talk to me as I was trying to get some water from the bartender.

"Your friend said something nice about you," she told me.

"What are you talking about? What friend?"

"Prince."

"*Prince!* What did he say?"

"Well, I asked him why he was in such a bad mood and he told me he was looking for something."

"Looking for what?"

"He said, 'I'm looking for that,' and he pointed at you."

"What did he mean?"

"I'm not a mind reader, girl. You're grown; you figure it out. I'm just telling you what he said."

"What did you say?"

"What was I supposed to say? I said, 'That's my girlfriend. Wanna meet her?' "

"What did *he* say?"

"Girl, he got really embarrassed. Then he got it together and said, 'Well, tell your girlfriend I like the way she moves.' "

For the entire rest of the night I was on cloud ninety-nine thousand. *Prince was watching me dance! Prince likes the way I move!*

I would liked to have met him, but it was a night that I would never forget. The attraction oil I got from Mr. K. was long gone by that point, but the effect it continued to have on me was really something else.

For my New Year's resolution in 1989, I joined Oprah in following the Optifast diet. Of course I was an avid watcher of her show, but I also identified with her struggles to gain control of her weight. One day, she dragged a wheelbarrow full of fat onto the set. It represented the sixty pounds she had lost on the plan. I vowed to replicate her impressive accomplishment.

Initially I struggled with the diet, which consisted of six seventy-calorie shakes spaced evenly throughout the day. I could also drink water, flavored seltzer and diet sodas—no other food. With my caloric intake so low, my aerobic exercise was limited to walking. I started by strolling about twenty-five blocks, then I increased it to thirty, then to forty. A couple of times I walked over sixty blocks from my office all the way home. It was difficult but the weight came off quickly.

After a short time, however, one big problem emerged: I couldn't afford the expense of $135 per week. The Optifast plan was so severe that it required weekly doctor's appointments. At that point I began substituting other shakes for Optifast. I worried that I might make myself sick. So after losing forty-five pounds in a little under four months, I started transitioning back to eating food, little by little, one food group at a time. I was happy with my thinner waist, but my thighs, which were always well toned from dancing, had started to jiggle. All in all, at the time it seemed a small price to pay.

Shortly before I finished the transition process to bring me off the diet, I started to get sick of my narrow dietary choices. One afternoon I was at home alone watching old movies on cable. I walked into the kitchen, opened the refrigerator and looked at its contents: Diet Pepsi, water, orange seltzer, raspberry seltzer, lemon-lime seltzer. I raised my eyes and called out to God, saying, "Lord, I don't need somebody in my life to complete me. I can go to dinner by myself. I can go to the movies by myself. I can entertain myself. I have crafts. I have friends. I enjoy my music. But I'd really like to have someone to share my life with. It can't just be about orange seltzer and raspberry seltzer. Please! And make it somebody nice, okay?"

I grabbed a soda, slammed the refrigerator door shut and headed back into the bedroom to watch TV.

Four days later I was at the 308 Bar on Fortieth Street between Eighth and Ninth Avenues, where I was singing background for Bert's band. The group members were milling about just before our set began, when a man walked into the club and caught my attention.

My God! He's beautiful! I thought. He had short, curly, black hair, beautiful eyes, and a turquoise T-shirt that perfectly complemented his almond skin tone. The man so captured my attention that I remembered the prediction. *Is it him?* I wondered. *I bet he's married.*

The man didn't look like he belonged there. In my mind he seemed like the kind of guy that had wandered in to use the bathroom. He probably had a station wagon complete with wife and child waiting for him outside. But the next thing I knew he walked over to Bert and the two of them started talking.

Oh my God, he knows Bert! I've got a connection.

I tried to be cool and play off the fact that I was staring. But as soon as he and Bert parted, I grilled Bert about the handsome stranger.

"Who was that?"

"My brother."

"Your brother? No, I met your brother, that's not your brother."

"Hello, Topaz. I have two brothers."

In the two and a half years I had known Bert, I thought I had met the entire Price family: Jeff, Nancy, Shirley and Karen. Now I was learning he had another brother—and a fine one at that!

"Would you like to meet him?" Bert asked, as I tried to figure out where my handsome stranger fit into the sibling hierarchy. "Gordon," he called across the bar. "There's someone I want you to meet."

Bert introduced us.

"Nice to meet you," Gordon said, as he took my hand and stared deeply into my eyes. "Topaz, is it?"

"Yes," I answered.

Throughout the night we flirted with each other. I watched him, asking myself, *Is he the one?* All the while I knew the answer, although I wasn't ready to admit it. For several days after meeting him, I wrestled with the idea of calling. Finally, I decided to ring Bert to ask him what he thought.

"Hey, Bert! What's happening?"

"Gordon's number is . . ." he said, and recited the number.

"How did you know I was going to ask that?"

"Call him."

"What am I going to say?"

"You'll figure it out," Bert laughed. "Good-bye!" Then he hung up on me.

I paced my apartment for hours before gathering the nerve to dial the phone. Fortunately, Gordon was delighted to hear from me. We hadn't been talking for long before he asked me a question.

"Topaz. That's not your real name is it?"

"No. It's just a name that I go by in the music business."

"What's your real name?"

"Lisa."

"If you want me to call you Topaz, I don't mind. But I'd rather call you Lisa if it's okay."

Wow! This is the one, I thought. *He is seeing the real me.* My heart swelled.

"Thank you for asking, Gordon," I answered. "I'd rather have you call me Lisa, too."

We stayed on the phone until the sun came up. It was a seven-hour phone call. We talked about everything about ourselves. Sometimes I wondered if we were sharing too much information. But that little intuitive voice that is sometimes hard to hear said, "Keep on talking. He's being honest."

That week, we conversed every day. Every time my phone rang and it was him, I was thrilled. We had many similarities: we both came from big families and had large extended families. His mom had adopted foster children, just as mine had, and in both of our homes, our sisters and brothers were our sisters and brothers, regardless of what brought them there.

At the end of that first week, we made plans to meet on Saturday afternoon. But early that day it became clear to him that he would be running late. He called my apartment to inform me, but I wasn't home. My roommate told him I was at the laundromat around the corner.

In the meantime, I was doing my laundry and getting nervous about our date. We had gotten so close over the phone I was anxious about being face to face. I was pulling a load of clothes out of the washing machine, when out of the blue I thought I heard his voice.

"Excuse me, but haven't I seen you somewhere before?"

I jumped and turned around, certain I must be imagining things. I wasn't. Gordon was standing in front of me in his full glory. It didn't matter what he was doing at my Laundromat, I was ecstatic to see his beautiful face. He looked gorgeous even though he was just wearing jeans and a jacket.

I just stared at him. I couldn't even speak, and I'm sure everyone in the place could hear my heart pounding. The next thing I knew we were kissing each other. Like we had been doing it for a long time. In the middle of the Laundromat. I had never done anything like that before. It was like a scene right out of a movie. When we finally finished smooching, he told me that he was running late for our date.

"How did you know where to find me?"

"Your roommate told me. I'll be back in a couple of hours."

I walked him to the door where we kissed again, briefly, and said goodbye.

"Was that your husband?" one woman asked when I returned inside.

"My husband? No," I said, blushing as I finished emptying the washer of my wet clothes, all the while trying to act like nothing unusual had happened.

"Your boyfriend?" she said this with a smile, as if to imply that this scenario was far better than her first supposition.

"Um-hmmm," I answered, savoring the thought of it.

"Nice," another woman commented.

"He's cute!" came the verdict from across the room.

Little did they know that they had witnessed our first kiss!

Later that afternoon, Gordon and I got together. We listened to music in my room. We kissed again and again and each time it was more electric. He commented on how good I smelled and while nibbling on my ear, whispered, "*Je t'aime.*"

"What did you say?" I asked and abruptly stopped kissing him.

"It's French."

"I know it's French. Do you know what you said?"

"Of course. I said 'I love you.' "

I looked at him in disbelief and said, "I love you, too."

With that, I was certain he was the one.

CHAPTER 9

Just Cos

Taken during the final taping of The Cosby Show *as I was listening to Boyz II Men sing*
"It's So Hard to Say Good-bye to Yesterday" to the Huxtables. While at Cosby *I learned that it*
is possible to love your job. I learned the joy and satisfaction that comes from working at what
you feel passionate about.

Things continued to get better and better between Gordon and me. I looked forward to being with him more than anything else each day. Gordon was the first man to really love and respect me for who I was, not for what he could make me into or what I might become. He loved everything about me. He pulled out my chair, he was affectionate in public, he kissed me on the subway. For once, I didn't have to be hidden. He wanted to shout his love from the rooftops!

I loved all those things about Gordon, but two of his characteristics in particular endeared him to me: One, he loved me even though I continued to struggle to manage my weight; and two, he didn't flinch when I told him about my miserable financial situation.

Going off the Optifast diet and trying to reintroduce food slowly without medical supervision turned out to be a problem. I had lost muscle from not eating enough. Now my body thought it was starving and had shifted into survival mode. It was holding onto every ounce of food I took into my body. Everything I ate caused me to gain weight—even salads and fresh fruit. Despite working out and eating right, I got heavier and heavier. Gordon loved me in spite of that.

He also adored me even though I had my money problems. And he, too, needed to do a little financial housecleaning. Now that I had a decent job and Gordon by my side, I was finally able to face my financial demons. I consulted a lawyer and started bankruptcy proceedings. It had become clear to me that I would never get out of debt. I owed $4000 less than my annual gross income. No matter how much I paid, with interest, my old bills kept going up. Even if I got a higher-paying job, I would be making payments forever. Bankruptcy seemed like the only way out. Like the choice I made to terminate my pregnancy, I would not advocate bankruptcy for anyone, except as a last resort. For me, I knew that there was no other way to restore my credit. I had lived beyond my means for far too long and it was time to pay the piper. At the time the choice was logical, and it was a relief to know that I no longer owed anyone any money. But, similar to abortion, a person never really leaves behind the stigma of bankruptcy. You can forgive yourself, you can move on, but you never forget, and you never really let go of the shame. If you're like me, you vow to yourself to never, ever get in that situation again.

In July of 1989, I moved into my own apartment. Gordon helped me financially. I got promoted to executive secretary that fall, which gave me a little more breathing room. At least I thought it did, until I realized that my boss was a tyrant.

"What the fuck is this?" he shouted one day as he stormed out of his office and threw a sheet of paper at me. I was stunned. Everyone at our company despised Samuel Lewindowsky except me. In my new role as his executive secretary, I catered to him and we got along well. I was his lifeline to the rest of the world that hated his guts. Now he had crossed the line by disrespecting me. All bets were off.

"You got the address wrong! What if I hadn't checked it carefully?" he ranted, thick eyebrows knit, and spit spraying from his lips. "Why can't you do your job?"

When the tirade stopped, I slowly reached down to the floor and picked up the sheet of paper he had flung toward me. My heart was pounding and my hands were trembling with rage. I felt humiliated. I wanted to jump up and give him a piece of my mind, but I was in bad financial shape and I couldn't afford to get fired. I would just have to suck it up and take it. At the same time I wondered, *What could I possibly have done that is so terribly awful that he feels he has to yell at me like this?*

I placed the piece of paper on my desk and read the letter carefully, comparing it to the handwritten copy he had given me earlier that morning. Mr. Lewindowsky was moving into a new apartment. He was sending the letter to notify people of the move. As I read the notes side by side, I finally saw what he had been screaming about—I had typed apartment number 1B instead of 1C.

"I see the mistake, Mr. Lewindowsky. I'm sorry. I'll fix it," I said, as pleasantly as possible under the circumstances.

He turned around and walked back into his office, muttering under his breath the entire way. I pulled out a fresh sheet of paper, placed it into the printer and quickly made the change. Then I got up, walked the letter into his office for him to sign, excused myself and headed straight for the ladies room. I refused to give him the satisfaction of seeing it, but once there, I cried.

Before this incident I used to pity Mr. Lewindowsky. I saw him as a small-minded and insecure person who had been put in a position of authority even though he didn't know how to communicate with people. Now, he had made me hate him just as much as everyone else. As I stood in front of the mirror, I stared into my teary eyes and made myself a promise: I would never let Sam Lewindowsky treat me this way again. I reached over to the dispenser, grabbed a paper towel and ran it under the cold water. I pressed it against my eyes until you couldn't see that I had been crying. When I had gotten myself together, I walked into his office and asked to speak with him.

"What is it?" he asked sharply.

"You were correct, Mr. Lewindowsky," I said to him. "I did make a mistake and had you not caught it, the letters would have gone out incorrect and the results would have been awful. For that, I apologize."

His eyes were widening. I could tell he was not exactly sure what to do or say.

"But I'm not in the habit of making errors," I continued. "I have never disrespected you and nothing warranted having that piece of paper thrown in my face. And I definitely did not appreciate being cursed at. I'm sorry for my mistake. But I deserve better than what you have given me."

Then I stood there silently, watching the crimson slowly rise up his cheeks. The tension was palpable. He looked down at his desk and ran his fingers through his thinning hair. Then he looked me in the eye.

"You're right, Lisa. I shouldn't have spoken to you like that. Next time just be more careful, okay?"

"I will," I said, and turned and left his office. My stomach remained in knots, and from then on, every time I heard his voice or had to look at him, my gut and teeth would tighten.

I stewed all day, trying to decide what to do. I had gotten myself into this predicament; I couldn't walk out on an abusive boss, because I desperately needed the money. But it certainly wouldn't happen again. I knew I'd kill him if it did. I told Gordon what had happened when I saw him that evening. Needless to say, he was outraged. We talked about how I should handle it and decided I should look for another job.

Later that week, just as my newly revised résumé was coming out of the printer, I received a telephone call. It was Delliah. While I was carving out my niche at HHC, Delliah was progressing through the ranks of the production team for the *The Cosby Show*. Now she was assistant to the producer.

"Fax me your résumé," she said.

"What for?"

"Just fax me your résumé. Right now. Here's the number . . ."

"Okay, but why?"

"Look, I can't talk long but they're looking for a writer's assistant for the new writing staff."

"What does that mean?" I asked.

"Don't worry, it's basically taking notes and typing."

"But I've never worked on a television show before."

"Don't you do those things as a secretary?"

"Yeah, but . . ."

"Lisa, are you interested?"

"Yes," I answered. "But don't you need a college degree? I don't have one, remember?"

"Don't sweat it, girl," Dee said. "You're used to reading résumés where people include their graduation year. Just leave it out."

"What do you mean?"

"Just put City College of New York Urban Legal Studies Program. Then don't put a year."

"Are you sure?"

"Yeah. Just take my word for it, Lisa. It's not like you have to bring in your diploma."

I left the year out as Dee had suggested, but I knew that if they asked me when I graduated I wasn't going to lie. That's where I drew the line. After all of the phoniness and duplicity that had come with Fedora, I wasn't going to deceive anyone. If it broke me, it broke me.

I knew that I was taking a chance by deciding to be honest. Gordon's truth-telling had cost him a shot on the *Cosby* staff a few months earlier. Mr. Cosby had needed a new driver. Gordon applied but ended up being the number two pick because he didn't have a degree. We weren't sure why you needed a college degree to be a driver. We assumed it was so Mr. Cosby would have someone interesting to talk to.

Choosing not to misrepresent myself was a big decision for me. Even though it was somewhat risky, I was proud that I had reached the point where I wasn't willing to compromise my integrity.

The next several days, as I waited to hear back from *Cosby,* I was on pins and needles—no, the waiting was actually terrifying. I wanted the job badly, even though I didn't know exactly what it entailed. I was nuts for *The Cosby Show* and had been a diehard fan from Day One. After spending all my life seeing shows like *Good Times* and *That's My Mama,* where black people were struggling as janitors and maids, I was starved for a television show where people looked and acted like my family—not that I had anything against janitors or maids, or that my parents were doctors or lawyers. But my mom did work in an office as a receptionist and bookkeeper, and Daddy did work as a social worker and youth counselor, wearing a suit and tie every day, my aunts worked in offices, one of my uncles was an artist and musician, and another was a captain of detectives. *Why aren't those kinds of black people on TV?* I used to wonder as a child. On *Cosby* I finally found a black family that was a little closer to my own reality. I watched the show every Thursday night like clockwork. I had taped the episodes for my brother Philip while he was away in college and would view them with him when he came home from school. In addition to that, I watched the reruns. I knew everything about all the characters.

After a few days I received a call inviting me to come in for an interview. I can't tell you how much of a relief it was when I saw that I was being interviewed by two plus-sized women. I had assumed that because the job was in television the people behind the scenes would be the same super-model types that you see on camera. I assumed everyone would be as beautiful as Delliah, who had the perfect figure and a fantastic face to boot. Don't get me wrong: they were beautiful women, but they didn't look like the women in the *Sports Illustrated* swimsuit issue. Making me feel even more comfortable, one of them, Judi, was black. The other woman was Brenda, a redhead who reminded me of Susan Sarandon, just plus-sized. The two women asked me about my work experience. As they read through my résumé, Judi seemed not to like the fact that I didn't have a TV or production background. Eventually they made it to the part that said where I had gone to college.

"What did you study?" Judy asked.

"Prelaw," I answered, and said nothing else.

They went on to the next question.

Thank God!

"Would working long hours or weekends be a problem for you?" Brenda asked.

"No. I don't have any children. I don't mind working late and I've been working on Saturdays for the past year and a half," I answered.

"Do you know how to take notes?" they asked. I went on to explain my job responsibilities and the things I did for Sam—taking minutes at his meetings, typing them up, preparing reports and corporate papers. I even attended the monthly meetings at the Hospital Health Corporation of New York and distributed the minutes to the entire board. They were impressed with that one.

By the end of the interview, both women seemed happy with me and I was ecstatic. As I left I felt like the job was mine. It occurred to me that all the painful experiences I had had in the last couple of years had prepared me for that moment. Suddenly, I loved Mrs. Gibson for making me work all of those Saturdays. I was pleased with myself for making good use of that time by teaching myself how to use the word processor. I didn't know if I would get the job, but I left feeling confident that I was qualified. And, worst-case scenario, even if they didn't hire me, I would still have a gig paying $25,000 a year until I found something better. This was the first time I understood that experiences build on each other. It was the first time I understood that everything that happens to you—good and bad—

prepares you for the next thing in life. My awareness of this truth has grown stronger over the years—to the point where I don't get as upset when things appear to be going badly; I know the "negative" circumstances are part of something larger that isn't yet visible to me. But this was the first time I became aware that so-called bad things can actually work out for good.

A couple of evenings later, the telephone rang at my home. One of the producers from the show called to offer me the job. The pay was almost exactly the same as my job with HHC—$500 per week, with overtime after sixty hours. They didn't offer any vacation, the insurance wasn't as good, the job would end at the end of the season and I'd have to wait and see if I'd be rehired. But the work would be great, if I got hit by a bus the hospital would accept me, and my GYN visits were covered. That's all that mattered to me.

"Are you interested?" the person asked.

"Yes!" I responded, barely able to contain myself.

"Do you think you could start a week from Monday?"

"Yes," I answered without hesitating.

But not everyone in my circle was as excited as I was. Several people around me couldn't believe what I was doing.

"You've just gotten back on your feet," one said. "Why would you give up the security of a position with the city for a job that isn't permanent?"

But I couldn't wait to leave HHC. The next morning I sauntered into the office and told Sam about my offer. To my surprise he was impressed and happy for me, even though I was giving him less than two weeks notice. Then he told me that he would be leaving the city in two weeks, as well.

On my last day Sam threw me a good-bye party, which was something he never did for anyone else. I thought Mrs. Gibson or one of my old bosses had put him up to it. But I found out later he thought of it on his own and they agreed to assist. The entire company was in attendance, there were balloons and cake, and they got me a great going-away present. I was stunned when Sam gave me his send-off.

"She is the best assistant I have ever had," he announced to everyone. "And she's got a new job at *The Cosby Show*. They will be lucky to have her." Then he gave me a big hug. I was stunned. This was the sweetest thing he had ever done. I cried, but this time it was a good cry.

I was reveling in my farewell party when someone ran into the room calling my name. "Someone's on the phone for you. I think it's from *The Cosby Show!*"

Oh my God! They've changed their mind.

I ran into the next room to pick up the call.

"Lisa," the voice on the other end of the line said, "I'm calling from *The Cosby Show.* I want to ask you if you'd mind doing us a favor."

Whew!

"What is it?"

"The writer's assistants have been working very long hours this week—from ten A.M. to two A.M.—because the writers were having a big meeting with Mr. Cosby today. They need to have the minutes of today's meeting transcribed by Monday morning, but everyone's fed up and tired and they were promised they could be off this weekend to rest. Would you mind coming in to work over the weekend to help transcribe the notes from the meeting?"

"Sure!" I answered. "I don't mind, but I have a doctor's appointment. Is it okay if I come after that?"

"Why don't you tell me where the doctor's is and we'll send a car to pick you up. And when you're finished, we'll have one bring you home. Here's the number you should call."

A car! I thought. *For me?*

"Okay, that sounds great," I said, trying to sound cool.

"And if need be could you also work on Sunday?" he added.

"Yep. No problem."

When I walked out of my doctor's office late the next morning, there was a pretty, black Lincoln Town Car waiting for me. *Wow!*

When I arrived at the office, Cathy, one of the writer's assistants, had already told the security guard to let me in and had left instructions on how to get to my desk. She also posted signs in the halls pointing my way. "Welcome to your first day of work. This way, Lisa," one of them said.

Later she called to check on me. "There's a refrigerator in the kitchen with snacks in it if you want them. There's also a menu book," she told me. "If you order anything, save your receipt and they'll reimburse you on Monday."

Again, I couldn't believe it. That afternoon I sat at Cathy's desk, placed the headphones on my ears and for the next seven hours transcribed the tape. I did the same thing for eight hours on Sunday. On Monday, all the writer's assistants were grateful to me for sparing them a miserable weekend. I felt as though I already knew the writers from listening to them converse on cassettes all weekend. I didn't feel as self-conscious about my lack of television experience, because listening to the tapes had given me a sense of how things worked. I knew I could do this job.

That first week was a hiatus week, the one week each month when the stage was dark and there were no celebrities around. This gave me an opportunity to get my feet wet, and get to know my coworkers. There were eighteen of us in the writing department. Seven were black and, of those, two were writers. Not knowing much about the business of television, I naively assumed that because the show had a predominately black cast, the staff—and certainly the writers—would be black, too. Wrong! To get those kinds of jobs you usually had to have an Ivy League background and connections, which excluded many talented African-Americans. Things are getting better, but the industry has a long way to go.

The Cosby Show opened the door for a lot of black actors and behind-the-scenes professionals. One of them ended up being my Gordon. In the days before I was hired, he received an unexpected call asking if he was still available; one of the show's drivers hadn't worked out. Even though he didn't have a college degree, Dee had somehow convinced the producers that he was perfect for the job. So now Gordon and I both had jobs at the most famous show on television!

During my first week, my training focused on taking notes as the writers discussed scripts. By Day Two, I was flying solo. Even though I had been nervous at first, my strong memorization skills helped a lot. Sometimes the creative meetings moved quickly, with more than one person talking at once. You didn't always have time to write everything down before someone would turn to you and ask you to read back what had been said. I could always remember even though I might not have had time to write it down yet. In time, one of the writers would begin to joke that I had a "seven-second delay." Early on, I could tell that I was good at this job. What made things better was that I loved it.

The following Monday morning the cast began to arrive. The actors sat around a table and read the script out loud with the writers and producers present. As they read, I barely noticed that television's biggest stars were standing ten feet away from me. I was more taken by the fact that I was standing in the Huxtable kitchen. On other shows they follow the reading with an all-day rehearsal, but Mr. Cosby rewrote at least part and sometimes all of the script, so the cast would go home for the rest of the day while he met with the writers.

The schedule was grueling. Monday, read-through and rewrite. Tuesday, second read-through and rehearsal. Wednesday was dress rehearsal. Thursday we taped two shows in front of live audiences. All the while the script was being revised until the last minute.

As a result we all worked a lot of long hours. I often left my house at ten in the morning and didn't leave the set until twelve or sixteen or even twenty hours later. Yes, that's right, I might not come home until six A.M. the following morning. I might only catch three hours of sleep before the driver returned to take me back to the set. I learned to roll out of bed, shower and dress in as little as fifteen minutes, but I was still a newbie, so it was all a lot of fun to me.

In time the writers began to turn to me to answer questions about the character bible. Every television show has a log where they record all of the pertinent facts about the many characters as they develop over the years— birthdates and locations, how many brothers and sisters they have, where their parents are from.

One day, I was sitting at my desk typing some notes, when one of the writers stuck his head out from a meeting and called out, "What's Rudi's formal name?"

That's easy, I thought and answered, "Rudith Lillian Huxtable."

"What the hell kind of name is Rudith?" came the reply.

"I've never heard it before either, but that's her name."

Well, of course, no one believed me so they went to the bible, to find out that it only said "Rudi Huxtable, youngest child."

That's when I had to go there with them.

"It's in the episode where Rudi writes a story for school," I told the team. "As Claire reads the cover of the book, she says her name."

That show had run several years earlier, but being the *Cosby* fan I was, I could still remember it. Of course, they didn't believe me. It took a while for them to locate the right tape in the archives.

"I'll be damned," one of the writers said, upon viewing the episode. "She knew something the bible didn't even know."

After that, no one questioned me. I knew the show by heart. I could even run dialogue for them. There was no need to open the bible; I became the character bible. Instead the writers would say, "Lisa, how many siblings does Claire have?"

"One," I would answer without looking up from my desk.

"Thank you," they would reply.

The Cosby Show was an amazing environment to be in. I had finally found my niche—television production. There was something incredibly energizing about watching Mr. C., as we often called him, walk in with an idea and have the story line build from there. An entire episode could develop out of something as simple as a new hat he had purchased over the weekend.

Working around Mr. Cosby, I got to see his genius and power. Being that close to someone that smart and funny and influential is an amazing experience, and Mr. C. is powerful in the true sense of the word. He would say things and there would be a ripple effect and *boom!* it would happen. From my child's-eye perspective, I had believed he was all about laughter and Puddin' Pops, but behind the scenes I saw him fight many battles to make sure black people were represented respectfully. He paid attention to every detail. All artwork had to be approved by Mr. Cosby. Black publications, such as *Ebony* and *Black Enterprise,* were always placed prominently on the living room table. He had high standards that everyone had to adhere to, and I never saw him treat anyone disrespectfully. In fact, he went out of his way to make people feel good, and he had that amazing ability to hold the audience in the palm of his hand.

By the time I worked on *Cosby* my father had graduated from law school and moved to Mississippi, where he is a professor at Jackson State University. Daddy continued his long-standing admiration of Mr. C. by watching the show religiously every week. He also hung on every piece of information I shared with him about my experiences working there. Mr. Cosby was known for wearing black college paraphernalia on the show. Daddy paid his respects to Mr. C. by sending him a Jackson State sweatshirt. He was gracious enough to wear Daddy's gift on the show. Naturally that made my father ecstatic.

The other members of the cast were wonderful as well. I especially admired Phylicia Rashad, who was reserved, peaceful, always smiling, and stunningly beautiful. She was some type of Buddhist and had music playing in her dressing room 24/7; it was never to be turned off, she said. Mrs. Rashad had an amazing mind and could memorize her script on the first day.

Malcolm-Jamal Warner was wonderful and very approachable. Yet, as well known as he was, Malcolm had this amazing ability to get lost in a crowd. Once I saw him out shopping for batteries on Steinway Street around the corner from the studio. He put his fingers to his lips to hush me so I wouldn't blow his cover. I pretended I didn't know him and he went about his business.

Lisa Bonet was rarely around by the time I worked on the set. The only direct encounter I had with her was on an elevator, where she was being stalked by a man who claimed to know her famous rocker husband, Lenny Kravitz. I watched the man move closer and closer into her personal space until he had backed her into a corner. When we reached our floor, Lisa raced off the elevator and down the hall. One of the drivers stopped the man, who apparently hung around until the end of the day, causing Lisa to take the back way out. For all her fame and beauty, I didn't envy the sister.

Keshia Knight Pulliam and Raven-Symone were adorable, sweet, and well behaved. I didn't know Tempestt Bledsoe well. Sabrina Le Beauf was quiet, until after the last show, when she got incredibly emotional and cried and hugged everyone in sight.

Working in the presence of this level of talent—both actors and the production team—was an incredible experience. Even though I never pitched any ideas or wrote scripts, I felt the contribution I did was important; it helped to make things happen. Because I knew my contribution was valued on the set, I was perfectly happy working in the background, helping out and not getting acknowledgment from the outside world.

After all the years I had spent hating my jobs, I was finally experiencing the enjoyment and satisfaction I had only dreamed of. While at *Cosby* I learned that it is possible to love your job. I discovered the joy and satisfaction that comes from working at what you feel passionate about. And I found that it could be okay to work hard and not get paid a lot. If you love what you do, you figure all that other stuff out. I didn't realize it at the time, but I was also learning the work ethic and commitment that was required to be an entrepreneur.

CHAPTER 10

Conjure Woman

Gordon was the first man to really love and respect me for who I was, not for what he could make me into or what I might become. We were married on Saturday, December 28, 1991.

As I worked on the *Cosby* set, my creative juices started flowing. Immersed in that incubator of creativity, I became really inspired about my own budding passion: making my own fragrances. By then, I was buying fragrance oils and creating my own "perfume" sprays. I was also adding these custom-made scents to unscented lotions and baby oil I'd buy at the drugstore. I'd do this on weekends and in whatever free time I occasionally had at night.

At that point I combined oils by instinct and based on what smelled good to me. I didn't know about or understand the aromatherapeutic and healing properties some of them have. For example, I wasn't aware that there is a difference between an essential oil, which is extracted directly from plants and flowers, and the fragrance oil I was purchasing, which is manufactured in a lab. I bought what I could afford, which meant it was man-made. I created what smelled good to me. Apparently, I did a decent job; people were always asking me what I was wearing. On the *Cosby* set, several staff members asked me to craft unique fragrances for them. As a result I experimented with a wider variety of scents than I would have if I had only been making them for myself.

In February of 1991, Gordon and I moved from Manhattan to Brooklyn. That April, we went for a walk through Park Slope, an upscale neighborhood bordering Prospect Park. As we passed by a New Age bookstore, I saw crystals in the window.

"Let's go in," I said.

I wandered around looking at the stones, the books on meditation, and other interesting and unusual items that caught my eye. Gordon headed off in another direction. As luck would have it, eventually I stumbled across a book on essential oils, *The Art of Aromatherapy* by Robert Tisserand. I sat down and started to read it. What I learned I thought was just amazing. On a practical level, I discovered there were better ways to blend oils than I was currently using. I also found out a lot more about how fragrance and essential oils are different. Lavender and rose don't just smell different; they have different effects on the emotions and physical health of the person who wears them. The book contained all kinds of great recipes for massage oils, pomades and other products. I also learned something very important: I had been getting cheated when I purchased my oils. This I wanted to share with Gordon.

"Hey, G.P.," I said after tracking him down. "The guys on the street have been lying about the oils they've been selling me. You can't get an essential oil from a pineapple."

"I guess they won't be able to take advantage of you now," he laughed.

I didn't think much of it at the time, but now I realize that afternoon was an important day in my life. I felt compelled to buy the book. Even though I'm not a big reader, I was so interested in its contents that I couldn't put it down when I got home. I tried some of the book's simpler recipes. It became my bible. But I couldn't afford to buy the ingredients or create many recipes; I was saving my money.

While I had been experiencing all of the wonders of the *Cosby* set, there were also wonderful things going on at home. Gordon had proposed to me. It wasn't the big and flashy getting-down-on-your-knees-with-a-big-ring proposal, but rather the kind of proposal that develops organically in the process of living together.

In June of 1990 Gordon's father had passed away. One morning shortly thereafter he rolled over in bed and looked me in the eye.

"I don't like introducing you as my girlfriend," he said. "You're more than that to me. I want to be with you for the rest of my life."

Nothing else needed to be said. At Christmas dinner that year Mommy announced to the entire family that Gordon had asked for my hand in marriage. We were to be wed one year later. Needless to say, after my previous history with men, several family members looked at Gordon closely, carefully, and over a long period of time. He passed the test with flying colors. Mommy loved him. My aunts liked him and saw how well he took care of me. He was also from a big family and family was important to both of us. Gordon and I knew the show would be on hiatus and we would have two weeks vacation over Christmas. It was the perfect time for the wedding. If family members visited for the holidays, they could attend the wedding without having to make a second trip.

Gordon and I planned and saved. We were financing the festivities ourselves. Since neither of us had a lot of money, I never expected a ring, but Gordon would always say, "I have to get you an engagement ring."

At one point, one of my maids of honor instructed me to pick a diamond ring out of a Tiffany catalog; her sister worked there and could get us a discount. Since every dime we had was going to the wedding, I picked out something that wasn't ridiculously expensive—a $400 ring consisting of a delicate gold band with two pearls on either side of a diamond. I wasn't quite certain whether he was thinking of it for a Christmas gift, a wedding ring or for Valentine's Day, but I was positive he didn't have any extra money to get it. Between our large families and the huge *Cosby* cast and crew, we had a guest list of over two hundred.

In August of that year, Gordon and I returned to work for what would be the final *Cosby* season. But the fact that it was the last year didn't make the season any less hectic. I had a little time to select a caterer in the wee hours, after the show.

A week before the ceremony, the annual Christmas party was held at the Supper Club, a beautiful, fancy restaurant located in Manhattan. By the time Gordon and I got there, the party was already packed. Cast members, the production crew, people from the industry and friends were there.

As much as I enjoyed the *Cosby* team, the last thing I was in the mood for was a party. The pressure of the wedding coupled with our heavy work schedule was making me feel stressed out. Unfortunately, many of the party guests knew that we would be married in less than a week. I know they were just trying to be nice, but all night people kept asking me about it—"Are you ready? Are you nervous? Is the dress done?" The questions went on and on. To make matters worse, there was an amazing spread of food that I couldn't eat for fear that I wouldn't be able to get into my gown. While other people were indulging themselves with Christmas sweets, I was stuck picking through the crudités. Before long, I started getting frazzled and wanted to go home.

At one point I was talking to a friend when I noticed a crowd gathering near us. The women were all giggling and grinning.

"What's going on?" I asked.

"I don't know," came the response.

Suddenly the deejay played "Diamond and Pearls," one of my favorite Prince songs, and I became aware that Gordon was standing next to me. I wondered what was happening when he grabbed me by the hand and knelt down before me.

"Lisa, will you marry me?"

It was only then that I really realized what was going on. All eyes were on us. He was sliding onto my finger the diamond and pearl ring I had picked out of the Tiffany catalogue several months before. I felt like I couldn't breathe.

I wanted to scream, *"How could you do this to me in public?"*

"Yes," I said, instead.

Of course, Gordon was trying to be very romantic. As everyone congratulated me, I tried to be gracious and hide the fact that I was pissed off. But after all the commotion died down, boy was I hot! All I could think about was, *"Why did you have to ask me in front of everybody?"* No wonder people had been bugging me about the wedding—they all knew what was about to happen! I felt like I was living in a fishbowl.

Gordon knew something was wrong; I wasn't acting like someone who had just been proposed to. But it didn't take long before my anger shifted from Gordon to myself. I was angry for being angry at him. *It was so romantic. Look at this beautiful ring!* I was acting like a spoiled brat and I knew it.

When we were in the car on the way home, I finally had a meltdown. I cried and cried and cried.

"I'm so sorry," I bawled. "I didn't mean to—"

"It's okay. It's okay," he answered.

On Saturday, December 28 at five P.M. sharp at the Cathedral of St. John the Divine in Manhattan, Gordon and I married. There were 187 guests and eleven people in the wedding party. It was a black and white wedding. Gordon wore a black tux with a white vest and shirt. My Aunt Norma made my dress, an off-white, Thai silk sheath with a sweetheart neck and a hip-length jacket embroidered with sequins. Gordon's brother Bert composed a song just for us. After the wedding we spent one night in a hotel in Manhattan.

After the New Year, Gordon and I returned to work on the *Cosby* set. For one year, almost everything we had earned went toward paying for the wedding and reception. Now that everything was over, I could afford to return to my beloved fragrances. I pulled out my aromatherapy book and started experimenting with the recipes.

Erika Alexander, who joined the cast and played the character Pam liked how I smelled and learned that I dabbled in fragrances. She asked me to blend some oils for her. Totally unbeknownst to me, when she went to Kinapps, a pioneering natural hair salon, she took the oil with her and had the stylist apply it. The folks at the salon liked it enough that they wanted to purchase it for the shop. I was so excited. Even though people were asking me to make items for them, it had never really dawned on me that anyone might actually want to purchase my fragrances.

In order to talk to the people at Kinapps my line needed a professional look—better packaging and a label. But before I could do that, I had to figure out what to call the product. I decided on Total Body Compliment, since that could mean absolutely anything. That challenge out of the way, I set about naming my company. At first I didn't have anything in particular in mind, so I used a trick I had learned from Mr. Lewandowsky. I wrote down a brainstorming list of who I was and what I wanted to become. Carol's Daughter just happens to be one of the things I am. When I said it out loud, I got goose bumps. I liked it and it stuck. Next, I had the printer around the corner from the studio make labels for me. I purchased some empty bottles from a place where I bought perfume. Then I bottled my blends. I was ready.

It turns out I wasn't able to strike a deal with the people at Kinapps, but the experience was eye-opening and got me thinking in that direction. I left the meeting with a new idea blossoming in my mind. *Maybe I can do this "scent stuff" to make money one day,* I thought. I have to admit that I was also feeling a little discouraged—like things would have worked out if I had been more prepared. Over the next year or so, I would gain and lose confidence in myself. The thought of doing fragrances as a side business would enter my mind, but then I would think I should stick to doing it as a hobby. I was very afraid of being rejected.

In April 1992, *The Cosby Show* came to an end. I made good-bye gifts for all the cast members. One was a perfume for Mrs. Rashad that I labored over for hours. I scented it with mango, honey, vanilla fragrance, and essential oils of sandalwood and black pepper. It was my attempt at an Indian scent, since I knew she traveled there and played Indian music in her dressing room.

"I *love* this, Lisa," she said, sniffing her wrists. "This is fantastic!"

"Thank you, Mrs. Rashad."

"This smells so good, I think you should go into business."

"Thanks, Mrs. Rashad. That's nice of you to say."

"I'm serious, Lisa. I mean it."

"Really?"

"Yes, child. And if you ever make it into a business, you should call me now, hear?"

"Okay," I replied, not thinking I would ever be a businesswoman, but knowing that if I did, I would be way too embarrassed get in touch with her. Like my fifth-grade teacher Mrs. Jackman, I guess she was someone who could see something in me that I couldn't see in myself.

After the show ended, Gordon and I knew we had found our place in the world and had what it took to succeed in television. There was no way either of us was going to return to a job that wasn't fulfilling. Our rent was manageable and our bills were low, and I didn't have any credit card debt because of my bankruptcy. One way or another we knew we could survive—and we were right.

Over the next two years, Gordon and I worked on a series of production jobs. As our careers advanced, I kept "playing" in the kitchen. From my trusty book, I had learned some basic recipes—massage oils, herbal

Fragrance Tips for Your Wedding Day

As with most women, making sure that my dress was perfect was one of the most important concerns I had about my wedding. Asking my Aunt Norma to design and make it for me left me with no worries as to whether or not it and I would be beautiful. That freed me to focus on other things, including making myself smell good.

Before I ever started to make products I was infatuated with scents. I have read that in ancient Egypt (also known as Khamit), people would massage various oils into their body when they prepared for a special occasion. For instance, sandalwood would be applied to the hair, rose to the feet and maybe frankincense on the thighs. This practice of oiling and scenting the body is carried out in many cultures. On the day before the wedding of an East Indian Hindu bride, her mother, aunts, sister, cousins and friends gather around her. They feed her sweet foods so she will speak sweet words to her new husband. They oil her body and hair with fragrant emollients so she will smell sweet to him. Her hands and feet are hennaed (nonpermanent tattoo). All of these rituals are performed to make her more beautiful.

It is important to give careful thought to the fragrance you'll wear for your wedding. If the flowers for your ceremony are lilies, you may choose to wear lily. To reinforce the positive energies of the day, I suggest you think of scents that make you feel good and remind you of someone you love. So if, for instance, you were standing under a magnolia tree when your betrothed proposed, you may feel partial to magnolias.

Then again, you may already have a scent that is your signature—the aroma your partner identifies with you and has become connected to. This was the case with Gordon and me. After he and I first kissed in the Laundromat, he marveled that the scents he smelled in my hair were different from the one behind my ear and that together they created an entirely different fragrance around me. Back then, I wasn't yet creating my own scents; I was wearing a combination of Halston, Lauren and Design. By the time we were married, I had crafted several fragrances; however, I chose to recreate the combination that had first entranced my mate. I accented this combination with rose.

Once you have selected the fragrance or fragrances that you would like to wear on your wedding day, you will need to have them in several forms—a body wash or soap, a bath and body oil, a moisturizer and a spray. You need them so you can layer your fragrance. If you layer your scents they will last longer. If you do so on your wedding day you won't need to freshen your perfume until the reception is over and you are on your way to paradise—in one form or another.

blends for conditioning the hair, and salves. But the one I wanted to master—a body crème—kept eluding me.

One day my girlfriend Anu, who owns a popular salon called Khamit Kinks, asked me to stop by her shop because she liked the smell of some blends I'd made and wanted to make a purchase. I prepared samples and headed over to her place. She was busy with a client when I arrived, so I started leafing through the magazines sitting on the office table. One in particular caught my eye. It turned out to be a catalog full of all of the essential oils and ingredients my aromatherapy book described. How fortunate could I be?

"Where did you get this?" I asked Anu.

"Oh, I get it all the time. The catalog just comes in the mail."

"Do you have another copy I can have?"

"Just write down the number and call them," she said. "They're a good company."

She was right. It wasn't long before I started placing regular orders for essential oils, fragrances, cocoa butter, shea butter, beeswax, and other ingredients I needed to master the body crème recipe. I had always been comfortable in the kitchen. From my early days with Nana, I loved to cook. Now, it occurred to me, instead of making food to eat I was trying to make food for my skin.

I purchased the pots and utensils described in my book and a postal scale to measure my ingredients. First, I placed pieces of beeswax, cocoa butter, and shea butter in a pot. Next I measured out and added several oils (back then my choice was a blend of soy, sweet almond, and wheat germ). As they melted, I stirred and sniffed the air, smelling the sweet, warm scents of chocolate from the cocoa butter and honey from the beeswax. To this day I love the scents this blend makes. Next, I added water. Then I would quickly spoon the crème into jars and place them in the refrigerator to cool. But much to my chagrin, time after time the crème would separate and oils would rise to the top.

It took a Duncan Hines commercial two years later to help me perfect the process. As I watched the cake batter being whipped with a hand mixer, I thought, *Maybe that will work.* I raced into the kitchen and set up my supplies. I melted my fats as I had many times before, but this time something told me to call on Nana's spirit, just as I had when I attempted to make butter cake without her. I pulled out her beige crockery mixing bowl, one we used many times to make butter cake. I thought it would bring me luck. I poured the melted wax and oils into Nana's bowl. The smells of chocolate and honey reminded me of Nana's kitchen. Then I added the water. This time, instead of spooning the mixture into jars after I added the water, I whipped my "batter" with a cake mixer until it was cooled. To my surprise it stayed firm. My crème didn't separate.

The joy I felt was unbelievable. I ran through my one-bedroom apartment, leaping through the air, screaming, "I made cream! I made cream!"

Since Nana's butter cake bowl had made it work, from then on my cream was called Body Butter.

That May it was time for the annual flea market at St. Mary's Church, Mommy's church. I had participated in the flea market the previous year, but it had rained for much of the day and my results were disappointing.

"Do you want to get a table for the flea market?" Mommy asked.

"I don't know. I didn't do well last year."

"Yeah, but it was fun hanging out with the family. I think everyone's thinking about doing it again. Maybe the weather will be better this year."

"I don't know. . . ."

"You could sell the new crème. . . ."

"That's true. What could I use for jars?"

"What about the baby-food jars I have?" Mommy had just taken in another child, my baby sister, Tura. "It would be like Mama used to do with her hair pomade."

"That's true. I could make the jars work. Do you think you have a few dozen?"

"Oh, yeah."

"How much is the table?"

"Twenty-five dollars."

That night I sat down with a pencil and paper and added up how much it would cost me to participate in the flea market. I already had some wax, oils, perfumes and cocoa butter, so I would only need to buy some shea butter. When I added up the cost of everything, I would be spending about a hundred dollars. It was a risk, but who knows what might happen.

My assortment of products included Baby Powder, Coconut, Cinnamon Bun and Rose Body Butters. I couldn't use my Total Body Compliment labels—they didn't fit the baby-food jar—so I pulled out some supplies from work and made my own. I used white file folder labels and drew flowers on them with colored markers. They were homey, but did the job.

On the day of the flea market, I felt a lot more confidence in my products and their presentation than I had the previous year. I added flowers and an antique tablecloth to my display table. The event was a total family outing. My cousin Karen was selling floral arrangements, Uncle Ron had T-shirts featuring his artwork and photography, and Aunt Norma sold her not-to-be-believed, delicious carrot cake.

Gordon suggested that I should also sell some of the fragrances I had been making.

"Put them in small bottles so that we can sell them for one dollar. This will get them to come to the table and at least try the creams. It should be easy from there." And so we did.

Gordon handed out fliers scented with the oils. They drew people to us like honey draws bees. Once people came over, they tried my other products, which almost sold themselves, just as Gordon had predicted. Before I knew it my table had sold out! During the show I received fliers for several more flea markets, so I reinvested the hundred dollars I had invested in ingredients along with the profit I made from the show. That summer I attended a couple of more flea markets. I found that not only were my customers coming back, they were bringing their friends!

I spent that summer attending flea markets and street fairs during the hiatus between television seasons. One August afternoon I found myself sitting on my bed labeling jars of body butter. At four, I switched from soap operas to *Oprah*. It was what I did; turning on *Oprah* was like breathing. But I rarely had time to sit and watch. The show would play in the background and I would listen.

"Today on *The Oprah Show*, women who started their businesses with little or no money."

When I heard the title I thought it was interesting, but I didn't associate it with myself—I wasn't a businesswoman; I was in television. But as the show progressed, the things they were talking about started to make me curious. I started to listen a little more carefully. By the middle of the show, Oprah ran a quiz so you could figure out if you had the personality profile to be an entrepreneur.

By now I was sitting still and watching because the show was resonating with me.

Oprah and her guests talked about what it took to be an entrepreneur.

The women talked about how they had started. One woman had begun with $300, another with $600. They were all "regular" people. One of the women stressed the importance of loving what you do.

"You know you're onto the right thing," she said, "if you will wake up in the middle of the night and go do that thing, no questions asked."

That's me! I thought. I loved my flowers and perfumes and butters.

So, on that ordinary afternoon when money was tight and I was waiting on my next job, a revelation hit me. *Maybe this can be a business and not just a hobby,* I thought. *This can supplement me in dry times. And maybe it will give Gordon breathing room to be pickier about his jobs.*

I was thirty-one years old when I had this revelation. After several years of dedicated self-improvement work, I had finally reached a point where I felt like my life was coming together. Now I was having a revelation that would have escaped me if I hadn't worked hard on myself.

On this seemingly average day the Universe brought me some amazing news. Using Oprah as the messenger, God revealed to me that my lifelong fascination with fragrances that had morphed into a hobby could also become a way of supporting myself. The revelation came to me in that simple way: no thunder, no lightning, no burning bush. Just me on my bed filling baby food jars and Oprah on TV.

After this discovery my sense of who I was shifted. Before long, my newfound business idea started developing a momentum of its own.

Lisa's Tips for Starting a Business on a Budget

My business was forced to grow slowly. Because of my bad credit, tax liabilities and inability to get a business loan, I had to be resourceful and spend money wisely. Here are a few things I learned:

1. Ask your friends and family for help when you have a lot of work to do. Something as simple as mailing out brochures can be made easier with more hands involved. Make your helpers a good meal or take them out afterward. The work will be done quicker and you'll have fun at the same time.

2. Shop at 99-cents stores. There are so many items available there for small, home-based businesses. For example, you may find storage bins that could cost three times as much as from a high-end store. Granted, the 99-cents bins may not hold up as long, but they will do the job until you have more money.

3. Read interior design magazines, or watch the many do-it-yourself shows now on television. (I didn't have those at my disposal back in 1994.) The ideas you will get from these resources can help you find space where you thought you had none, set up your office, decorate your salon, make curtains for your shop windows—things that would cost a lot of money if you hired a decorator.

4. Check with the small-business development program in your area to find out what free services may be available to you. You may be able to speak with lawyers, accountants and other consultants free of charge. If these services are not available gratis, invest in an hour with an attorney that specializes in your type of enterprise.

5. Barter. Why spend money when you can trade services? Swap cookies for typing, babysitting for alone time, cooperate with a friend and organize your offices together.

6. Invest in an accountant. Don't try to do your own taxes. The money you spend on a professional will be far less than what you might pay in penalties and interest because you didn't know the tax laws.

7. There are great finds in value-oriented stores that are in your area—like Ikea for furniture, storage, lighting, and display. I can't tell you how many times people have come into my shop and asked, "Where did you get that?" and my answer was Ikea. Another great resource is Wal-mart. I love their selection of candle holders and trays. They also have good deals on towels and washcloths, which come in handy if you own a spa or nail salon. Lastly, Marshall's for beautiful baskets, if you are in the gift-basket business.

CHAPTER 11

Working It

*Every night when I came home from work, I would make one of my products.
My customers liked that my products were made by hand in my kitchen.*

U ntil this point in my life, I had taken other people's direction and
had carried out their vision. After watching that Oprah show, I
started developing a vision of my own. I had thought of my career as TV
production and this "scent stuff," as I called it, as my hobby. Now, slowly
but surely and one day at a time, I began to realize my love of fragrances
could be so much more.

Actually, a quick look around my bedroom proved that my so-called
hobby had been occupying a larger and larger place in my life. Ingredients
that were once confined to the back alcove of the room had spread and

were now occupying storage tubs under my windows along with a fold-away table and chair. My hobby had actually become like a second job.

Things were unfolding wonderfully! Now the only challenge was to figure out how to keep them running smoothly. At this stage, I began to learn two important lessons. First, when you set a firm intention, as long as that intention is honorable, you have an almost magical ability to attract resources you need and people who can help you. If you have less than honorable intentions, you'll attract a lot of stuff all right, but much of it won't be good. And, second, many of the things I needed were already accessible to me in my environment; I just hadn't recognized them.

Now that I had a vision for Carol's Daughter and my life, I was always thinking of different ways to grow and succeed. Because of my experience with Mrs. Gibson, I knew that it was possible to do more at work than just my job. I just had to be up front about it, so I didn't get in trouble. Working in television provided a perfect opportunity to do side projects, since the nature of the work is often "hurry up and wait." It's okay to be reading a book or working on something else, as long as you're ready to go when you're called. So I started looking for opportunities to work on Carol's Daughter. Before long, I realized how many resources at work could be applied to my own business. This is a strategy I'd recommend for any budding entrepreneur or person pursuing a dream.

Here's an example of how things started coming together. In 1994, I was working on a start-up company called Café USA, which wanted to supply a television network to food courts in malls. Because it was a new company our team was small: the office manager, several business executives and me. By this time, being with higher-ups no longer intimidated me. After spending hours in writing sessions with the executive producers of *The Cosby Show,* I had no problem striking up a conversation with bosses over a coffee break or lunch. Because our team was so small, I ended up working more closely with them than I had with business types before.

For the first time in my life, meetings I attended as the resident executive assistant/production coordinator started becoming interesting. I began paying attention as the team talked about venture capital (I was broke; I would need money to start my business), planned advertising strategies (I needed to know how to reach new customers), and any other business-related activity that came up. I started to read the trade publications that came into the office with my company in mind. These were resources and opportunities I wouldn't have recognized in the past. I would have seen them as relevant to somebody else. With my new mind-set, I started taking notes about anything I thought might pertain to Carol's Daughter.

The more time I spent with the business team, the more I got to know them and they me. I worked with seven former advertising executives.

One day, I found myself in the lunchroom with Steve Bowen, one of the vice presidents. It dawned on me that since I was always around these business "whizzies," maybe I should ask their advice about my company. So I struck up the conversation, and, yes, I was nervous.

"Steve, can I bounce some ideas off of you about the products I'm developing?"

"Products? What type of products?"

"I make body care products in my kitchen. Right now it's mostly moisturizers, but I've made bath salts and I'm working on a shampoo, shower gel and hair products."

"You make them? That's fantastic. How'd you get into that?"

As I told him my tale of butters and scents, I became more relaxed. He listened and laughed with me. He then went on to tell me how much money there was to be made in hair care products; the key was knowing how to sell them.

"Basically, you have to show an unattainable standard of hair. Perfect hair."

"Perfect hair?" I asked him, confused.

"In advertising, we use Asian hair because it's thick and shiny."

And straight, I thought.

Overall the conversation was good, but "Asian hair" was not going to help me sell my products. It did, however, give me a clue that there was a gap. An African-American woman will damage her tresses trying to obtain advertising's version of "perfect hair." To me that meant that black women were not even being targeted. Needless to say, I ramped up development of my hair care line immediately. Ironically, it was a white man who helped me figure this out.

In between testing my new hair oil and making hair butter, I made certain to do my nine-to-five job well. Since my bosses knew about my side business, it would have been catastrophic to my career if I let Carol's Daughter interfere with my ability to excel at work. By then I may have wanted to stay home and make butters all day, but balance was key and I knew it.

Sometimes, my job required that I run personal errands for my bosses.

Over the years, I learned not to fuss when I was asked to do these types of tasks. I enjoyed getting out of the office, even if it was to exchange a frozen yogurt with nuts for one with sprinkles. By then, life had taught me that experiences you think are meaningless can become important later on— my trip to Sam Flax, for instance.

Sam Flax is a stationery store where I was sent to purchase a pen for one of the men in my office—at least that's what I thought. When I was in the store, I discovered that the Universe had sent me there for another rea- son. Sam Flax sold all sorts of paper—with flower petals in it, linen blends, card stock. In the past I wouldn't have paid much attention; I would have gotten the pen and left. But now as I browsed through the store, these ex- quisite papers began to resonate with me. I envisioned the Carol's Daughter brochure on printed coral and lavender linen paper.

After developing that vision, it didn't take long until the Universe hooked me up with an opportunity to make my brochures at work. In the past, I would have been a little pissed off when the team needed to go to Las Vegas for an expo and chose the blond secretary to accompany them instead of me. In their defense, they did ask me if I minded. But with an expanding vision of Carol's Daughter taking root in my imagination, I told them the truth—I couldn't care less. I kept to myself the fact that I had my own agenda.

With the team out of the office, I would be free to work on my own stuff uninterrupted. I crammed and finished the project they left for me to do and spent much of the week working on my brochure. I got to experi- ment with the new, off-the-hook fonts that came installed on the new computers that had just arrived in the office (thank you, God!). By the time the team returned, in addition to completing the work they assigned me to do, I had also designed and printed 250 coral and 250 lavender Carol's Daughter brochures on beautiful linen paper. I shared my new style with the guys and they loved it.

Not too much later, another resource became available. Bill Perkins of- fered to take me to breakfast and let me pick his brain. Bill was another ad- vertising executive, whose office was right near my desk. Bill had tested my Cool Mint shower gel after his basketball games and liked it. He was very excited about the look of the brochure and the potential of my products. Bill's feedback bolstered my self-confidence.

"From an advertiser's point of view, you have the lingo down," he said. "And the labels and brochures look fantastic!"

Bill filled me in on how to improve upon and maximize the potential of my fledgling customer database. He suggested that I send samples to magazine beauty editors as a way of getting some press. When I was ready, I should consider purchasing a portion of *Essence* magazine's mailing list and sending out brochures and samples.

I couldn't afford to follow up on many of his suggestions, but it did help me expand my vision of who I was and the things I could do to expand my company. He made me feel as if I had something real to work with, and he was the first one to sense the important role *Essence* would play in helping me grow my business.

By this point in Carol's Daughter's existence, many nights when I arrived home from my day job the telephone would be ringing.

"I'm glad you're home," the caller would say.

"Who's calling?"

"My name is Cynthia. You don't know me, but I bought your Cinnamon Bun Body Butter at the African Street Festival. I'm running out. I want to know where you'll be vending this weekend so I can come and get some."

"I'm not going to be vending this weekend. But if you're about to run out, you can come by my house."

"When can I come?"

"How is Saturday morning?"

"I'll be there at ten."

"I look forward to seeing you."

The sisters would always show up, sometimes with friends. Before long, people started coming unannounced. At times it got a little weird, but given my financial situation, it didn't make sense to turn away money. I didn't have the resources it would take to have a real store.

Word-of-mouth among African-American women is a very powerful thing, and news of how to obtain Carol's Daughter products had found its way onto the grapevine. More and more people began to show up at my door on Saturday mornings to shop. Before long Gordon and I were forced to move into a larger apartment. The daily dance around the sprigs of eucalyptus that seemed to be growing in the bedroom was getting to be a bit much. We moved to a fourth-floor walk-up and it was then that Carol's Daughter really began to take off.

Every night when I came home from work, I would make one of my products. That way I would have enough on hand for what soon became the Saturday rush. In our new apartment I had a room that was all for Carol's Daughter. It was my office, workroom, storage room and show-room. Shelving that acted as walls separated the various areas. I hung chimes outside my window. The shopping area was decorated with baskets, flowers, shells and a Balinese mask that had been a wedding gift.

Gordon thought what was happening was just amazing. He used to joke with his brother Jeff that people would come over and give his wife money. We never talked about safety and, thankfully, I was never harmed. I suppose that the Universe didn't want those kinds of thoughts clouding our thinking. At that time we needed the money and didn't have a lot of options. In time the dollars started to add up.

I couldn't always guarantee that I would be home on Saturdays. Sometimes people would leave nasty messages on my answering machine when they came and I wasn't there. If you were one of them, I apologize, but there were times that I had to work.

In November, my mother amazed me by bringing another baby into our fold. Khoret Amen-Tera joined our family shortly after her birth. She was such a blessing to us and my mother truly honored me by giving her my name. It was a perfect sign that my "differences" were understood and accepted.

When the holidays came that year, there was more good news and also some bad. First the good news: After three years in good standing with one credit card with a secured balance, I was approved to lease equipment that would allow me to process people's credit card payments. Making payment more convenient for people would really help Carol's Daughter grow.

Also, that season my products were mentioned in *Essence* magazine. It wasn't a big mention; it was a short beauty story with a quiz that helped the reader match their personality type with the right fragrance. It said something like, "If you're a B type person—a bohemian girl—fragrances you might like are . . ." There was a list of products and one of the choices was Carol's Daughter Fresh Peach. That little sentence on page 232 helped boost my business. Every Saturday, more and more sisters trudged up the four flights of stairs to my apartment. Fortunately, the landlord and neighbors didn't seem to mind. I was very, very grateful.

But right on its heels came the bad news. For five years my accountant had been trying to get the IRS to respond to our numerous letters about my case. Now their answer was hard to face. With interest and penalties I no longer owed the $14,000 I once did. My debt had more than doubled. I now owed $33,000! *Thirty-three thousand dollars!* The news was devastating.

I called my mother and Gordon in tears and both of them encouraged me. Gordon actually had the presence of mind to find a blessing in the situation.

"Thank God you were approved to process credit cards before the IRS got back to you," he observed. "Otherwise, you wouldn't have been able to accept those sales until after they were paid off."

Gordon was right. If things had happened in reverse order my business would never have been able to get off the ground and grow in the way it has. Now that I look back on it, as painful as it was at the time, everything worked out perfectly.

"Write this down!" the voice said to me as I lay in my bed.

"Huh?" I said, sitting up and looking to see who was talking. No one was there. I had been dreaming again. It was four A.M. and even though I had been asleep, I knew I had heard someone speaking to me. It was as loud and clear as if someone was lying in bed next to me.

"Hurry up and write it down before you forget."

I grabbed a pen and paper and started scribbling as fast as I could. My holiday sale, which had become an annual open house in my apartment, was scheduled to begin at noon. Yet the voice in my dream was telling me to make a *Waiting to Exhale* gift basket before I opened up shop. It even told me what to put in it—Silk Body Milk, Champagne Body Spray, Sister Fragrance Oil and Fresh Peach Body Cleansing Gel. Some of its contents were fragrances I hadn't even made yet.

Even though they had been very popular, I hadn't yet read Terri McMillan's book nor had I seen the movie. But I knew everyone was raving about them. Fortunately, by now I really trusted the different ways my intuition would speak to me. Dreams had become an important way that Spirit spoke to me. So even though it was the middle of the night, I knew what I had to do. I got up from bed and started making the products and baskets it told me about.

"Whatcha doin', honey pot?" Gordon asked during a middle-of-the-night bathroom run.

"I had a dream and had to get up and make some baskets."

With that he smiled, nodded and went about his business. Messages in my dreams were something to which he had become accustomed. By the time he woke up at eight A.M., I had created thirty *Waiting to Exhale* gift baskets.

It didn't take long for my effort to pay off. That afternoon one woman walked in and bought twenty-four of the thirty baskets I'd made! Her sale alone made it a phenomenal day. I couldn't believe it. I kept thinking, *What if I hadn't had that dream?* It became another sign for me to keep going forward even though my huge money problems made some days very difficult.

Even though business was going well, the size of my IRS debt would frequently depress me. So I followed Mommy's advice.

"Don't think about it," she suggested. "Pay as much as you can as often as you can and pay it down. That's all you can do. Stressing over it is not going to make it go away."

"But Mommy, it will take forever to pay it off."

"No, it won't. I don't believe that. Just pray."

I knew she was right. I prayed and still do for strength, clarity and patience.

Work in television continued to come for both Gordon and me. Gordon had advanced from driving and production assistant jobs to doing camera work. Eventually he landed full-time work with a shopping channel. Most of my jobs ended up being temporary, but that was okay with me. Even though the gigs came to an end, another would start within days of it, so my income was pretty consistent.

I left Café USA to work on a show for Hearst Entertainment and *Redbook* magazine. Even though I was working someplace else, I still had permission to come back to Café USA to use their computers to print labels and brochures. This was back when only rich people had computers at home because they cost so much money.

When that project ended, I did a few other jobs and eventually landed a job as script supervisor on Lifetime Television's *Our Home,* a home show. I had an assistant who was eager to learn, so I taught him. For the first time in my television career I had normal working hours, which left my evenings and weekends free for Carol's Daughter. During my second sea-

Facing Money Problems and Restoring Your Credit

When I was forced to declare bankruptcy, not only was I ashamed of myself, I thought I had ruined my life forever. I mistakenly believed the "conventional wisdom" that a bankruptcy on my credit report would prevent me from enjoying my life forever. Well, having credit problems did cause me to have to sacrifice, exercise discipline and "behave" financially in ways I hadn't when I was younger. Occasionally, my history of bad credit still comes back to embarrass me, even though the problems occurred in the mid-1980s. Still, I can't tell you how glad I am that I didn't let money problems stop me from pursuing my passion. Remember, I started my company with only one hundred dollars. I built it and generated enough income to support my family while I was still bankrupt. If I had adhered to "conventional wisdom," that should have been impossible!

Here's what my experience has taught me: when you take responsibility for your choices and always strive to "do the right thing," little miracles take place in your life. They happen every day, so keep your eyes and heart open to them. Over time, they build on each other and create momentum in your world. If you're short on resources, over your head financially and/or feeling hopeless for whatever reason, I encourage you to pray for guidance and never lose sight of your dreams. God can—and as I have learned, does—move mountains, even for ordinary people. The contribution our Creator put you on this planet to make is between you and Him. Humans are not powerful enough to stand in your way; that is, unless you let them.

These commonsense financial strategies helped me take responsibility for my spending and get my financial house in order. You may find them helpful.

- If you are spending to make yourself feel better, you may have a problem that needs to be addressed in counseling or therapy. If you just buy things on credit because it's easier for you than paying cash, then you need to put credit cards on a time-out.
- Nowadays, many people are using credit cards more than cash. If this is you, get a card with a fixed spending limit. Or use a checking or debit card that will only allow you to charge what's in your checking account. Use this one card for gas, food, dry cleaners, etc. If it doesn't have a high spending limit, you won't be tempted to buy things you don't need.

- Leave your credit cards at home or, better yet, cut them up and pay cash. Even though it was difficult in the beginning, being without credit cards after my bankruptcy forced me to think about whether I really wanted something. Impulse shopping was a thing of the past.
- Read your credit card statement and take notice of how much you are paying in interest charges. If you just keep paying the minimums on your cards, the interest really adds up. Take the time to do the math. Multiply the monthly interest by the number of months it will take you to pay your credit card off. You would be surprised at what you could do with that money. And I'm sure you'll be hard-pressed to locate the items you purchased that made those interest charges.
- If you are coming out of bankruptcy, get a secured card in order to begin building good credit. Use it to purchase the things you need each month—groceries, gas, items you would normally pay cash for—and pay off the whole amount at the end of the month. But don't go overboard. Remember, you have to pay the balance in full each month.
- If you are having serious financial challenges, call the consumer credit counseling service in your area.

son Lifetime cut back my workweek to four days. I thought they would reduce my pay, but they didn't. I took advantage of every minute of it.

During a weekly production meeting, the team discovered that there was a hole in the show's lineup.

"Lisa, why don't we do the segment on you?" the executive producer asked.

"What would you like me to do?"

"Well, can you do a segment on making potpourri?"

"Sure, I can." Potpourri was something I had learned how to make to help decorate my gift baskets. Here was a chance to do something I loved and get free press for my business at the same time. Once again, telling my bosses about my side business proved to be a good idea. And once again the resources I needed to help my company were very close at hand.

And just like that, "Lisa Price, the owner of Carol's Daughter, a homemade body care company, based in Brooklyn, New York," showed housewives across America how to make potpourri. It was my first television appearance promoting Carol's Daughter.

After all those years working in television behind the scenes, doing my first work in front of the camera was very exciting. Shortly thereafter, I received a phone call from *Essence* magazine. *Essence* wanted to photograph some of my products for the December 1995 issue. I was thrilled! I had been an *Essence* reader my entire adult life, so having my products featured in the magazine was a real honor. Once again, I knew that God was in my corner; I hadn't gone looking for free publicity from *Essence*.

For the photo shoot, I made a holiday gift set called an Angel Basket that I sold for fifty dollars. Several people talked to me about the tremendous number of orders I would receive after appearing in the magazine. They recommended that I have 1,000 baskets ready to sell. But no matter what they told me, my intuition told me not to make them. *I can't do that. If no one buys them, what am I going to do with all those products?* So instead of spending money on baskets when other holiday items needed to be created, I got organized. I wrote down everything I would need if I had to make 1,000 baskets quickly.

Thank goodness I listened to my gut, because I only received three phone calls. Two were from people trying to sell me something and one was from someone who said she wanted to buy the basket—but only if she could get free samples first. The response was disappointing but the magazine clipping would look great in the press kit I envisioned having in the future.

The next month *Essence* did a big hair story that covered straight, braided, natural and locked hair. On the lock page, there was one line that read, "To keep locks moisturized try Carol's Daughter Loc Butter," followed by my phone number. I got 500 requests for catalogs from that one line alone. It worked out well because the issue was on the newsstands in December, just in time for Christmas.

Between my first time on television and Carol's Daughter's first appearance in *Essence*, Gordon and I learned some exciting news. We were pregnant! We found out while we were attending his family reunion. Since so many important people were present, we made the announcement then and there.

Right away I started getting morning sickness. I know that many women experience it, but when your job is to make fragrances and those very smells make you sick, it is not a good thing. Scents that I had created and loved before, I now could not stand. Yet I kept working through it.

Stop making Mommy sick, I would say to my tummy. *Mommy's got a business to run.* Eventually my baby listened.

Ever since that *Oprah* show three years earlier, when I realized Carol's Daughter could be a full-time business, I had worked hard in the hope I could stay home with my children. Now I was in a position to do it. Gordon was advancing professionally and I knew that we could live on his income, and Carol's Daughter had gotten to the point that it could sustain itself.

In February of 1996 I left my television career behind. In March I became a mother. I was admitted into the hospital three weeks before my due date because my blood pressure was high. When I checked into the hospital that morning, Mommy was with me. The doctor needed to decide if he was going to induce.

"Don't be nervous," Mommy said, encouraging me. "It's so exciting. The baby will be here soon."

She was smiling that smile I loved so much. The same one she gave me when I was a child. I looked at her face and thought, *She's so pretty.*

"I know that everything will be okay," I said. "But you know me, this is not on schedule. I haven't made all of my plans yet. I was supposed to have three more weeks."

"Don't worry. I'll take care of everything," she promised. "Aunt Ruby and Karen will help. You just focus on that baby and don't worry about anything else."

And with that my Mommy allayed my fears and calmed my spirit. I rested my head on her shoulder and felt safe in her arms. The doctor decided to induce labor, but the baby was turned the wrong way in my uterus. After three days of Pitocin, ice chips, pushing and several moments which my husband would later describe as alien possession (there were feats of athleticism that I performed during labor that frightened him), our son Forrest entered the world by C-section. Up until that point, I thought my wedding ceremony was the most perfect thing I had ever beheld. Then I looked at that little face, held his tiny hand and smelled the top of his head. It was magical.

Deciding to work on my business and stay home with my baby was very liberating. It wasn't a top-of-the-mountain moment, but more of a natural progression. I loved my television career very much, but I loved being independent more.

CHAPTER 12

Take This Job and Love It!

My sons, Ennis and Forrest.
I can't tell you how many community baths I had when they were toddlers.
Being their mom is such an amazing feeling.

When the phone rang I was melting cocoa butter in a pot on the stove.

"Aunt Syl is going to closing today," Mommy told me.

"Oh. Really?" I responded.

Even over the phone, I knew that Mommy could hear the disappointment in my voice. Aunt Syl and Uncle Robbie now lived in Georgia, but they still owned the house next door to Aunt Ruby and Uncle Stan's, where Nana and Gramps used to reside. I wanted both houses to stay in the family and with them all my wonderful memories.

When Mommy and I hung up, I burst into tears. I had messed things up once again. I wanted that house. I wanted Gordon and I to live in it and raise a family and share memories of the house with my children. But I couldn't work up the courage to even ask about it. I felt so guilty and ashamed about my finances, I couldn't even fix my mouth to say the words. I didn't think I had enough money for a down payment, not to mention the perfect credit I believed you needed to qualify for the mortgage. And there was no way I would ask Aunt Syl for a favor. But I couldn't wallow in it now, I had Healthy Hair Butter cooking on the stove.

Later that day my luck turned.

"You're not going to believe this, Lisa," Mommy said.

"What happened?"

"They didn't sell the house."

"What? What happened?"

"Would you believe those people came to the closing without a check. After they knew Syl and Robbie flew up from Georgia. Sylvia is hot. Now, she's refusing to sell them her house."

This time when I hung up the phone, I had a different reaction. This was the second closing that had fallen through. It was a sign—I was certain. I felt like the Universe was telling me "Hello! The door is open. Will you walk through it?"

Could the answer be as simple as gathering the nerve to ask the question?

I asked Gordon if he would be interested in living in the house. He responded with an overwhelming yes. Because the business was creating so much traffic in our building, the landlord was pressuring me to rent a studio to use for the business. We were running out of space in our apartment, so Gordon and I had been considering his offer. I knew Aunt Syl was anxious about the house being vacant—not to mention the fact that between the two failed closings one of the pipes had burst.

We may not qualify for a mortgage, but we can certainly afford to pay rent. Maybe that option would be good for both of us.

My intuition kept telling me that at the least I should start a dialogue with her. The worst she could say is no, and I'd be no worse off than when I started.

"Aunt Syl," I asked the next morning. "Do you think you and Uncle Robbie would be willing to rent the house to Gordon and I?"

"I didn't know you were interested. Why didn't you say something sooner? Let me discuss it with Uncle Robbie."

Once again, the Universe intervened. I learned that being willing to overcome my fear and merely ask the question could open doors I hadn't been able to envision opened when I was afraid. Together, Gordon and I discovered an unexpected solution, and in June of 1996 we were able to move into our new house—a three-story brownstone.

There was a basement we could use for storage. On the ground floor were a dining room, kitchen, full bath and laundry room. We could use the dining room as the showroom for Carol's Daughter. The company would use the kitchen to produce product during the day; at night our family could use it. On the parlor floor was a very large living room and two rooms we could use as bedrooms. On the third floor was a two-bedroom apartment we could rent out. Carol's Daughter would have room to grow, and we would be landlords for the first time. Even Forrest could have his own room. Everything was perfect.

But even though things were great, it didn't take long before I was feeling overwhelmed. I have never for one day regretted leaving television production, but in those early months after I left my job, I did feel the pressure of losing that steady income. When I quit working, Carol's Daughter was generating just enough revenue to pay for itself. Now that I didn't have a regular check from my TV job, I felt pressure to grow the company quickly to make up for my lost income—especially because my IRS bill was like an albatross around my neck. I was terrified of the IRS. I wanted to do everything I could to get them out of my life.

During that same time I also learned how difficult being a homeowner can be. Owning my own home sounded so romantic when I was living in apartments. It had never occurred to me that when something went wrong—when a toilet wouldn't flush, the roof leaked or a faucet wouldn't stop dripping—and you're an apartment dweller, you just call the landlord. Now Gordon and I were the landlords. When something in the apartment went wrong, our tenants would call us. When something went wrong in our own living quarters, we had to rely on ourselves. Deep down inside I felt that Aunt Syl and Uncle Robbie would be there for us if we needed them, but I didn't want to need them. I wanted to stand on my own two feet and do things on my own. I had the "need to please," too much pride and fear of failure all going on at the same time.

That's on top of the incredible pressures I felt being a first-time mom. Naturally I wanted everything to be perfect. I worried about the normal things, like dropping him on his head. But then there were the irrational things. *If I choose the wrong mobile for his crib, will he develop a psychosis and need therapy as an adult?*

From the beginning nothing about motherhood seemed to go as I had planned. For starters, I had envisioned myself having a natural delivery, but Forrest was turned face first and had gotten stuck. After three days of labor, I couldn't take it anymore and had a C-section. Even though I endured incredible pain, there was a part of me that felt I had failed Forrest. I thought that childbirth should be natural, that everything that occurred during childbirth was for a reason, and that a C-section deprived him of coming into the world in the way that nature intended. That made me even more determined to give him a healthy start by breastfeeding. But that, too, proved to be elusive. Fortunately, the Universe sent my girlfriend Kim.

I had known Kim for several months. She's nurturing, funny, beautiful and strong—one of those people who always has a light emanating from her. When I was pregnant I shared with her that it was vital that I breastfeed my babies. Breastfeeding became important to me when I was in Ausar Auset. All the women in that organization fed their children naturally. I thought it was beautiful. I hadn't been breastfed. Mommy told me that back when she had me, many doctors were encouraging women to take a pill to dry up their milk so they could feed their children formula instead. But unlike Mommy and many of the women of her generation who were lied to about the importance of breast milk, I knew about breastfeeding's health benefits for both the infant and the mother. I wanted to breastfeed my babies for a minimum of two years.

Forrest seemed to have another idea in mind. Because my labor was induced three weeks early, my breasts weren't yet engorged. Also, since the delivery process took so long, I was exhausted after he was born. By the time I was able to sit up to feed him, he had already been put on a bottle. After that Forrest just wouldn't nurse. That's where Kim came in handy. For one full week Kim called several times a day with information and tips to encourage me.

"Hang in there, girl," she would say. "You've gotta keep trying."

"I can't tell how much he's drinking," I'd respond. "It's making me nervous that he's not getting enough."

"Here's how you tell. If he's crying he's hungry. If he urinates he's eating. If he goes to sleep, he's not hungry."

"But I don't think he's eating," I'd answer, on the verge of tears. "I don't want him to waste away. I thought babies just knew what to do."

"It can be hard, Lisa. So just keep trying. I'm not going to give up on you, sis."

Sometimes I wished she would. In that postpartum state my perspective was skewed; one week felt more like a month. Yet I also felt in my heart that Kim knew what she was talking about. When I first brought Forrest home I fed him some formula. However, the things she was saying made sense to me. So I cut out the formula and we waited on my breasts.

"How's it coming?" she'd ask when she called later on.

"It's not. I'm having a hard time," I'd bawl. My hormones were fluctuating wildly.

"Every time he cries stick your breast in his mouth. He'll learn what he's supposed to do."

"I've been trying that and nothing happens. I'm afraid he's going to lose too much weight. Maybe I should go get some formula."

"Don't do that. Keep trying. I remember the person who talked to me during her pregnancy about how important breastfeeding was."

Why doesn't she leave me alone? I'd think.

"I know you're getting frustrated with me because I keep bugging you," she'd continue.

Um-hmmm, I'd think.

"I'm only bugging you because I know how much you want to nurse your child. If you're mad at me, it's okay. You'll love me for it later."

And I did. After a while I could feel my milk start coming in. I had needed the action of the baby's sucking to stimulate production. The first time Forrest pulled away from my breast, belched, and a little bit of milk ran down his chin, I was ecstatic. From then on I was fine. It was very empowering watching him grow and knowing that my own milk was nourishing him.

In many ways I loved being a new mom. I would just stare at Forrest's face or look into his little eyes and just totally love him in a way I hadn't loved anyone before. But filling all these different roles was very, very difficult. First of all I had to work a drastically different schedule. Before Forrest was born, I could work all the time. I'd get up every morning when Gordon went to work. I'd work all day until he came home ten or twelve hours later. We'd eat and then I often did a little work later that night.

I was always very organized and efficient. I'd set my pots on the stove and start melting down my butters and oils. As they cooled, I'd label the products I'd bottled the night before. After that I'd do paperwork and filing. At the time I didn't have regular orders, so I'd do shipping whenever I had to, but I'd try to get it out of the way because I hated it. Sometimes I had to work on weekends, but it wasn't that big of a deal because I wasn't taking time away from somebody else. Of course, things started to shift when I was pregnant. I had to rest sometimes, and it seems like you're always going to the doctor. That's when I started realizing how much my life would have to change.

After Forrest was born, carefully planned and organized days went out the window. All I could think about was *How am I going to juggle all this?* Like all new mothers, I was awake 'round the clock. I had so much more to do than before. But one thing I think happens to women when they have children is they learn to get to a deep sleep quicker. Because you can't sleep through the night, I believe your body gets you there faster. You are better able to catnap throughout the day.

Forrest would awaken at two A.M. to nurse, but then he would want to stay up. So I'd nurse him, then take him down to the basement, put him in his bouncy seat and start working. He'd coo and laugh as he watched me. When he'd get fussy, I'd nurse him again and we'd both fall asleep at about four A.M. I'd get three hours of sleep before he awakened. At that point one of the women from Aunt Ruby's church would come over and help me with him for a couple of hours. That way I could get another hour or two of rest. This was how I got sleep and kept my business running.

Breastfeeding became an activity that helped give me balance. Even though the business was really busy, I was forced to stop to feed him. I admit that at first I sometimes looked at it as a disruption to my work. Before long, I realized it was a benefit. In addition to giving Forrest and me an opportunity to bond, breastfeeding forced me to slow down. I had to be still and take a breath—something I would never have done if left to my own devices. If I didn't become a mother I suspect I would have burned out trying to keep up with all the demands.

But my child needed me, my husband needed me, my customers needed me. I felt like I was always being pulled in different directions, which didn't leave much time for me. Plus, physically I didn't feel so great about myself. I had gained back thirty of the forty-five pounds I had lost prior to getting pregnant. I felt like I had failed again. I was even having a hard time looking in the mirror. I would make plans to exercise or eat a certain way, but it was too hard to be perfect in all those areas. Expecting myself to do everything right, I was setting myself up to fail and didn't even know it.

While my business continued to grow and on the surface my life looked good, on the inside I felt like I was spiraling out of control. Eventually I hit the wall. Gordon and I spent several months in counseling to get back on track. As demands had begun to pile up in my life, I became angry with him and angry with myself for being angry with him. I never would have believed it if someone had told me it would happen, but we reached a point where we did not know how to talk to each other.

Initially, I hated the idea of counseling. That was something rich folks did to waste their money. I learned how wrong I was. Marriage counseling did wonders for us. After our couples counseling was finished, I continued to get help for myself.

My therapist helped me see that I was the only person who could change my out-of-control life—since who was the one controlling it? Me. *I* made the choices that kept me so busy, *I* had to learn to make time for myself. I've made a lot of progress, but I'm still learning that lesson.

The therapist would ask, "So, when have you scheduled your next massage?"

"I haven't."

"Well, when are you going to book it?"

"Hmmm . . ." I'd think. "Well, it's not far from here. I guess I can book it for the next time I come to see you."

"That sounds like a good plan."

Without the therapist all these voices would race around my head: *I don't have the money. I don't have the time. I don't have enough time with Forrest as it is. I can't possibly leave him to book a massage.* But when I saw my therapist the voices would recede into the background. Everything he said about taking care of myself seemed to make sense, but I needed his support to make myself a priority. I couldn't have done it alone.

Once again, I learned that asking the question about something I thought was impossible led me to a good answer. I became more willing to consider difficult questions rather than ignore or turn away from them. To tell the truth, I don't schedule enough massages even now, but engaging the issue makes things seem a lot simpler. Sometimes just admitting that I can book a massage will make me say, "Or you can just take some time off and go see a movie." I often have more choices than I may be willing to see or take responsibility for.

During my saddest days, when counseling, meditations and affirmations just weren't doing the trick, I decided to get a reading. The reader told me that I was out of balance. I wasn't honoring the energy of Oshun within me. She said that being a good wife, mom and businesswoman was important, but I needed to learn to lighten up, let go and enjoy my life. She suggested I spend more time with friends, go for walks and just relax.

"You know what Oshun does when she has a lot of work to do? She goes out to dinner."

"Huh? What do I tell a customer when their order isn't ready?"

"Call your customer. Be very sweet and tell her you won't be able to meet the commitment you made to her for Friday. Tell her, 'I'll have it for you on Sunday morning and I'll give you a free bottle of crème to accompany the oil.' Trust me, she won't complain."

I hadn't thought of negotiating like that before. Of course, when I tried it, it worked.

The reader also told me that I should bathe in honey that week.

"Your life will be sweet if you bathe in sweetness," she said. "You will speak sweetly if you pour honey into your mouth. If you pour sweetness into you, sweetness will flow out of you."

She instructed me to take baths in honey for five nights in a row. Before I got in the tub, I was to put honey around every orifice. This extreme application of honey was a symbolic way of tipping the scales into balance. But it only works if you pray and make changes in your lifestyle. You can't take any shortcuts. Honey, of course, was a metaphor for how I was to take care of and treat myself.

"For the first couple of times you may cry," she said. "Your spirit will realize how long it has been deprived of sweetness and weep. But after two or three baths, you should feel better."

The first time I did this I started sobbing uncontrollably. After that first bath I felt better already. By the fifth bath I felt sexy, hot, and confident. About a month later I learned I was pregnant. Our second child had been conceived during the week of the honey baths. Even though motherhood was proving to be difficult, I was excited to be pregnant again. This time I had the same pregnancy-related issues as I did during the last one—only worse. Last time I couldn't stand certain smells; this time I couldn't tolerate *any* of them. Smelling almost anything made me sick to my stomach. I spent much of my second pregnancy in my office with towels stuffed under the doors. Friends and family members came to my rescue and helped me make products in the kitchen. I also developed high blood pressure again and was put on bed rest for a while. I would have to do stuff like sit in bed and box and label things. Sometimes it was frustrating. I was sleepy and nauseous at the same time, especially during my first trimester.

During the time I was pregnant, *Essence* magazine contacted me again. They wanted to take my picture and include it as part of a "People to Know" story. The photographer came to the house and took a photo of me pregnant, standing in front of my mantel wearing a black batik dress. Back then, I had short natural hair (I had just cut off my locs). The story was scheduled to come out in October, which is when the baby was due.

The same month *Essence* took my picture, Gordon lost his job. He went into work on a Thursday and was told that seventy-five percent of the company was being let go. He was told he wasn't being cut. But over the weekend he got a call telling him not to report to work the next day. When

Honey Healing Bath

Honey—pour a generous amount into a decorative bowl
Full-length mirror
Candles, preferably pink or yellow

1. Close the door to your bathroom and draw a hot tub of bath water.
2. Light candles.
3. Stand in front of a full-length mirror. Look at your body, loving its curves, dimples and droopy places.
4. Ask God to send a healing energy to your spirit. Let the Universe know that you are willing to let go of pain and accept health and wholeness.
5. Dip your fingers into the decorative bowl, covering the tips with honey.
6. Smear honey around both eyes, your ears, your nose, mouth, genitals (upper thighs) and anus. (Note: Be careful not to allow honey to enter your vagina.)
7. Slowly get into the tub, being careful not to burn yourself.
8. Pray. State to our Creator the thoughts, habits and behaviors you are willing to release. Also let God know that you are open to having your spirit healed. Say it like you mean it.
9. Be still. When you finish praying, crying, praising God or whatever emotional reaction you may have, spend a few moments in silence, taking in the peaceful energy you have drawn into your life.

his check was due to be deposited on Wednesday, not one penny hit our account. He wouldn't be getting paid for the work he had done over the prior two weeks. Of course, we were panicked. We already had one baby and another on the way. We didn't know how we would make it. But we cut back on our spending and survived, somehow. In the meantime, Gordon joined a class-action lawsuit filed by the employees of his company.

One morning toward the end of the pregnancy, I was scheduled to see my doctor. My intuition told me to get up early that morning and finish writing the new brochure before my appointment. Good thing I did. The doctor realized that I was contracting and sent me straight to the hospital.

Our second son, Ennis, was born that day, also by cesarean. He was amazing—eight pounds, nine ounces and beautiful. The *Essence* "People to Know" story appeared on the newsstand the following day. Gordon bought one and brought it to me. When I saw it I was surprised. I thought I was going to be included on a page with several other women. As it turned out, there were only two of us, and there was a short article written about me and my business. I was happy about the story, but my new bundle was more important and I promptly forgot about it. Ennis, unlike his older brother, latched on with no problems and nursed at the moment of our first encounter. I didn't need Kim this time. I was an old pro.

The next day, Gordon told me that the Carol's Daughter phone line was ringing off the hook. I just assumed he meant it was ringing more than usual, which I would expect since the magazine was out. So I kept telling him not to worry about it, that the messages would go into voicemail and we would pick them up later. But I didn't realize that he really meant the phone was ringing nonstop. I didn't find that out until Sunday, when Ennis and I came home. It also wasn't until Sunday that I realized that voicemail can actually fill up. When I finally checked, I had forty-seven new messages. Whenever one of us emptied the voicemail, it would be full again two hours later. Every time we put the phone down, it rang again. So I'm sure that while I was in the hospital there were probably thousands of people calling to request catalogues who were unable to leave a message. Those opportunities were lost, maybe even for good.

I swear that God sent me home from the hospital early so I could start catching the calls, because I actually wasn't supposed to leave the hospital until Monday. But out of the blue, some doctor came by on Sunday and said, "You can go home today." Even though it was good for Carol's

Daughter, I felt like I left too soon. I was moving around slowly and really couldn't walk yet. I felt like my body had betrayed me. Ennis was about four days old when I got the courage to look in the mirror. I was accustomed to a round, full body. I was accustomed to my soft belly, curvy hips and thick legs, but what I saw in my reflection scared me to death. My stomach appeared to be pointing downward. I looked like a Who from Whoville in the Dr. Seuss classic *Horton Hears a Who.*

I felt depression looming over me, but God had other plans: "No self-pity for you, old girl. You've got work to do!" Since the brochure was already written, all that had to happen was photocopying, collating and assembling it. The response from the *Essence* story was so good that we had to double the number of catalogs we normally printed from 3,000 to 6,000. Once again family and friends pitched in. Our living room looked like a makeshift printing press, replete with folding machine and industrial stapler.

While the collating was performed on the parlor floor, the first-floor showroom was a hub of activity. There were many more customers coming by the house to shop, and they had some unusual requests. People wanted to have their picture taken with me next to the mantel I had posed in front of for *Essence.* They didn't care what I was wearing. Mind you, they sometimes caught me in a sweatsuit, which in my house also means pajamas.

I have two babies, no sleep, and you want to take a picture with me? I thought I looked awful, but they didn't seem to care. They wanted to know where I got my dress and earrings and who did my hair.

"You look like such an approachable, everyday person," the women would say. "Not how I thought you would."

Women liked that my products were made by hand in my kitchen. And now that they knew what I looked like, they felt they had made a personal connection with me.

I just thought the whole experience was amazing. After spending much of my life feeling like my appearance didn't live up to what I wished I looked like, suddenly there were all these women identifying with me and accepting me for who I was—no hair weave, no makeup, and dried mashed bananas on my shirt. They gave me a true lesson in self-acceptance. The lesson was invaluable.

Now that I had two children I really had to change the way I worked. I had to stop often to nurse them. I had to stop to cuddle with them. I had to stop and change diapers. Sometimes it was frustrating because I often thought I was supposed to be doing something else—working. I was still feeling pressure about my IRS debt and I needed to bring a certain amount of income into our household. (Gordon had found work on the stage crew at *Sesame Street,* where he still works today.)

Prior to becoming a mother, I'd had nothing to focus on but Carol's Daughter. If a label was crooked, I'd straighten it. If something wasn't done right, I'd do it over again. But now that I had two babies, what could be more important to focus on than them? Being their mom was such an amazing feeling! But I couldn't just let everything go so that I could fingerpaint all day; I still needed to work very hard. Christmas was coming and the company had grown and somehow we'd have to keep up with the business. I needed to keep learning how to work differently.

I learned to incorporate their personalities and schedules into my work life. For example, Ennis always wanted to be held, so I would work while I held him. Forrest, I could put in a rocker and he would be fine. Sometimes when the babies got up to nurse at night, I would stay up and work until the next time they needed to nurse.

It was during this time that the business really took off. I remember being up one night nursing, and being really tired. Both boys drifted off to sleep. I tucked Forrest in by his sleeping dad and Ennis between my pillow and my shirt, hoping that their radar wouldn't go off and make them notice I was gone. I decided to go process orders that still needed to be run through the credit card terminal. As I put the orders through, I realized how many orders needed to be shipped. Knowing that there were customers waiting for their products gave me the energy to work.

You can do it. You can keep working, I'd say to myself. *These people are waiting for their orders.*

Thank God I could rely on family during those days. Mommy would always find someone to help me out. If it wasn't one of my younger brothers—Little Phillip, Sean or Christian—it was a teen from her block looking for something to do after school. My brother Aerol was one of the first helpers I had. He would do whatever I asked of him. My cousin Michael and Uncle Stan both had full-time jobs, but in their spare time they set up a shipping department in my basement. It was truly a family affair.

That Christmas season we scheduled our annual holiday sale in a room in Aunt Ruby's church. At the last minute the church venue became impossible for us to handle. Making the products, assembling the baskets and filling holiday orders on time became paramount.

"Why don't you clear the furniture out of your living room and hold the sale up there?" one of my friends asked.

I Love You Just the Way You Are

As a woman who has been overweight most of her life, runs a company whose products show up on the beauty pages of magazines, and has spent time in the television industry, I felt it imperative to address the subject of self-image and the importance of accepting who you are. Unfortunately, we live in a society that places a disproportionate amount of emphasis on external beauty, and it's very narrowly defined. To find true health and happiness, we must find a way to make peace with our appearance, no matter what we look like.

Now, I am not advocating that if you are fifty pounds overweight and have health issues like high cholesterol and high blood pressure that you just ignore that and say to yourself, "I am beautiful," as you chug down a Coke and eat a bag of chips. But I also don't think it's helpful to live in a body you don't love, wishing for one that may never come. When we focus on having unattainable looks or don't accept the body we have, there is a tendency to create unrealistic goals that set us up to fail. You may go on a quick-fix diet. You will get results, but they won't last, and more than likely you will put the weight back on and then some.

Even if you reach and maintain your goal weight, that doesn't guarantee you'll feel better about yourself. The years I've spent in television have taught me a lot about looks. Some of the most insecure people I have met in my life are "beautiful" in the cover-of-a-magazine, supermodel way. I would look at them and think, "Why is she so worried about what people will think? If I looked like that, you wouldn't be able to tell me anything." Then I realized, "Wait a minute. I actually have something important that Miss Perfect Tummy doesn't—confidence!" I noticed that when I was in Fedora, I was always more outgoing than either Dee or Taylor, who I felt were much more beautiful than me. I couldn't understand why they were shy. When they walked into a room, heads turned and everyone wanted to talk to them. What I didn't realize was that I had a gift that they didn't—the ability to take the first step.

As you look at the pictures in this book you will see me at varying weights. When I was in Fedora in 1987, I was a size fourteen or sixteen and thought I was fat because I didn't wear a six like the other women in the group. Years later, in my postpartum days, I wore a size twenty-six. Trust me when I tell you that the heavier me longed for the days when I could wear a sixteen. Even today, if I could go back to being a size sixteen, I would appreciate that woman and love her rather than think she was inadequate. This makes me understand that I need to accept Lisa as she is today, imperfections and all.

This particular lesson was driven home to me quite clearly in the fall of 2001. Back then, I didn't use my image on Carol's Daughter promotional materials. It's really sad to admit, but I did not think I was attractive enough to be on the cover of my own brochure. But I reached a point where I was no longer able to use a particular picture and did not have the time or budget to schedule a photo shoot. That's when it dawned on me to substitute a photo of myself. For the first time in the history of Carol's Daughter, my own face was on the brochures, the web site, the gift boxes. Everywhere I looked it seemed I was smiling back at myself. To my surprise it seemed completely natural. After a while I even liked it! My spirit said, "Duh! Why in the world did you ever believe that anyone other than Carol's daughter should be depicted on Carol's Daughter literature?" It was an important lesson to learn. And I'm happy to say I have never felt inadequate again when it comes to promoting who and what I am.

Accepting who and where you are is the first step on the road to changing for the better. When we learn to love ourselves, we feel centered and powerful. We focus on what we *do* have rather than what we don't—bodies that perform millions of calculations each second, allowing us to see, breathe, smell, touch, think, eat, walk, work and bear children, for instance. We value the beauty of our bodies to help us create each day—the wonder of our lives, our loves, our families and our contribution to the planet. We consider the possibility that perhaps our behinds were made especially curvy to attract our perfect partner, or that our droopy breasts helped our children grow strong and healthy, or that our ebony-colored skin allows us to age wrinkle free. It makes no sense to question God's wisdom or struggle against the flow of the entire Universe.

Before you begin any weight-loss or exercise program, look at your body in the mirror and say "I love you." I know it's difficult; I struggle with this still, but it's important. Remind yourself of all of the things that are wonderful about your body or that it allows you to do well. For example, I love my hair. Its curly texture is perfect for all sorts of natural styles—locs, braids, twists, wild and free. My legs are big, but they are strong. Strong legs are a gift with which my Mommy was not blessed. In my entire lifetime I never saw my mother run. She couldn't. Watching her fall and struggle to walk as her legs got weaker and weaker made me appreciate my legs, big or not. I have always been a very good dancer. That means I have a wonderful sense of rhythm. I am graceful, well coordinated and flexible. When I was six, I nearly died from a perforated appendix. I have lived with an appendectomy scar all my life. It never bothered me. When other children teased me about it, I laughed. To me it was a badge of honor. Even at that young age, I knew that I had cheated death. Because of that experience, scars don't bother me.

And even though I have been overweight, this body and spirit has drawn some very attractive men to me—inside and out—up to and including my husband, who is no slouch in the looks department. Not all men want supermodel types. Not that there's anything wrong with looking like a supermodel. I will be the first one to stand up and applaud a beautiful woman, but don't we all really want a partner who sees our inner beauty, regardless of the packaging?

Those of us who are overweight learn to make jokes about ourselves before others do. But it would be much more productive to stop making jokes about ourselves and appreciate the good sense of humor that we have developed. We learn to accept that certain things are not just going to come to us; we have to go out and get them; sometimes, demand them. That sharpens our skills, teaches us to work hard, persevere and if necessary take rejection and move on. These are all assets—character-building moments that I am sure many of you have experienced. Love these things about yourself.

When we constantly nitpick, criticize or even hate ourselves, we pit our mind, body and spirit against each other. Only disease and discomfort can result. We can't wait on the world to love us for us. True validation must come from within.

"That's a really good idea," I answered, "but the people will be at the church. We sent out over a thousand invitations telling them to go to St. John's."

"Shuttle them over to the house with a van."

"Oh, that's a great idea!"

Another friend volunteered to drive his minivan back and forth between the two locations. Two of my customers arrived at nine A.M., three hours before we were to open at noon. We were still setting up when they arrived. They let their dissatisfaction be known.

"This is exactly why I don't like doing business with my people," one of them complained to a friend who had volunteered her time to help me. "Black people can just never get it together."

"The change in venue was unavoidable," my girlfriend offered. "But we put signs up at the church to tell people what was going on. And we can drive them back and forth between the two locations."

Tips for Creating Balance for Working Moms

Take my word for it: these tips will help you clear hours in your day. Well, perhaps that's a bit of an overstatement. But they will give you a little bit of space and a lot of sanity.

1. Learn how to say "No." When they ask for volunteers to run the concession stand at your child's preschool winter carnival, don't say "yes" if you've got a job, another infant on the way, and you're trying to get that back room converted into your office so that you can work from home after the baby comes. It's just too much. "No" is one of the most important words to master as a mom. Embrace it.

2. Have a lock installed on your bathroom door, high enough that only an adult can reach it. I can't tell you how many community baths I had when Forrest and Ennis were toddlers. Not that I'd trade those times—they are precious—but sometimes you need to be alone in the tub and you shouldn't have to get up at three A.M. to get some time to yourself. A simple little latch will keep them out for a few glorious minutes . . . until someone has to pee.

3. When the second-grade class at your daughter's school has a bake sale to save the rain forest, don't feel bad that you didn't make the brownies yourself. When your child says, "But Billy's mommy always makes her own brownies and she puts nuts in them and smiley faces on top," I want you to walk into that bake sale with your head held high. Be proud that you had the good sense to go to Costco. It's a good thing.

4. Make time. Time for you and time for you and your kids. Do time for you first; it will lessen your tension level and then you will have more fun with your children.

5. Carve out a quiet space for yourself. I used to go into a small room in my house, where I kept all of my clothes, and I would sit in there and be still. I would turn on some quiet music, light a candle and be still for five minutes. Then, I would invite the boys in and we'd read a book or sing or just talk. The key here is the word "invite." Let them know that the space is Mommy's. Even if it's just a beanbag chair behind the laundry room in the basement. It's yours.

"Well, this is shoddy, just shoddy," the woman responded. "And you're supposed to be open by now and you're not even set up."

"I'm sorry, Ma'am," my friend responded, "but I think you may be mistaken. We don't open for three more hours."

The woman didn't know it at the time, but I was sitting less than six feet away behind a piece of fabric that had been hung to divide the room. I can't tell you how grateful I was that my friend was there to handle the situation. I had been up for days on end tending to my babies, cooking product and getting people's orders out to them. I was absolutely frazzled. The more the women went on complaining about my business, the more I wanted to reach around and grab them by their store-bought hair. But I wasn't raised that way, and I had the presence of mind to know that it was exhaustion that made me think those thoughts.

"Well, we're not quite ready, but if you'd like to purchase something, I'll be happy to help you."

"Terrible," the woman continued. "This is just bad business."

"You see, this is why black folks don't have anything," her cohort added. "So trifling, I tell you. . . ."

At that point I couldn't take it anymore. The roller-coaster ride that my hormones had put me on pitched from anger to despair. Tears welled up from my gut and I burst into sobs. I ran out from behind the divider and raced upstairs.

"What was all that about?" the woman asked, startled.

"Oh, that was Carol's daughter, the owner. She heard everything you said."

After I stopped sobbing I was able to tell Gordon what had happened. Naturally, he made a beeline to the living room to give the women a piece of his mind. Fortunately, they had left by then.

My experience with the women was instructive: retail is a very difficult business; it is not for the faint of heart. I had to learn to develop a thicker skin, while at the same time being open to input and criticism. I found that this ability was particularly important because most of my customers were black. Black consumers often have very high expectations of black business owners. Sometimes those expectations are justified; they are often a reflection of our pride and desire to see people like us succeed. But sometimes we're extra hard on each other, penalizing our own for things that would go unnoticed in a mainstream establishment. I had to learn how to discern between valid criticism and when the customer might be imposing upon me some of the stereotypes about black people she had unwittingly internalized from mainstream culture.

"I agree we need to handle this better, and we will," I eventually learned to say. "But I challenge your assumption that black businesses are shoddy. If I accepted that premise there would be no reason for me to get up and try to do a good job every morning."

Tough feedback from customers is just a regular part of running a company. I'm not always up to it, but I've learned that on the heels of a challenging interaction God often sends me some encouragement.

After one particularly difficult day of feedback, I was taking a breather in the basement when Aerol came downstairs singing, "Badu, Badu," a hook line from one of the office's favorite songs on Erykah Badu's *Live* CD.

Aerol liked to tease his big sister, so I didn't pay much attention when he said, "Badu wants to talk to you."

"Lisa," he repeated, singing, "Badu, Badu wants to see you." And, no, my brother cannot sing.

"Aerol, I have had a bad day," I replied. "What are you talking about?"

"Erykah Badu is in your living room, shopping in your store and wants to talk to you." He could barely contain his grin. He knew I was stressed and he knew this would make me smile.

"Erykah Badu! Get out of here. Are you serious, Aerol?"

"For real. I'm not kidding."

I did my best to get myself together. A couple of years earlier, before her first album came out, I heard about her and sent her a basket of strawberry-scented products. Back then, she had called to thank me. Now Erykah Badu was a star. The woman's music played on and on at Carol's Daughter so often my babies were even known to hum a line or two. Now she was upstairs in my house. We would finally meet. God is good!

When I walked into my living room, I almost didn't recognize her because I had only seen her with her head wrapped. This day, her beautiful, long locs were cascading over her shoulders.

"Sister, I just love your products," she told me.

"Thank you," I replied. I felt like I had a lump in my throat—me, the woman who worked for Mr. Cosby and shot the shit with Malcolm-Jamal Warner. I was nervous.

"Can I show you some of the new things I've made?" I asked. And with that the lump went away and we chatted and sniffed our way through the various products around the room.

As the company continued to grow, I started receiving another type of encouragement: letters from customers who had used my products. Sometimes their notes spoke of how much they loved them. Other times they described more serious situations. I learned that some of my customers had serious health or personal problems and used my products to nurture themselves. One customer said she was on chemotherapy and Carol's Daughter was the one thing that made her feel better.

As I sat there reading such letters, I would reflect on the times when I knew all my customers by face and name. I had sold or packed and shipped every single order. Now I was getting letters from people telling me that my products were the highlight of their day and I didn't even know who they were. The butters and crèmes that I made by hand in my little kitchen were making an impact out in the world that I hadn't even dreamed of.

This fact was underscored when I overheard Michael talk to a woman about her order. It dawned on me that not only were the products being sent to people I didn't know, one day in the not-too-distant future I would have employees. This was not just the house of Lisa and Gordon and Forrest and Ennis; people came to work here. Granted, they were family members and friends helping us out. But it dawned on me that one day this could be their full-time job. That realization was a real turning point for me.

Even though I didn't have a vision for the business when I started it, Carol's Daughter had taken on a life of its own. Now it was serving a more important purpose than I had ever imagined. It was a place where people could come when they needed to rejuvenate their spirits. It was a place where people could earn money to support their families. Even though it was my company, Carol's Daughter had become bigger than me.

I realized I had to take a major leap forward in my personal and spiritual development. The business could no longer be about Lisa earning money so she can support her family and pay off her debts. It was incumbent upon me to make good business decisions for the people who supported me. I needed to give back to them so they could provide for their families and take care of themselves. The business was growing and it wasn't okay for me to get stuck in my fears and weaknesses anymore. A lot of people were counting on me to move past my insecurities.

CHAPTER 13

Facing My Fears

Carol's Daughter's first retail store, opened on August 21, 1999.
Our products are also sold online and in gift shops and beauty salons across the country.

On a cold and rainy December night in 1998, I was presented with one of many pivotal dilemmas that would challenge me to grow. The company was in the middle of our holiday rush. I had worked a long, exhausting day and felt like I was on the verge of catching a cold. All I wanted to do was go home and crawl in bed. But I had made a commitment to restaurateur B. Smith to do a product demonstration at a launch party for her new magazine, *B. Smith Style*. Already the host of a successful cable show, B. was now putting features from her show into a magazine. She wanted her former guests, of which I was one, to demonstrate the crafts that would be featured on the magazine's pages.

I really didn't feel up to honoring my commitment. Plus, Gordon was at work, I don't drive and I didn't have a ride to Manhattan. I would have to haul a bunch of heavy boxes by myself in a cab. I can't tell you how much I wanted to stay home. Did I mention the rain?

There was a time when I would have called, claimed to be sick and begged off of the event. After all, I wasn't being paid or anything. But the new and improved Lisa vowed to keep her promises, even when she didn't want to. I knew that people were counting on me to be the best person I could be. I fantasized about acting like the old Lisa, though. I could be warm in bed, snuggle with my babies and maybe even get a good night's sleep. But every time I indulged those thoughts, the little voice inside of me said, *But you said you would be there, so you have to go.*

On top of that B. Smith had been so nice to me when I was on her show, I couldn't let her down. So after a lavender bath, some goldenseal, and lots of sniffling, I dragged myself and my boxes across the city to her restaurant in the cold rain. Good thing. Little did I understand at the time just how connected everything is and how many amazing doors that one little demonstration would open.

Once I arrived at the restaurant I knew I had done the right thing. A friend from high school was playing the piano and I got to hear his music, which I interpreted as a sign that I was supposed to be there. The crafts being demonstrated at this party were quite diverse. One woman was doing embroidery, another was giving people henna tattoos and I would be making Rose Milk Bath with Vodka.

At my table I made the rose milk bath in a large glass vessel set into a bowl of ice and strawberries. I placed roses in vases at either end of the table and scattered rose petals all over the tablecloth. The presentation was beautiful, and the milk bath was a really big hit with both men and women. By the end of the evening, they were so jazzed about it that they were digging empty bottles out of the bartender's recycling bin so they could take samples home with them. People were also really excited about the other products I brought. It was amazing. I was so glad I dragged myself to the event.

In the weeks following B. Smith's party I went about my business. Back in September I had initiated the paperwork to incorporate the company. On December 10, 1998, I became a corporation. That made the company more real to me. It was further confirmation that Carol's Daughter wasn't a hobby anymore; it was a corporate entity. At that point we started hiring. People who once worked for free now became our employees.

We worked diligently through the holidays and our family looked forward to spending a relaxing Christmas in Florida, visiting Grandma Hilda and Grandpa. Grandma Hilda had Alzheimer's disease, which made visiting her a little depressing, but I was looking forward to being in her company and relaxing with the family.

Several days before we were to leave, we received a devastating call. Grandma Hilda had passed away. Instead of traveling for a Christmas visit, we attended her funeral. Though it was all very sad, in a way I was relieved—not to lose my grandmother, but because I had been to visit her in September. Even though I knew the family was planning to get together that Christmas, I felt the need to go sooner. Grandma and I spent quality time and for the first time I talked and she listened. When I asked her if she knew who I was, she sang, "la, la, la." I took that as a yes. Grandma Hilda remembered that I sang. I didn't realize that would be our last time together, but it was precious and beautiful and I wouldn't have changed one moment of it.

A couple of weeks later, I was working in my office when the telephone rang.

"Hello, I'm looking for Lisa Price."

"This is Lisa."

"Oh, hi, Lisa. My name is Jakki Taylor. I'm a producer for the television show *The View*. I saw your product demonstration at B. Smith's launch party, and I was wondering if you're comfortable doing live television?"

The View! My heart leapt into my throat. It was one of the hottest new shows on television. *Live!*

"I've never done a live show before," I admitted. "But I've recorded live to tape and didn't need a second take. I'm pretty sure I can do it."

And just like that I was booked to appear on *The View* in February of 1999. As I hung up the phone, my first thought was, *What if you had bailed out on B. Smith? This never could have happened.*

Even though I was excited about the opportunity, I was terrified about doing the show. We would be live in front of an audience and I couldn't make a mistake—no stopping and starting over if you messed up. The studio audience would see me and depending upon how badly I flubbed, so might the rest of the world.

Lisa's Rose Milk Bath—Fresh Version

With its sensual and aphrodisiac qualities, rose oil is known as the queen of all oils. It soothes the emotions, uplifts the spirit and boosts the user's self-confidence. Excellent for skin care, it nourishes dry and/or aging skin.

1   quart whole milk
1   fifth of vodka
2   tablespoons vanilla extract
5   roses
50 drops rose fragrance oil
Strawberries, sliced and strained of juice (optional)

1. Sit in a comfortable chair, preferably one with arms or pillows to embrace you. Bring roses to your nose, close your eyes and inhale deeply. Let the aroma take you on a journey. Be careful not to lose your balance.
2. Gently pull the petals off the roses, throwing away the center and stem.
3. Toss the petals into a large mixing bowl, saving some for floating in your bath or in a bowl near your bath.
4. Pour in the milk (smoothes the skin), followed by the vodka (tones the skin), then the vanilla extract (an aphrodisiac). Stir.
5. At this point you have the option of including sliced strawberries to add alpha hydroxy acids (improves skin texture, cleanses pores).
6. Add rose oil fragrance. Be creative if you dare by adding gardenia (uplift-ing), honey (attracts and retains moisture) or sandalwood (calming, aphrodisiac, aids in meditation).
7. Close the bathroom door, turn the shower on "hot" and allow bathroom to steam up. Shift water to bathtub nozzle, reducing temperature to warm so as not to dry out the skin.
8. Gather remaining rose petals in a decorative bowl. Put some John Coltrane in your CD player, light your favorite candle, dim the lights and sit on the side of the tub. Slowly pour rose mixture into bath, swirling the ingredients in the water with your hand. Set bowl of petals alongside your bath or sprinkle petals atop the water, asking them to help you draw out your most loving feelings. Stick your big toe in the water to test the tem-perature. Adjust the water as necessary. Slide in.

Before I even thought about what I would do, I had to think about what to wear. Since I spent much of my day making products whose base consisted of fats and oils, I didn't dress like the kind of business owner who is out in front of her customers. I only wore clothes I didn't mind getting ruined. In fact, between the babies and the business many of them were messed up already. And in my size, it wasn't always easy to find something that I really liked and felt comfortable in, and that would also look good on camera.

For Christmas, Gordon had given me a two-hundred-dollar gift certificate from a company called Blue Fish. Blue Fish was a wearable art clothing store whose styles I had admired since my days at *Cosby*. Some of the cast wore Blue Fish clothes on the show. Back then I could never afford to buy any wearable art. Now I could, so I did.

Next, I focused on hair. Alake (formerly Erica), my sister-girl of fifteen years, twisted my then shoulder-length mane into curly locs that were just perfect.

On the morning of the show Gordon accompanied me to ABC studios. I was a nervous wreck and not too happy about him chronicling the entire event on camera. When I arrived I learned that Star Jones would host my segment. She and I were in makeup together. Although we didn't talk, I overheard her conversation and wicked sense of humor. I felt comfortable with her instantly.

But during the commercial break before my segment, I can't tell you how badly I wanted to leave and go home.

What if you mess up? the old, doubting voices inside of me asked.

Gordon said to me, "It's your choice. You can leave if you want to. I'll take you home right now."

He knew exactly what he was doing, of course. His reverse psychology worked. I thought about how my staff and my family were gathered around the TV, toasting the screen with mimosas. I thought about Forrest and Ennis, now almost three and eighteen months old, respectively, propped up in front of the TV waiting to see Mommy.

You can leave and go home if you want. The producers will be angry, but they'll fill in the gap with something else. But won't you be disappointed in yourself if you don't go through with it?

Of course the answer to that question was yes. So I looked my husband in the eye and said, "I can do this."

He said, "I know."

And I did it.

Star Jones—Miss Fierce in her taupe, two-piece pantsuit—led me through the segment. She was fantastic, guiding me very subtly. If I was looking the wrong way, she'd gently tap my hand. Or she'd point at something and the next thing I knew, my eyes were looking into the correct camera. I realized that if I just relaxed and allowed myself to follow her lead, I would be fine. Before I knew it we were talking about spa treatments and natural remedies you can create in your kitchen. I made Honey Almond Sea Salt Scrub in front of the audience. I remember pouring the honey on top of the salt in the jar. I recall putting some flowers in a bottle and making an aphrodisiac bath oil. I might have made a milk bath, too. As I cleaned up between making products we made "girlfriend" jokes. But I don't remember much else; Star was so good that my five minutes of fame felt like fifteen seconds.

Afterward I was exhilarated because I had pushed past my insecurities and done the show. I was learning that every time I faced my fears they just evaporated, and it seemed like I was always rewarded for my effort. There was always some benefit just around the corner that I hadn't been able to see because it was obscured by apprehension. Going on *The View* was another important step in Carol's Daughter's growth. I was proud that I hadn't let my company or myself down.

Shortly after *The View,* another wonderful thing happened. I have no idea how she found out about me—it was another piece of the Universe's magic that I interpret as encouragement for doing the right thing—but Halle wanted to send Oprah a Carol's Daughter gift basket. Yes, Halle, as in Berry, and Oprah, as in Winfrey!

Needless to say, I was floored. Halle Berry was one of my favorite actresses, and Oprah was my hero. She was one of the first women on television who actually looked like me. I was honored to have the opportunity to share my products with her.

Naturally, I wanted everything in the basket to be perfect. Halle had already selected the products she wanted to send Oprah, and I added a few special items of my own. I had just seen an Oprah segment where she said she loved how cucumber and grapefruit smell. This gave me a clue as to what fragrances she might like. I actually wished I could hand-deliver the basket so I could see if anything had shifted during shipping. Of course, I couldn't. But while it was in my hands, I placed each flower and each seashell in the basket with precision. Then I let it go.

Next, I made a gift basket for Halle and wrote her a note thanking her for honoring me with the opportunity to do business with both her and Oprah. The basket I sent her was beautiful. It was like Little Red Riding Hood's, a small little thing with a handle and I decorated it with berries. After I shipped Halle's basket, I didn't think about it again. I went about my business, unaware that the Universe was working more magic.

In the meantime the business kept growing and growing. In the summer of 1999 we developed the Carol's Daughter web site. Now people who didn't live close by could do business with us easily. We moved the store up to our living room and expanded our offices on the ground floor. Our tenants had moved out and our family now lived in the third-floor apartment, but it was starting to be clear that even the living room would be too small to use as a showroom. Even on an average Saturday, when we didn't have a special event going on, the living room would be crowded and women who were waiting to shop would be sitting on our stoop. When we had a sale, the line would extend out to the sidewalk. We knew that at some point this would get on our neighbors' nerves. Gordon and I started talking about moving the store into a retail location, expanding production and keeping the offices in the house.

One day I was in the apartment. Alake had come by to do my hair—our excuse for getting together sans children and talking girl talk. In the middle of one of our juicy tales, the phone rang. It was a Realtor.

"I was reading the bio on your web site and noticed you said you always wanted to have a store in Fort Greene," the man said. "I have a place I'd like to show you."

Immediately I was skeptical. Fort Greene was a nice neighborhood in Brooklyn, in the process of gentrification. Because it had become such a popular address, people in adjoining neighborhoods that were not as nice had started to claim their neighborhood as Fort Greene. I suspected the Realtor was doing the same.

"Yeah, where?" I asked cynically. "Fort Greene East?"

"No, in Fort Greene itself." He gave me the address.

"When can I see it?"

"Well, I don't have the keys to show it right now. It's still being worked on. But when they're finished, I'd like to take you by."

That evening I told Gordon about it. We wanted to have the store in the Fort Greene/Clinton Hill area because that is where we lived when we started selling products out of our home and we had done well there. We drove over and looked in the window of the store. The space was nice, affordable and the same size as our living room. From the window we could see that it would only take a couple of days to paint and move in. Our family could have our living room back and also expand our production area downstairs. It was a no-brainer.

But it took forever for the realtor to get hold of the keys. In the meantime a friend mentioned in passing that we should sign a ten-year lease so we could build our clientele. That statement was a godsend. I had no idea that commercial leases could be as long as ten years. Nor had it dawned on me that we would become identified by our location. I had assumed we should think of the space the way we thought of an apartment. After a year or two, we could move on if we needed more room. But ten years in a space that we knew would soon be too small? We needed to keep looking.

During the time Gordon and I lived on Washington Park, I would often go walking with my friend Marlene through Fort Greene Park. While we were walking we would look over at a store, Spike's Joint, located on the corner of DeKalb Avenue and South Elliott Place. Spike's Joint was a retail clothing store owned by filmmaker and director Spike Lee.

"Have you ever been in there?" Marlene asked one day.

"Yeah, it's a cool place," I responded.

"One day you're going to have a store like that."

"Ummm . . ."

Marlene always used to say that the two of us could make things happen by talking out our magic. Boy, was she right. Eventually Spike decided to close his store so he could move on to bigger and better things, like starting his own ad agency. The space was empty for a year or so. One night, I had an interesting dream. In it the realtor called me.

"Sorry I haven't been in touch with you," he said. "I still don't have the keys to show you the other space. But I have a couple of ideas. What do you think about Spike's Joint?"

When I awakened I noted the dream, but didn't inquire about the space because I was sure I couldn't afford it and was afraid of being embarrassed. Several weeks later, after walking with Marlene, I shared that we were going to pass on the first space.

"Why don't you ask about Spike's Joint?" Marlene asked.

"I can't. I don't have enough money," I answered. "Look how huge it is compared to the other place. If that place is $1,100, this has got to be three or four grand, easy. Plus, since it was Spike's, it might be even more expensive."

"Well, it doesn't hurt to ask."

At that point I decided to share my dream with her.

"You have to call him today!"

"It's Saturday."

"He's a Realtor. He's working," she replied. "You need to call him right now and at least leave a message. You and Gordon need to be looking at that place on Monday morning."

"You think?"

"I know," she responded. "Let's go look at it right now."

I knew she was right. I should call the Realtor, but I didn't feel very confident about it. I was willing to go to the store with her, though.

When we arrived I realized the store's doors were red and black, the colors of the Yoruba deity Elegba. Elegba stands at the crossroads of everything you do and controls whether doors are opened for you. But Elegba is also a jokester, and I had been having dreams where someone was playing games with me. Maybe I was about to make a fool of myself.

Then I thought about the address: One South Elliott Place. I liked that—Number One for my first store. Maybe it, too, was a sign to move forward.

"Oh, yeah, Lise. This is you," Marlene said.

"It's nice isn't it?"

"Yeah, and look at the colors—he's telling you he's opening the door. This is it!"

But back then, I believed that if you had to ask the price, it wasn't for you, so I had to work up the courage to inquire. I called the Realtor that same day. As Marlene predicted, he was in. Then the most amazing thing happened: Our conversation began the exact same way as it had in my dream.

"Sorry I haven't been in touch with you," he said. "I still don't have the keys to show you the other space. But I have a couple of ideas."

At that point I interrupted. "What's up with Spike's Joint? Has it been rented out yet? It might be out of my league, but I have to ask."

"Hmmm . . . You know what?" he said. "That's not a bad idea. That space *is* still available. Let me make a call. Last I heard some people had expressed an interest in opening a restaurant there, but I think the deal has fallen through."

After we got off the phone, the Realtor talked to the building's owner. The rent was $3,500 a month. It was a lot, but we felt confident we would do more business there and could cover the extra cost. Unfortunately, the owner was, apparently, not too excited about me. That didn't matter; I wanted to see the place anyhow, and the owner was willing to give the Realtor the keys.

I could feel that the place would be mine as soon as he opened the outer door to the property. As we were standing in the vestibule a sudden chill came over me. My inner voice said, *This is going to be your home.*

As we walked about the store, the Realtor pointed out its features. Gordon and I realized that it was ideal for a retail store. Spike had invested a lot in features that we could never have afforded on our own, allowing us to store some items here that were taking up space in our house. The space had been well maintained; basically, all we would need to do is paint and we could move in.

As we were walking through the shop the Realtor started talking.

"I was trying to explain your business to the owner and I really couldn't," he admitted. "Could you put something together for him—a press kit and some products or something—to let him know who you are?"

Well, as they say, I sat on that basket. I learned that his wife liked body care, so I made a hellified basket I knew she would love. I filled it with skin care products, candles, incense—everything wonderful I could think of. Then I put the press kit together along with a letter of introduction, and dropped it off at the realty office.

To hear the Realtor tell the story later, apparently his wife loved the basket so much the man was like, "Restaurant, what restaurant? We want Carol's Daughter in here. That's it!" I was ecstatic, although still a little anxious about whether I could afford it.

A couple of days later, the owner, Realtor, and I sat down to put faces to names. That's when he dropped a major bomb. I would need to put up four months' rent to get into the store.

Say whaaat!

I held on to my chair to keep from falling off. I started doing the math in my head. Four months' rent was $14,000.

I don't have $14,000!

At the time I didn't know much about commercial real estate. I didn't realize that it operated differently than residential property. I had figured I'd have to come up with $7,000—the months' rent and a months' security I was accustomed to for residential locations. I didn't know that commercial real estate would cost me twice as much in up-front costs. Nor did I know that I'd be charged higher rates for gas and electricity. I'd learn that later on. But by now I had claimed the store in my spirit. I realized I needed to have it. It was the only way Carol's Daughter would grow.

I hung on for dear life during the rest of the meeting. Afterward, Gordon and I drove over to the store and stood out in front of it.

"Nice, isn't it?"

"Yeah, Lisa. It is."

"See this window over here?" I said, walking to the DeKalb Avenue side of the store. "Couldn't you see it decorated with seashells and sand, and blue silk draped behind it?"

"That would be beautiful . . ."

"I can't believe how expensive this is going to be, but we have to get this store, Gordon."

"Then that's it. It's ours."

Now I had to figure out how to come up with the money. I decided to put some feelers out to see if I could get an investor. I knew I had a couple of clients who had access to people with money. Maybe I could get one of them to loan me $20,000. I knew I could pay them back by the end of the year.

It was a big deal for me to think about asking anyone for money. When I was in the singing group, I had asked some family members for money and was told no, and that I had screwed up my life. The idea of borrowing reminded me of that time, so I hated even thinking about the idea. Yet I pushed forward and got over my fear. I persisted in talking to people I knew. One customer asked me to put together a business plan, which I had no idea how to do. Fortunately, my accountant gave me one to use as a guideline. I got really intimidated when I looked at it. Even though the accountant was going to help me, I didn't really have the kind of financial information you need to put in a business plan. I procrastinated until I was up against the wall. The night before I was to meet with my prospective investors, the proposal finally made sense to me. At one A.M. I figured it out and stayed up all night to get it done.

That evening I had a dinner meeting with my potential investors and their accountant. I was really, really nervous. On top of that, everybody was name-dropping and talking about how they wanted to do more than loan me money; they wanted to be business partners. With their combined influence, they said, they would be able to pull a lot of strings in terms of obtaining product endorsements from celebrities, and support when the store opened.

I wasn't prepared for this kind of talk. I was just looking for a loan; I had never considered a partnership. But I really needed the money so I decided to be open-minded. Then the conversation took a turn I wasn't comfortable with: I felt like I was being interrogated.

"What makes you think you'll generate enough revenues to pay your monthly rent?" the accountant asked.

"Based on what I am currently doing in my living room, I think I'll be able to handle it."

"But why do you think you'll be successful?" he persisted.

Huh?

This man was not my customer. He had never been to my home to shop. He didn't see how crowded it was and how long the lines were during the holiday season.

"Well, I really don't mean to sound arrogant, but I am Carol's Daughter." On second thought, yes, I did mean to sound arrogant.

"I'm sorry, I don't see how that answers my question."

"Right now, I have a store in my living room inside a brownstone in a residential neighborhood with no signage. If I have a store in a place like Fort Greene, with three display windows, people will simply come in to see what is there. Then they will smell my products and then they will buy them. This is how it has been for years, except I have been doing it from behind closed doors." My words did not sound as confident as I would have liked. I was really uncomfortable.

"But DeKalb Avenue isn't a commercial shopping strip. What makes you think you'll make it?"

Wait a minute! What's up with these people? What makes me think I'll make it?

I started this business from scratch and had grown it to a respectful size out of my home, using only my own money. I was proud of what I had done. In some ways I had already "made it." But to hear them talk about Carol's Daughter, it was as if I hadn't accomplished a thing. I felt like they were ganging up on me to make me feel small. It was working—I was so intimidated that I just wanted to leave. But then I thought, *Don't be emotional, Lisa. Maybe you've been put here to learn something.*

Well, I did learn a lot of important things. It turns out that in exchange for the $20,000 I needed, they wanted to become partners.

"We would need to determine the current value of the company. The size of the investment you need would determine our level of ownership."

"Ownership?"

"Yes, arrangements can be 40/60, 70/30 or, depending on the size of the investment, it could be 49/51."

"You would own 49 percent of my company?" That made the hairs on the back of my neck stand up.

"The process is not as simple as that. The first step is determining the current value of the company. . . ."

He continued to speak, but I could no longer hear him. *Do you really think I'm going to sell you half of my company for $20,000? I'll stay in my living room before I let that happen.* Rather than let my emotions rule me, I smiled and told them I would think about it. But I was absolutely, positively outraged.

I didn't understand it at the time, but the questions my prospective investors were asking were smart business queries. Even though I thought that the opportunity was obvious, from their perspective they were risking their money. This was a business proposition. They had a right to ask tough questions, and I couldn't answer all of them.

Back then my ego was still fragile, especially where money was involved. All the scrutiny made me feel small. But in this difficult situation the Universe was also presenting me with an opportunity to examine my worth. Buried in my outrage were the seeds of understanding that my company had value, and that my prospective investors were not valuing it enough. It's possible that I had not appropriately articulated this worth, and this was being reflected in what I perceived to be a lowball offer. Then again, as I would later understand, this was business, and starting low is a negotiating tactic. I had much to learn and many areas in which to grow. Among other things, this experience taught me that balancing your head and your heart is a smart tactic for women in business.

But at the time I was angry and also feeling down. I knew that I couldn't go into a partnership with them, and if I couldn't find the money I needed, there would be no store. When I got home, I recounted the story to Mommy.

"Are they out of their goddamned minds!" she shouted.

Even though she was my mother, I was surprised by how outraged she was. Mommy rarely cussed like that. Her reaction made me think that maybe this deal was as horrible as I sensed it was. As much as I thought I needed the money, perhaps what I needed more was to walk away from the offer.

That night Gordon and I stayed up late doing some serious thinking. I made a list of the pros and cons of staying in the house, and they clearly came out in favor of moving. I also wrote out what I thought my income and expenses would be if I opened a store instead of staying at home. According to my calculations, even if our sales were only mediocre, we should be able to handle the expense of the shop.

I still felt pretty bad when I went to bed that night, but going through that whole exercise made things really clear. *I'm not going to partner with anyone. This is a family business and that's that!*

In the meantime, and without my knowledge, my mother had shared her upset with my Aunt Marilyn. Aunt Marilyn had been Mommy's best friend since they were teens. She called me after speaking with Mom.

"Hey, baby. Your mother told me what's been going on. Uncle Whip and I want to help you." Uncle Whip was her husband.

I can't believe this.

"Thank you, Aunt Marilyn," I cried.

"It's okay. I'm proud of you, girl. You know this."

Aunt Marilyn then talked to her brother Larry, who called me up and asked to see my business plan. Between the money the two of them loaned me I had enough. It wasn't $20,000, but it was enough.

The next day my lawyer called, telling me that the owner's wife was about to deliver a baby. They wanted Gordon and me to sign the following afternoon. We wouldn't have the money from Aunt Marilyn and Uncle Whip by then, but we agreed to come to the closing. I didn't have a clue how we'd come up with $14,000 in the next twenty-four hours. We needed to figure something out quickly.

Gordon and I began to gather our assets. We emptied the savings account and the checking account. When Gordon lost his job before Ennis was born, he and his coworkers filed a class-action suit and were awarded a huge settlement. Gordon's share after taxes and legal fees was just over five thousand dollars. We were supposed to use it to open up a college fund, but that would have to wait. I called our two credit card companies to see what I could get in cash advances. We scrounged around everywhere. We were like Lucy and Ethel when they needed to raise money to join Ricky and Fred in Europe.

After all of the drama, on a hot Friday afternoon in July, we signed the lease. We had a total of sixty dollars left in our bank accounts. Not only did the boys no longer have a college fund, they didn't have a piggy bank either. There wasn't a coin or postage stamp to be found in any of the sofa cushions. But now the store was actually ours and life would never be the same.

Carol's Daughter's first retail store opened less than one month later, on August 21, 1999. The night before we had a private reception for family and friends. Only Mommy didn't make it. Her health had deteriorated and she needed a walker to get around—not a fact she was willing to admit at the time.

"I'm sorry I can't make it for the party," she said. "I'm just not strong enough." I knew it was a matter of pride and I chose to leave her with it.

"Mom, it's okay. I'll tell you all about it after and I'll save you some cake. Love you."

"I love you too and I'm proud of you."

The following morning, the day of the grand opening, Gordon and I were at home, gathering products to take to the store, when the telephone rang. It was the store manager.

"There's already a line down the block and it's only nine thirty," he told us. The store wasn't scheduled to open until ten A.M.

"Oh my God, Gordon!" I shouted. "There's a line down the block! We'll be there as soon as we can."

Gordon and I arrived at ten fifteen, and we couldn't believe what we saw. The store was absolutely mobbed. There was no clear passage from the front door to the back. It was filled with a sea of people. Happy people! Shopping people!

The promotional bags filled with free products for the first fifty customers were gone by the time we arrived. Business was so busy that by the end of the day, almost all of the products in the entire store were gone! We made more money on our first day than we had ever made in the house. And I didn't have to give forty-nine percent to anybody!

Face Your Fears Ritual #37

I'd like to tell you that overcoming your fears is a simple process. Unfortunately, in my experience, it's not. This will take time, so be patient with yourself. Repeat it as often as necessary.

1. Review your past and chronicle the times you overcame a fear. Write them down. You will surprise yourself as you look at the long list of situations you have survived.
2. Going forward, keep a journal to record these "victories" as they continue to happen. The more often you sit down and read them, the more your fear will dissipate. You will be forced to admit to your spirit that you are tough.
3. There is nothing to fear in asking for help or for something that you want. A lot of times we don't ask because we are afraid of the rejection that comes with "No." Don't be afraid of this. If you ask a bank for a business loan and they say no, you are no worse off than before you asked. But if you didn't ask, you wouldn't have learned that there's an old bill sitting on your credit report that you need to have removed. Or maybe you don't qualify for a business loan, but you're in good standing for some other type of credit option. Best-case scenario, you get everything you asked for and then some. You won't ever find out if you don't ask.
4. Don't be upset with yourself for being afraid. Remember, you only have courage when you stand in the face of fear. If you don't experience fear, you can't be courageous.

CHAPTER 14

A Rose by Any Other Name

A few of our gift baskets. We have a theme with regard to our body products: butter (Mango Body Butter), milk (Almond Milk), jam (Cocoa Butter Body Jam), jelly (Ecstasy Jelly). I believe we feed our bodies and in turn feed our spirits and have kept this in mind when creating and naming our products.

In August of 2000 I celebrated three things: the one-year anniversary of the store, seven lucky years of being in business, and freedom from my IRS debt! The morning I wrote my last check to the IRS, I wanted to run through my house singing at the top of my lungs and do the Caribbean butterfly dance on top of my desk. Of course, the Carol's Daughter employees working one floor beneath me prevented me from being that expressive, but I could finally move on without a black cloud over my head.

Despite my elation, there was some anger. I was angry about how much I had to pay in interest. I was angry that though I had been diligently paying the bill over the past five years, the interest had continued to mount. But mostly I was angry with myself for ever letting things get so out of hand in the first place. It was a lesson I would never forget.

After I addressed and stamped the envelope, I reflected on the unexpected turns my life had taken. I took in a deep breath and exhaled. *Ah, black vanilla and lemongrass.* As luck would have it, our Herbal Hair Rinse and Oily Skin Toner were created on the same day. I loved when this happened. The two scents created a heavenly duo.

How lucky am I? I thought. I was twenty-eight when I filed for bankruptcy and thirty-two when I started paying back the IRS. The trials and challenges of the past decade had shaped me into a very different person. I was no longer the insecure young woman who was afraid to face her problems or make other people unhappy. I knew I still had plenty of growing to do, but I was satisfied with myself. I had learned to develop my strengths and work on my weaknesses instead of using them as excuses. I learned to listen to my spirit. Doing so led me out of a deep, dark place and into a fantastic life. I was married to a wonderful man, had two amazing boys and had discovered work that I loved.

At that time about fifteen people worked for me, between the house and the store. From the top of the steps outside my office door, now located on the parlor floor of my home, I could listen to what was going on below me. My staff was like a mini–United Nations, and the Spanish I learned while I worked there was coming in handy. I sat on the top step and closed my eyes. From the sounds and smells I could tell what was happening on the two floors below me.

Gordon's mother, my dear, sweet mother-in-law, Elmira, was stirring the pineapple and watermelon fragrance into a fifty-quart, stainless-steel pot of body balm.

To the left of Elmira would be Nellie, a native of Venezuela who came to New York via Alabama. She was not only a godsend in the early years when my babies were actually babies, but also a godsend in the kitchen. I envisioned her seated on her blue pillow atop a bucket that was about the same height as a milking stool. Between her knees she would be holding the huge industrial mixing bowl she named "Samantha."

"¡Qué rico!" Nellie said to Florencia about the richness of Jamaican Punch Honey Butter she was spooning into jars.

"*Si, yo quiero alguno para mí,*" responded Florencia, a brown-skinned Honduran woman with dimples so deep you could dive into them. She knew that Nellie would save her some of the scrapings from the bottom of the bowl. Florencia would put the lids onto the jars as Nellie filled them. Their speech flowed with the same rapidity as their hands. As their lips moved, their fingers flew.

In the next room, Ana, a Colombian, was labeling bottles being brought up from the basement, where I could hear the thump of hip-hop music. As long as the work got done, I didn't mind the music; with Debbie around, the work was sure to get done. Debbie is of Trinidadian descent, like me. She lived on Mommy's block and helped me out from time to time when she was a teen. Now, she is in her twenties and working for me full-time. I walked down to the ground floor and stood at the top of the basement steps to take a peek.

"Be careful not to stir too quickly," Debbie warned. "It will spill out the sides." Debbie was speaking to Marie, giving her instruction on the proper way to add oil to sea salt scrubs.

"If I spill can't I just wipe it off?" Marie asked.

"Yes, but the jar will be slippery and the customer might drop it."

That's my Debbie, I thought.

As my production team worked, the sounds of Mary J. Blige blended with Placido Domingo and Mario Bauza as smoothly as shea and cocoa butters, as naturally as the plantains and black beans and garlic and tortillas my employees brought for lunch, as easily as coconut and ginger and mangoes back in Nana's kitchen.

The sound of the telephone ringing interrupted my reverie. I reached into my pocket and pulled it out. *Thank God for cordless phones.*

"What's up, poopaloops?" Mommy asked.

"Guess what? I just wrote my last check to the IRS. I thought I'd never finish paying them."

"Oh, Lisa! That's fantastic. I know you are relieved. It wasn't even my bill and *I'm* relieved. That's great."

"Thanks, but you know, I couldn't have done it without your help."

"Okay, cut it out. You're going to make your mother cry. How soon before you call your cab?"

Oh my goodness, I'd promised Mommy that I'd go to her doctor's appointment with her. Mommy's health was not so good these days. Her legs were growing weaker and weaker. Thankfully, she now admitted it to herself and she wasn't stuck inside all the time. These days she was willing to use her walker in public.

"Uh, fifteen minutes?" I answered, hesitantly.

"You have to shower and get dressed don't you?"

"Yes. I'm sorry. I forgot. Am I going to make you late?"

"Of course not. I called you early to remind you. Now get dressed. Can you be here in forty-five minutes?"

"Yes. Thanks, Mom."

"That's what mothers are for."

Since the store's opening, business was increasing so rapidly we knew the days of making products in the kitchen of our house were drawing to a close. Carol's Daughter needed an industrial kitchen. Ironically, we were in danger of collapsing under the weight of our own success. I knew we needed help in a number of areas, so we hired some consultants. Each of them had the same message for me: You have to pull yourself back from the business, or the company will be unable to grow. There was only one problem—I couldn't see when or how I could do it.

After Christmas we began building inventory for Valentine's Day 2001. I didn't have a chance to take a breather between holidays. On top of that, I was planning to attend an International Beauty Show in Frankfurt, Germany. Gordon had to work and couldn't go with me, so I was traveling with my cousin Karen, who has a nine-to-five at the phone company but also has a passion for decorating. Silk floral arrangements, window treatments—you name it, she can do it. Our Brooklyn store has two walls of windows, and Karen designs them for us each and every holiday season. While in Frankfurt, I thought I'd visit my Aunt Judy and my cousins. I hadn't been to Frankfurt since I was eleven, when I went with my Dad for a month one summer. The trip would take me away from the business for five full days. I had to set up work for ten people to do for a week.

In the process of trying to handle everything I ran myself into the ground. When I left for the trip, I prayed that I wouldn't get sick. I was terrified I'd spend my whole time abroad in bed. I made it through the trip fine, but within days of returning home, I came down with the chills and a fever that lasted for four days. I was too weak to speak. For me, that's saying something; I can always talk.

For two weeks I was confined to bed, unable to communicate about the business. My condition scared both my husband and mother. Forrest and Ennis spent time at Mommy's house, so that they would not be worried when they looked at me.

In my delirium I dreamt about my Nana. She told me, "Call Aunt Ruby to come and rub your head. You need some Watkins on your head." Watkins Salve was Nana's cure-all, a camphor ointment that she used for headaches, mosquito bites, fevers, you name it. I wished I had some, but I was too weak to tell anyone about my dream.

Well, Nana must have spoken to my mother as well. Mommy called Aunt Ruby and asked her to come over and look at me. Back then, Aunt Ruby still lived next door. She came over and brought the Watkins.

"I'm sorry, baby, my hands are so cold," Aunt Ruby apologized.

She had no idea how happy I was. My head was on fire and the coolness of her touch mixed with the icy hotness of the salve brought me the first bit of relief I had had in days. Aunt Ruby continued to apply the salve according to Nana's instructions and tied up my head in a scarf. I slept like a baby. The next day my fever began to break and I was strong enough to go to the doctor. *Thank you, Nana.*

While I was sick and at the height of the Valentine's rush, my company almost collapsed. When all was said and done, I had spent fourteen days in bed. Fourteen! I gave birth to two babies and was back on my feet quicker than that. I didn't realize it until disaster almost struck, but for all these years everything about the business had remained in my head— recipes, ingredients and packaging costs, everything. I had never taken the time to write them down. I had a successful company and nobody knew how to run it but me.

As I lay in bed, barely able to move, I realized that the consultants were right. I had to change how I functioned. Twenty-odd employees and their families were relying on me. I needed to take better care of myself. I needed to learn how to delegate. I didn't really think I was going to die, but it did occur to me that the company needed to survive whether or not I did.

After I got better I started documenting my business so others could run it in my absence. I learned to embrace technology I previously shunned. I had been "old school." I used to work on a typewriter with carbon paper; I didn't need these new gadgets. But not only did my new, more open-minded way of thinking get me out of the day-to-day activities of the company, divesting myself from the minutia of the business helped me to be a better mom and a more involved parent. I suddenly had time to attend school plays, dance recitals, and conduct potpourri-making workshops for my sons' classes. Gordon and I could get away, even if only for five days, to our favorite place, Miami, without engaging in a crazy, one-month, "gear up to go" work schedule. Having more time also made me available to Mommy as she needed more help.

That spring I received a wonderful bit of recognition. I became a regional finalist for *Working Woman* magazine's Entrepreneur of the Year Competition in the home-based business category. I was invited to a luncheon held in our honor.

I knew that I was being considered for the *Working Woman* award—they had called me about entering the competition back in November. But now that I was diligently documenting my business, creating recipe books, working on inventory protocols and finalizing copy on a new brochure, I really didn't have time to go. Still, I felt I should.

On the morning of the luncheon, everything went wrong and Gordon was unable to go with me.

"Don't worry about it," I told him. "It's just a networking thing. Do what you need to do. I'll go by myself."

Truth be told, I thought a lot about bailing out, but that little voice kept telling me, "*Go.*"

This is part of the new you, it said. *Let go of what's going on here at the house. You could use a break and a nice lunch. You don't want to get sick again.*

That was all the impetus I needed to get out the door.

I arrived at the Marriott hotel at the World Trade Center late. I had missed the breakfast and morning networking, but was right on time for the luncheon. I surveyed the banquet hall for brown faces and joined the table with my sisters. Just about everyone else at the table had done the same thing—looked for friendly faces.

Before long the mistress of ceremonies started to announce the finalists. There were various categories of winners—home-based businesses, overcoming adversity, bouncing back from financial ruin. The women's stories were very inspirational—they had overcome abuse, breast cancer, rape, money problems, the loss of several family members. A couple of the winners were seated at my table. Before long we were all in tears and hugging one another.

I was scrounging around in my bag for another tissue when the winners in the home-based business category were announced. I was curious about who would come in in first place; I wanted to hear the woman's story. But as soon as I heard the first sentence, I knew the winner was me! As she read my bio, I thought about all the crazy things that had happened that morning. I thought about how I figured this would just be another networking event. I remembered how I was overcome with the competitive energy to win when I first arrived. Then just as quickly, as I heard the stories of the women being awarded, I was honored just to be in their company. Now I was the one being honored. I was speechless. Even more tears streamed down my face. I was frozen in my seat until I heard them call my name: "Lisa Price."

I walked to the stage absorbing the love of all the cheering and smiling faces. *They like me. They really like me!*

Wait until I tell Gordon, I thought, and for a moment I felt a little sad that I had come by myself. Gordon had been such an important part of my success. But as I wove my way between the tables and headed to the front of the ballroom, I realized that in a way it was appropriate that I was alone. He was somewhere in New Jersey picking up coconut oil—doing what he always does for me, being my biggest supporter, loudest cheerleader, and staunchest defender. I would thank him later; for now, I needed to revel in this moment. In some ways it validated my worth. I had already experienced a good bit of success among my own people, but now I was being accepted by the mainstream business world—a world that was predominately white and didn't always value women like me. I deserved it.

When I finally reached the stage I was trembling and crying and could hardly compose myself to speak. After the ceremony ended the first thing I did was call Gordon and left a message on his voicemail. Then, I called Mommy.

"Mommy, I won," was all I could say as I clutched my plaque. "Mommy, I actually won!"

The good news about Carol's Daughter continued to spread. By now I had many celebrity customers—Erykah Badu, David Sanborn, Gary Dourdan, Edie Falco. The list was growing longer and longer, and those were just the ones that I knew of.

In June, representatives of a major investment firm approached me. They had a minority- and community-business investment fund, and they wanted to know if I was interested in applying. By participating Carol's Daughter would be eligible to receive a large influx of cash that we would never be able to generate in one lump sum on our own. In five years we would buy back their portion of the business.

I knew the company was about to outgrow our ability to create product in my house. What we had to do to qualify for the investment was to continue to document our business. But somewhere along the way, my instincts started kicking in. This was a business that grew based on faith, and operated in a humane way. If we accepted the investment money, we would be accountable to people who were nice, but didn't necessarily share our values. When we talked it felt like a bunch of experts were trying to tell us things that make sense in the mainstream business world that didn't make sense in ours.

I didn't care about opening franchises in every major city. I longed to create a great quality of life for myself and my family. I wanted to be able to provide the occasional job to a person transitioning from welfare to work. I remembered that when I was young and stressed out it calmed my spirit to work with flowers. I thought it might make another person who was experiencing a challenging life feel good to make a product that smells good, and it was a way for me to hire affordable labor. I wanted to be able to employ the boys my mother sent to help me after school, rather than watch them hang out at the corner of her block. And being able to provide jobs for my family was the most amazing feeling of all. Aerol was running the store and cousin Michael—the same Michael who lent me sixty-six dollars to get my phone turned on fifteen years earlier—was now my general operations manager.

"I don't know about this investment thing," I said to Gordon late one night after the boys had been put to bed.

"I'm having that same feeling," he responded.

"Remember what happened to Blue Fish?" I asked.

When Gordon and I visited my favorite clothing store earlier in the year, it was no longer Blue Fish. Blue Fish, started by a woman barely out of her teens with a love for art, painting and designing clothes, went out of business in April of 2001. One of her ten-year employees shared the story with us when we finally located the store, now operating under the name Barclay Studio. Its owner, Jennifer Barclay, had lost ownership of the store's original name and had to start over.

"Don't listen to the consultants," she said. "You may gain international sales, but you can lose control of your business."

I didn't know what circumstances caused Blue Fish to go belly-up (no pun intended), but the woman's advice haunted me. It echoed in my head.

Plus, I was proud that we were a black-owned company. I wanted it to stay that way. I longed for my children to have a legacy.

Where will my boys work? What will they own? Who will they know in high places?

When I thought of my black friends, none of their families owned businesses. Many of my white friends' families ran little candy stores or plumbing businesses, for instance. They weren't wealthy, but they had a sense of ownership of something. I needed to have that, and I wanted my business to reflect my values. Carol's Daughter doesn't operate in the regular business world—it never has and never will.

So Gordon and I reached an important decision: the business must continue to grow and we must increase our production, but we would walk away from the investment offer. There had to be a better way. I knew the Universe would bring it to us.

In the meantime we investigated warehouse options. Gordon located the perfect space in an industrial strip along Atlantic Avenue. Our plan was to lease the building, renovate it and install an industrial kitchen to make our products. We thought we could do this for $30,000. Boy, did we have a lot to learn. The ball was rolling and we really didn't know what we were doing.

Before it was over the project we thought would cost $30,000 was going to cost ten times that much! We would spend all this money to make these improvements to the facility and wouldn't even own it in the end. Needless to say we were sick to our stomachs, but we had to keep moving forward or the company would collapse. So, just one year after clearing my credit report, I went out and got a bunch of credit cards and took out cash advances against them. That, too, made me sick, but I needed money to pay the contractor who would renovate the space. Every Friday for the next five weeks, I would need to pay him approximately $20,000. Whatever the store didn't generate, we would have to pay with high-interest loans from my credit cards. I knew we would be able to pay back the money. It would just take us a while. Still, this was a tremendous leap of faith, even for me.

Shortly thereafter, September 11 happened. When I first heard what had taken place, I realized that only five months earlier I had been inside of Three World Trade Center for the *Working Woman* luncheon. *But for the grace of God go I.* Fortunately, for me, everyone that I hold near and dear was unharmed. Tragically, that wasn't the case for thousands of unfortunate people. September 11 is Gordon's birthday. It has never been quite the same since, but somehow he gets through it.

Seemingly oblivious to the happenings of that day, people continued to shop at the store. Our boys were frightened because we could see the black smoke from our neighborhood in Brooklyn. Out of respect for the loss of life and my staff, who needed to check on loved ones, we closed the store and stopped production for several days. Sales were okay for a few weeks but by October our business began to plummet. I didn't know what would happen to our company or how I would be able to pay back the loans I had taken out against those credit cards. But I knew too many people relied on us for us to go out of business. I prayed that the Universe would bring us another miracle—soon.

"Hello, I'm looking for Lisa Price," came the voice from the other end of the phone.

"I'm Lisa."

"My name is Manie Barron. I'm with the William Morris Agency. Have you heard of us?" the man said.

I wanted to jump out of my chair. Of course I knew William Morris. They represented Mr. Cosby. *Why is he calling me?*

"Yes, I am very familiar with the William Morris Agency. What can I do for you?"

"Well, I was just wondering if you had ever thought of making the Carol's Daughter story into a book?"

"Well, yes, as a matter of fact I have, but I'm not a writer. I just write stories in my brochures."

"Well, if you'd like to have lunch and talk about it, we'd like to represent you."

"But I'm really not a writer."

"Oh, don't worry, I would put you together with an author and you would collaborate."

William Morris wanted *me* as a client? They represented the biggest names in the world. How did I show up on their radar screen? Before long,

Manie introduced me to a writer. Hilary and I clicked right away. We started meeting on Fridays and I told her my tale. I wanted the process—and money—to be quick, but it wasn't. Like everything else that happened in my life, writing a book had a rhythm and timing of its own. I prayed that we would still have a business by the time the book came out. I didn't know what Christmas sales would be like. We badly needed to have a decent holiday season and with the recession spreading I didn't know what would happen. But sales spiked at the last minute and we beat 2000's sales by a hair.

In February 2002 I received a telephone call from a national women's magazine that wanted to include me in a feature on women with jobs that were fun. Perfect! It would help generate additional sales so I could pay back these credit cards.

The photo shoot went well and the story was scheduled for the May 2002 issue, which meant it would hit the stands in mid-April. The timing posed a real dilemma. If we got a ton of phone calls about our products and production was still in our house, we wouldn't be able to handle the business. And we might not just lose our new customers; if the volume of calls was really high, we might have a hard time keeping the store stocked and meeting orders for our existing clients. Either scenario could prove disastrous.

The kitchen in the warehouse wasn't ready, but we could at least move in the shipping and customer-service departments. We pulled out all the stops to make this happen in time, but everything imaginable went wrong. The worst of it was that there were issues with the telephone and computer systems. Given the volume of calls we were told to expect, that was a tremendous problem, so we spent even more money we didn't have because we didn't want this opportunity to backfire.

The magazine finally came out. For some reason it hit the newsstands in Mississippi before New York subscribers had their copies. My brother Philip picked one up and called me with some unexpected news.

"Lisa, I don't know how to tell you this, but I have some bad news."

"What?"

"I've gone through the whole issue of the magazine and you're not in it."

"What?"

Tears welled up in my eyes. We had jumped through hoops and spent extra money so that we would be ready. Someone from the magazine had called me to fact-check the story. I had appeared in enough publications to know that that's usually the sign your story will run.

"I know you're upset. I am too," Philip continued. "I want you to try and not let this bother you and I'm going to pray on it. I just don't think God intended for this to happen."

I was stunned. I hung up the phone and walked through the warehouse. Aerol saw me first. He already knew. Philip had called Mommy and Mommy told him to be there for me.

I crumbled into his arms and burst into tears. My baby brother, who was now twenty-one years old and six feet three inches tall, held me as I sobbed.

"It's all right. Everything will be cool. Look at what's going on with the phones and computers. We're not ready. That's all it means—nothing else. It will happen when we're ready."

I knew he was right, but I was so disappointed. Michael walked over and joined in the group hug.

"I just got off the phone with Gordon. He's on his way here. Don't cry."

I couldn't stop sobbing. I was so glad that they were there for me.

"Thanks, guys," I mumbled as I sniffled.

"Don't worry, yo," Aerol said as they held me tight. "We were here before they called us and we will be here after. Now go in the bathroom and clean up."

"Yeah," Michael added, "you're getting snot on our clothes."

In the days that followed, I actually got a little depressed. I felt like I had failed. My insecurity about my appearance immediately kicked in. The first thing that came to my mind was that my picture didn't look good enough. I was too fat. I was also embarrassed because I had told so many people that I was going to appear in the magazine. Plus the company really needed the boost. Our cash reserves were now depleted. Money was really, really tight. I knew there must be a reason this had happened, but for the life of me I couldn't imagine what it was. Eventually, we got a call saying that they'd hold the piece for a future issue. That gave me a little bit of hope.

By June we were able to relocate the labeling department to the warehouse. I decided that I would move my office downstairs from the parlor floor to the ground floor. Gordon would turn my old office into his home office. For some reason I couldn't explain, I felt a sense of urgency to get out of his space and have my new office set up within one week's time. It was like I was obsessed. I asked my brothers Sean and Christian to help me move my furniture downstairs. I had my new office painted, and bought a carpet because I couldn't get the hardwood floors finished in time.

In time for what? I didn't know. I just felt like I had to get it done. Two days later, Gordon and I headed off for the Natural Hair Show in Atlanta.

While I was in Atlanta, unbeknownst to me, the Universe continued to work wonders. Jakki Taylor, the producer from *The View* that I met at the B. Smith party, had traveled to Chicago to visit a friend. But this wasn't a visit with just any friend. Her friend happened to be a producer for *The Oprah Winfrey Show.*

One day over lunch they were sharing story ideas they were working on. The *Oprah* producer shared that they were shooting a show about women with home-based businesses.

"Have you called Lisa Price?" Jakki asked.

"Who's Lisa Price?"

"You don't know who Lisa is? She's the owner of a business called Carol's Daughter. You've got to get in touch with her."

When I returned from Atlanta I received The Call. Philip and Aerol were right—from their mouths to God's ears. As Aerol had said, "It will happen when you're ready." Now the Universe's plan was clear to me. I never felt disappointed about the magazine article again.

Oprah's people moved quickly. Just two days after they called us there was a television crew inside my home filming background footage. Now my obsession to move my office quickly made sense to me. While my old office was lovely, it was smaller than my new one. It would have been difficult to do a photo shoot there. Somehow my spirit had known that I would need to move.

So, on a Tuesday afternoon, only six days after receiving The Call, Gordon and I were flown to Chicago. Aerol and cousin Michael accompanied us. The next morning a limo picked Gordon and me up at the hotel and we rode to the studio with one of the other guests—the woman who created the popular *Baby Einstein* video series—and her husband. When we arrived at "The House That Oprah Built," Aerol and Michael, who came by cab, were whisked off to audience holding. Gordon and I were escorted back to the green room, where I met the other guests appearing on the show. They were everyday women just like me and I felt comfortable with them immediately. We laughed, joked, encouraged each other and swapped stories to keep from being anxious. I kept hoping that my mouth wouldn't go dry as cotton when Oprah was talking to me and my lips wouldn't stick to my teeth. (Even though I make all sorts of lip balms and moisturizers, would it surprise you to know that I didn't have any on me?) But while we were laughing I also was thinking, *Thank God I'm here; I'm the only sister. Black women with businesses and dreams need to know that they can succeed, too.*

The show seemed to be running a little late. To alleviate my anxiety I wandered out into the hallway to look at the photos of Oprah and her guests that lined the hallway: Oprah and Maya Angelou, Oprah and Tom Cruise, Oprah and Sidney Poitier, Oprah and Denzel, Oprah and Dr. Phil, on and on down the wall. It was an impressive display of some of the world's most popular, accomplished and influential people.

"Good morning!" A warm and familiar voice resonated behind me. *Oprah? No way!* I tried to be cool but I'm sure my eyes were bugging out when I turned around just in time to see her brush by.

Oprah breezed on down the hall and around the corner and was gone as quickly as she appeared. Although she is a commanding presence on TV, she actually is a petite woman—I'd guess five feet four inches without her heels. But even though she's of average stature, I felt like Power had just walked by. The air had shifted and I could feel it—the strength and spirituality emanating from her lingered long after she was gone. And I could tell that she wasn't a diva, which helped me feel relaxed. (You never know which celebrities will be charming in front of the public, but flip a switch and become less than pleasant in private.)

I returned my gaze to the celebrity lineup on the wall—Oprah and Halle Berry, Oprah and Jill Scott. As I looked I realized that I felt like a different person. Suddenly, it dawned on me that many of the stars in the photographs were also my customers. They had either ordered products directly or someone had sent them a gift basket. I counted eighteen in all, including Halle, Jill, Will and Jada Pinkett-Smith, Patti LaBelle, Alicia Keys, the Dixie Chicks, Brian McKnight, Brandy. . . . *These are my people!* I said to myself. Some have been incredibly supportive through the years— walking up four flights of stairs when I sold products out of our apartment, writing notes about how they loved them, shopping at my store. . . .

Looking at their familiar faces made me realize that I belonged. A peaceful feeling came over me. I was *supposed* to be on *Oprah*! It was my destiny. I had done nothing to be invited. In the nine years that I had been in business, I had not done so much as send her a press kit, yet here I was. God must have orchestrated a million events for my name to end up in her hands. I had just literally been minding my business. I worked hard, tried to better myself, ran my company honestly and lived the best life I knew how. This opportunity had to be an affirmation that I was doing the right things. If God thought that I deserved to be here, who was I to disagree?

Soon it was time to go on air. A woman escorted us into the studio.

The crew members began to move about the set and the familiar *Oprah* theme song started playing. Gordon leaned over and whispered in a choked-up voice, "I am so incredibly proud of you right now." My eyes welled up and I took two or three deep breaths to push the tears away. Then the queen of television talk shows swept into the studio looking fabulous—all made up, every hair in place, wearing a cream-colored pantsuit and tuxedo-style shirt, smiling and high-fiving her way onto the stage.

Oprah interviewed the first couple of guests and dispensed big-sisterly business advice. Then the next thing I knew she was doing the lead-in to introduce me. During the commercial break that followed, Oprah smiled and called my name in a singsong way, "Lisa, Lisa, Lisa, Lisa, Lisa." Who knows why she did it, but I interpreted her playfulness as her way of giving me love, of communicating to me that she was glad to have me among her stay-at-home-mom success stories. The attention made me feel at home and even more confident. Then the break ended and she began her lead-in to my story.

"Lisa Price was a successful career woman, but always had hoped to stay home once she had children. Now she is doing both and it all started with a childhood passion for perfumes," she announced, shooting me an encouraging, girlfriend kind of look out of the corner of her eyes.

I watched the videotaped segment about my life, family and business play on the screen in front of me. Seeing how the producers had spliced my life into a two-minute video was like having an out-of-body experience.

"Lisa's career path led her into television and film," Oprah's voice-over continued, "but she always kept her favorite hobby on the side. For fun, Lisa started selling her products at flea markets and out of her apartment, but kept her day job to pay the bills . . ."

When I heard her warm voice saying, "When Lisa decided she wanted to have children, she knew she wanted to find a way to stay at home," I started blinking back the tears. That was a risky choice and life-changing decision and I was very proud of myself.

"So she took a gamble on her hobby and made it a full-time home-based business. Nine years later, with just a hundred-dollar investment, Lisa's home business is making over $2 million a year."

Wow! It sounds so amazing. And she's talking about me! When the tape ended I couldn't stop grinning from ear to ear.

"Wow, that's wonderful," Oprah's voice resonated warmly. She clapped and the audience followed.

"You won't guess who introduced me to Carol's Daughter," she said, like we were longtime friends. "Halle Berry gave me my first basket. . . ."

"I remember that day vividly!" I exclaimed.

"You remember?" she responded, her voice rising incredulously.

"I had been out all day and I came home," I told her. "And the person who was working with me at the time held up a sheet of paper and he said, 'This person works for this person who called for this person because they need a basket for this person.' And all I could see was Halle Berry, Oprah." I pointed to the top and then the bottom of the imaginary list I held in the air.

Suddenly she was beaming and the audience behind me was in stitches. Oprah's eyes twinkled and she laughed, too.

"Well, you say you had just filed for bankruptcy right before you started your home business?"

There. She had asked it. Now millions of people around the world knew my big financial secret. I could easily have hidden it from the show's producers, but decided to reveal this personal tidbit because I knew that there were thousands of women like me—women who had lost control of their finances for one reason or another. I wanted to share my not-so-stellar financial history in order to give them hope. Surprisingly, I felt calm after Oprah said it. *Now it's out in the open and can't hurt me anymore.*

"Yes," I admitted. "I was one of those people who thought that using credit cards was the way to pay bills and buy more than you can afford. In 1990 I had filed for bankruptcy, and I started my business in '93. So I had to do it without credit cards, without bank loans, going slowly, and I learned a lot doing it that way."

As the interview continued she asked about my lifelong struggle with the "disease to please." I shared how hard it had been for me to shake it, especially when dealing with complaints and angry customers.

"What would they be angry about?" she asked, sounding astonished. I gave her an example—and then the unthinkable happened.

"Send them the foot cream, which is fabulous!" she said. "You won't have any problems."

YES! Oprah Winfrey had answered the prayer that I had been afraid to utter: she had endorsed one of my products! Even before that lucky occurrence, the day ranked as one of the best in my life. But this made the experience even more incredible. After the show I fielded some questions asked by the women in the audience. Then all of the guests and their spouses got the chance to meet and be photographed with Oprah. When my turn came, she shook my hand and hugged me warmly. "Lisa, Lisa, Lisa, Lisa, Lisa . . ." And then in the most casual, girlfriend kind of way, she admitted that she almost didn't tell the story about receiving the basket from Halle, because she thought it might sound kind of silly. She was surprised that I remembered that day and thankful that I had even made it funny.

Oprah was amazed that I remembered? In 1998 when Halle sent her my gift basket, I was a wife and mother of two young babies running a small business out of my home. Back then I didn't have a web site or a retail store. How in the world does someone like me forget something like that? In my universe, you don't forget it—ever. What I found so awesome was that *she* remembered even though it happened three years ago and she must receive a tremendous number of gifts. Needless to say, I was on cloud nine. Everything was perfect. . . .

Or so I thought. Totally unbeknownst to me the company was having a big problem. Even though we had spoken with our Internet service provider several times during the weeks before the show, after it aired and viewers headed to our site, it couldn't handle the volume of people who visited. You could get on, but you couldn't place an order. Needless to say, I was outraged. For weeks our ISP had been promising us it wouldn't be a problem. Our money was tight. We couldn't afford to lose potential sales. We desperately needed the business.

Fortunately, many viewers kept trying. We got a tremendous sales bump following the show and again when it aired a second time a few months later. Between those viewings and the repeat business from our new customers, we received the financial breathing room we needed. Carol's Daughter had survived a close call. The company would be okay!

That September, Carol's Daughter moved the final aspects of production out of the house and into the warehouse. Our family finally had our home to ourselves. Gordon celebrated the occasion by walking through the entire house in his underwear.

"I'm in the kitchen and I'm wearing my drawers," he announced. "Now, I'm walking through the office in my drawers." He continued throughout what had previously been the "public" areas of the house.

Shortly after production moved, *People* magazine decided they wanted to write an article about me.

"We want to do a photo shoot in your kitchen."

"In my home?"

"No, didn't we hear that you have a warehouse?"

"Yes, I do."

With that, I knew the Universe had shifted again. The warehouse was now officially the home of Carol's Daughter's production department.

As if being in *People* magazine was not enough exciting news, in September I found out something else glorious: I was pregnant! From day one I knew it—I was going to have my girl. Of course I love my boys, but after a while you get tired of rugby shirts, khakis and baseball caps. I was longing for lacy dresses with daisies and a matching purse. I couldn't have been happier.

The news was particularly wonderful because I had spent the previous year reconciling myself to being told by a doctor that I shouldn't and probably couldn't ever have a baby again. Now, the test strip was pink and my new ob/gyn quickly dismissed the previous doctor's advice, claiming that he had decided prematurely—after only a routine pelvic exam—that I should no longer bear children. She said I was fit to carry my pregnancy to term.

Gordon and I told everyone. The boys were happy that they would have a little sister. Even though I woke up every morning and felt nauseous, emotionally I still felt great. I was so happy to have that feeling of life growing inside me again. As far as I was concerned, it was a miracle.

Two weeks after finding out the good news, I was scheduled for a dating sonogram. When I went for the test it showed that no fetus was present.

"Lisa," my doctor explained, "this isn't a good sign. We had an image two weeks ago. We should be able to see something now."

"But I don't understand," I answered. "I have no pain, no bleeding—nothing. I feel great."

Could my baby just be gone?

My doctor sent me home while she did blood work and told me to keep her posted if there were any changes. I went home and waited. I clung to every wave of nausea—hoping. I knew that I had to pray, but I didn't know for what. I felt that if I prayed for the baby and for some reason it wasn't meant to be, then I'd be praying for the wrong thing. At the same time, I couldn't just give up on my dream—my miracle.

"I accept whatever is your will," I said to God. "I pray to be at peace with whatever is your will."

And with that I felt something pull away from me inside my abdomen. It wasn't painful in a physical sense, but it was a painful separation nonetheless. My dreams of my little girl faded away. My grief was overwhelming.

But as sad as I was, I wasn't the only one having a difficult time. In January 2003 Mommy received some difficult news. She had lymphoma on the lacrimal gland of her right eye. It was a very rare and nonaggressive lymphoma, but it was lymphoma nonetheless. While it wasn't expected to be life-threatening, due to her preexisting illness, polymyositis, all sorts of doctors were consulted on how to treat it.

The radiation treatment would start in about two weeks and would probably be intensive—five days a week for about five weeks. First, Mommy wanted to go to Atlanta to visit Aunt Sylvia. She could spend ten days in Georgia.

Once Aunt Sylvia learned that Mommy planned to visit her, the family began to pull together as it always did in times of crisis. Aunt Sylvia asked Aunt Ruby to come along with Mom. Aunt Ruby had lost her husband, Uncle Stan, the year before. The holidays had been rough for her, to say the least. She also invited Aunt Joanie from South Carolina. The sisters planned activities they would do together.

When Mommy and her siblings got together, their behavior could be amusing; everyone reverted to their childhood roles. Being the youngest, Mommy would get babied—"Carol, do you need this? Carol do you need that?" But a little pampering was just what she needed right now. Everybody thought it was a good idea for Mommy to get as much love and rest as possible before her treatment. I couldn't provide it in the same way that her sisters could, and I had way too much work to do to join her. Or so I thought.

"The only thing that would make it perfect would be if my little girl was there," Mommy sighed during one of our morning telephone coffee breaks.

Creamy Love Cakes by Lisa [massage bars]

Massage bars are a very economical way of making massage oil because the packaging is minimal. The bar is its own bottle, and as you rub it between your hands, it melts into an oil form.

> ¼ lb. or 4 oz. liquid measure of cocoa butter
> 12 drops gardenia perfume
> 3–5 dried rose petals
> 2 tsp. table-grade sea salt
> Candy mold or nonstick muffin pan

1. Melt cocoa butter in a double boiler, or over a very low flame.
2. Allow it to cool for 10 minutes.
3. Place one teaspoon of sea salt into the bottom of your mold. The salt will give the bar a light exfoliating capability. You can skip this if you want your bar to be smooth and used strictly for massage.
4. Add rose petals and rosebuds to the mold. These are for decoration only and are purely optional. If you were making a peppermint bar, you could add mint leaves or leave it plain. The choice is yours.
5. Add your essential or fragrance oil to the melted cocoa butter, stir and pour into your mold. This recipe calls for gardenia, but you can make it any scent or combination of scents that you like.
6. Place your mold in the refrigerator to cool.
7. After 30 minutes, remove the bar from the refrigerator, and carefully add the second teaspoon of salt on top.
8. Place back in the refrigerator until firm, about 2 hours.
9. Remove from fridge and pop out of the mold.
10. The bar is now ready to be used. During warm months or in places with high heat, keep refrigerated. If you give this as a gift, you can wrap it in wax paper and tie it with a bow.

This woman is good, I thought of her not-so-subtle hint.

"Gordon," I asked later. "Would it be okay with you if I went to Georgia with Mommy?"

"Of course. You need to be there. It will be good for you and for your mom."

Mommy and Aunt Ruby traveled together. I followed five days later.

Aunt Joanie came from South Carolina as planned, but had to leave when I got there. Uncle Ronnie, who also lives in Georgia, joined in the festivities, too. Uncle Sonny and Uncle Hugh couldn't make it, but called often. Before my arrival, Philip came with his wife and four children. The youngest, Matthew, had never met his Grandma Carol and she was so happy to see them all. My aunts and uncles described the time together as a ten-day fete, a West Indian term for a party.

Mommy made traditional codfish cakes and I brought treats from Allen's Bakery, a West Indian sweet shop located in Brooklyn. We cracked jokes, walked in the woods (I had to rescue Mommy; she walked too far and her legs gave out), watched old movies on cable and sat on the porch talking about the future. Mommy said she wanted to move to Florida.

We all had a ball watching *Drumline* at a movie theater together. Mommy and I ate Twizzlers and pretzels and she drank a huge Diet Coke. Afterward we all laughed hysterically as Mommy and I raced through the lobby together—she in her wheelchair and I pushing as fast as I could—so she would make it to the bathroom in time.

The next afternoon I played Gloria Estefan's *Mi Tierra* CD. Mommy loved Latin music and she particularly loved this CD.

"Remember when you were younger and used to hang out at Roseland?" Uncle Ron asked her.

"Yeah, that was a long time ago. We would dance and dance until the sun came up. That was fun, huh?"

"Yeah, it was."

Mommy looked at me and extended her hand.

"Come here, let me see if I can still bolero."

I took Mommy's hand, and helped her balance as she stepped away from her walker.

"You all right?" I asked.

"Yeah, I'm fine. Just don't let go."

As Gloria sang "*Con Los Años Que me Quedan*" ("With the Years that I Have Left"), Mommy led me in our dance.

"*Y con los ãnos que me quedan por vivir/Demonstrare cuanto te quiero.*"

("And with the years that I have left to live/I will show you/How much I love you.")

Afterward, I rushed into the dining room so I could cry discreetly.

"What are you crying for?" she asked when I returned.

"That was really cool!" I managed to say through my tears. "It reminded me of when I danced with Nana at my thirteenth birthday party."

"What are you trying to say—that I'm old?" Mommy retorted.

After a few more magical afternoons with the aunts and Mommy, Aunt Ruby, Mommy and I flew back to New York. Gordon and the boys met us at the airport. During the trip back to Brooklyn, Forrest and Ennis regaled us with tales of their activities in first grade and prekindergarten. As they chattered I said, "Uh-huh" a lot, but wasn't hearing all of their dialogue because I was preoccupied. There was so much going on. The company was gearing up for the Valentine's Day rush. We had to toughen ourselves for Mommy's battle with cancer. And I had a lot of work to do. Fortunately work wouldn't be as consuming as it had been in the past. Since the near disaster I caused when I got sick two years ago, I had made a lot of changes in how I ran the business. These days, I involved myself less in day-to-day activities. That freed me up to be more creative and focus on the long term. It seemed to be working well for everyone. My staff was doing a fantastic job in their expanded roles, and I was able to spend more time concocting new creations—which was the passion that drove me to start Carol's Daughter in the first place.

"Did you remember to get roses from Fairways?" I asked Gordon as the kids goofed around in the backseat.

"Did you ask me to get roses from Fairways?"

"Yes. But did you?"

"Of course, I did. What, do I look like I'm new here?"

"No, honey. Thank you."

"Did you get—"

"Yes, I got the hot pink roses."

"Thank you, dear."

The next morning, Gordon drove the boys to school and headed to work. I was at home alone. Alone! The house was silent. I had forgotten how quiet it was these days. After years of hustle and bustle all day, I was still getting used to the silence.

I walked into my office and looked around. Everything was in order. My hot pink roses were in a vase on my coffee table. I turned on my fountain and smiled at the sound of water trickling over seashells. A tuberose candle called me. As I lit it I closed my eyes and inhaled the sweet fragrance. I sorted through my CD folder. Prince was calling my name. So was my kitchen. It had been way too long since I'd had creative time in the room that had given me so many fond childhood memories. I wanted to formulate a new product—Sweet Love Crush. I sang and danced as I wound my way into my favorite room.

In the kitchen I washed my hands before reaching into the cabinet and pulling out a large stainless-steel pot, which I placed on top of the stove. Above my head in the cupboard was a bucket of cocoa butter. I reached up and grabbed it, along with a container of salt. I scooped out a piece of cocoa butter with a cooking spoon, weighed it and placed it in the pan. It needed to melt slowly, so I turned the flame on low. As the butter softened, the smell of chocolate filled the air and I slowly poured salt into Nana's measuring cup.

Then I turned away from the stove to the flowers on the counter. One by one I plucked off their beautiful petals, singing and dancing along to Prince all the while. Before long the chopping block was covered with vibrant pink velvet. I picked up one petal, chuckling as I remembered how long I held onto my rose petals after Aunt Judy's wedding so many years ago. But there would be no saving these beauties. It was time to work my magic. I raised my wooden mallet about six inches above them. I crushed them and the petals released their sweet fragrance. Valentine's Day was around the corner. Love was in the air.

Epilogue

My mother, Carol Frances Hutson, taking care of me as she always did.

In my dream Mommy was rubbing the center of her chest—her heart chakra, the energy center governing the circulatory system. I was holding her other hand and kneeling at her feet.

"It hurts. It hurts," she was moaning.

"I know, Mommy," I replied, looking up at her. She was wearing a beautiful pink robe. "It will be over soon."

When I awakened I tried to figure out what the dream was telling me. Mommy would be treated for lymphoma soon. I interpreted it as telling us what to do to prepare.

My mother didn't own a pink robe. I felt the dream was a sign that pink could be a healing power in her life; pink is a calming color associated with the heart chakra. So together we wore pink. We burned pink candles and prayed. We prayed for God to heal her body as well as my heart, which was still broken from the miscarriage I suffered only a few months earlier. Before long we felt that we were ready.

Before Mommy's first treatment date, Gordon, his mother, the boys, and I left on a short vacation we had previously booked at Universal Studios in Orlando, Florida. When we arrived I immediately called home to check on her.

"She doesn't want to talk to you," my stepfather answered.

"What do you mean Mommy doesn't want to talk to me?" Even when our relationship was strained back in my early twenties, Mommy had never said anything like that to me. Then I realized that she must be feeling really bad. I felt powerless, helpless, and so far away. I wished that I was with her.

What shall I do? I asked God.

"*Pray,*" came the answer.

"Dear God, please take my mother in your arms and ease her pain," I implored. "Since I am not there, please comfort her for me. Let her know that I love her and, Lord, ease her pain until I can see her again."

I poured libation into the hotel sink, then put on my pajamas and drifted off to sleep. In the early dawn hours the shrill ring of the telephone awakened me. Gordon answered.

"Oh, no. . . .," he said. Then he hung up. My husband walked across the room, placed his hands on my shoulders and looked me in the eyes. "Lisa, your mother passed away this morning."

"What do you mean?"

"I'm so sorry."

"No, that can't be."

I don't understand. This doesn't make sense.

"I need Philip," I said.

When you talk to Philip and Aunt Syl, they will want details. Get the information, I told myself. *I can't cry yet. I can't lose it.*

Before calling Philip, I got to my feet and dragged myself to the bathroom. My legs trembled as I walked. Gordon tried to comfort me. *Why is the bathroom so far away?* Along the way I must have picked up my cell phone. When I reached the bathroom it was in my hand.

I sat on the side of the tub and called my stepfather. He was crying. I had never heard him cry before. As his tears flowed he told me about Mommy's death.

That Valentine's Day morning at five thirty A.M. my mother died of a massive heart attack. For this I was not prepared. We knew that cancer was threatening her health, but as far as we knew her heart had been fine.

Why wasn't I there for her? I thought as he talked. *Why can't I wake up from this? Does it have to be real?*

When he finished explaining I said, "You go and tell Aerol. He needs you and you need him. I will call Philip."

Philip's voicemail picked up. *Leave a message? Don't tell him in a message. Just tell him to call you.* Next my fingers dialed Aunt Syl. It was 6:36 A.M. *She goes to the gym at six thirty every day. Maybe she'll be a little late today.* But I got her voicemail too. I tried to disguise the tremor in my voice as I asked her to call me right away on my cell phone. *How can I tell her that her baby is gone?* My whole body felt as though it wanted to turn to liquid. I couldn't stop trembling. *I can't cry. Not yet. I still have work to do.*

Then my phone rang. It was Aerol. He was wailing. Finally, I lost my composure and started screaming. As I grieved I remembered the dream I had had over a month earlier. I recalled her hand rubbing her heart. *Was this a clue that I didn't decipher?* I thought of all of the pink therapy. *Didn't it work?*

I returned from Florida right away to make arrangements for Mommy. When I arrived at the airport, I called my stepfather and asked him to please not touch anything in her room. "Don't make up the bed, please," I begged. He assured me he would shut the door and leave it be. I didn't know why, but I had to go to her bedroom. I knew she was no longer there, but it didn't matter.

Michael met me at the airport and took me to her house straightaway. When I arrived I climbed the steps to her room as quickly as I could. There was still a dent in the pillow where her head had been. I climbed into her bed, lay in the folds of her sheets and inhaled deeply. I could smell her! It was as close to a farewell hug as I was ever going to get, and it was wonderful. The sheets smelled of lavender and eucalyptus, peppermint and geranium—all of the scents I had made that she used over the years. Fragrances that made her feel better.

All of the sudden Aerol appeared in the room and climbed into bed beside me.

"Can you smell her?" he asked as he cried.

"Yes," I said between my sobs. "I can."

I don't know how long Aerol and I lay in her wake, absorbing what was left of our mother, but the scent that lingered in my mother's sheets is indelibly etched in my spirit. In the days following her death, I questioned why Mommy had died.

I am not ready for this, I told God. *What am I supposed to do now?* Mommy was not just my mother, she was also my sister-girl, my buddy, my dog, my ace-boon-coon, my boo, my heart. She was the one who told me what to do. Now I would have to move forward in this world without her. *How?* I remembered my prayer in the hotel bathroom on the evening before she transitioned—"Please take my mother in your arms and ease her pain." I realized that is exactly what had happened. God had answered my prayer. It's just that I wasn't expecting that particular answer.

The pink color I hoped would heal my mother I now made the theme for her burial. Pink candles burned in the homes of as many of her loved ones as possible. We dressed Mommy in pink silk. The funeral parlor was awash in pink roses. When black mourning clothes became too heavy for my spirit to bear, I wore pink instead. I later painted the walls of my store pink in her honor. In addition, our family displayed Mommy's picture prominently in our homes. We set up shrines in our living rooms, bedrooms and hearts.

I knew Mommy's funeral would be a large one, but the turnout at Woodward Funeral Home was even greater than I had anticipated. This was particularly surprising because in the days before the service there was a tremendous snowstorm that dropped two feet of snow on the city. You could hardly get around.

All of her children paid tribute to her. Together, the eight of us read one of Mommy's favorite prayers. Philip read the Valentine's Day card he had sent her and that the mail carrier delivered on the morning of her death. Aerol read her a beautiful letter. During the service, I began to realize that, as the oldest, I was also the luckiest. I had my mother for forty years; my youngest sister, Khoret, was only eight.

As I stood in front of the congregation reading my tribute, I could see how tightly the pews were packed. People were standing in the aisles, and among the familiar faces were many I didn't recognize. Later I realized that Carol had become much more than just our mother. In some ways making her name and identity such a prominent part of my business made her the community's mom, as well. Many people I didn't know sent cards and spoke to me of her strength, her pride in her children and her love of her family. It was clear that I was not the only one grieving the loss of this magnificent woman.

Mommy has "visited" many family members in one way or another to let us know that she is fine. I always talk to her and sometimes I even receive messages back. One of the messages she has sent to Philip and me is to take care of our younger siblings. Christian is now living in Mississippi with Philip, his wife, and their four children. Khoret and Tura are frequent guests in our home, and I keep as close an eye as I can on Sean and Little Phillip.

Every day I burn a pink candle in Mommy's honor. It has a wonderful rose, geranium, and sweet-grass fragrance. She never got to smell this one. I wonder, *Can spirits smell?* I am not sure, but I'm certain that Mommy can see my candle and knows it's in celebration of her. Equally, I know that she sees how radiant I am when I wear pink. It is the glow I received from her smile, her love. And when I am tired or overwhelmed and don't know what decision to make, I have only to remember my mother and the smells of lavender, peppermint, and geranium in her bed. That's when I remember why I do what I do. After all, I'm Carol's daughter.

In memory of Carol Frances Hutson
September 29, 1942–February 14, 2003

Appendix

RESOURCE GUIDE

Here are the uses and definitions of key ingredients used in the recipes and rituals to get you started on your own journey. Also included are lists of suppliers for some of the ingredients as well as book and Internet resources that were helpful to us in writing the book.

Name	Latin Name	Definition	Uses/Properties
Base Oils		Deepen oil mixtures and draw oils into the skin. They have rather faint smells, and often release their fragrance for several hours.	**Uses:** Base oils are usually combined with fragrance and essential oils. They include sweet almond, soy, corn, olive, sesame, etc.
Candles	*Candela*	Usually molded or dipped mass of wax or tallow containing a wick that may be burned for light, heat, scent, or for celebration or votive purposes.	**Uses:** Burn them to release aromatic essential oils and to achieve good physical, emotional, mental, and spiritual health and balance.

Name	Latin Name	Definition	Uses/Properties
Candy Molds			**Uses:** Soap making.
Chamomile Herb	*Anthemis nobilis, Anthemis mixta, Chamomilla matricaria, Ormenis multicolis*	A composite herb from Europe and North Africa with strong-scented foliage and flower heads that contain a bitter medicinal substance.	**Properties:** Anti-inflammatory, antispasmodic, anticonvulsive, anti-depressant, emmenagogue, antianemic, febrifuge, sudorific, antiseptic, analgesic. **Uses:** Pain relief: muscle aches and pains, rheumatism, headaches, migraine, neuralgia, toothache, ear-ache; Skin problems: acne, eczema, rashes, wounds, dermatitis, dry itchy skin, and allergic conditions in general; Relaxes and soothes: the nerves, digestive system and gynecological conditions, an irritated and teething baby, colic, diarrhea, and gastric spasms.
Cinnamon (Chinese, ground)	*Cinnamomum cinnamon*	An aromatic spice prepared from the dried inner bark of a cinnamon tree.	**Properties:** Stimulant, antiseptic, antibiotic, astringent, carminative, digestive, emmenagogue, stomachic, insecticide and antispasmodic. **Uses:** Relieves infection of the respiratory tract, rheumatism, arthritis and general pains. Stimulates the glandular system thus easing menstrual pains; tones the whole body.

Name	Latin Name	Definition	Uses/Properties
Cocoa Butter		A solid fat used to soften and lubricate the skin and often used in place of wax to harden creams.	**Uses:** Aids in combating blemishes, itching, sunburns, dry skin.
Coconut Oil		A white saturated fat obtained from coconut that melts at body temperature.	**Uses:** Excellent for lubricating and smoothing the skin.
Coconut Oil, virgin		A fatty oil or semisolid fat extracted from fresh coconuts and used especially in soap and food products.	**Properties:** Antimicrobial and antiviral properties. **Uses:** Apply directly to the skin for conditioning. Also eliminates dandruff.
Cowrie Shell		Shells that are commonly found in warm seas and have glossy and often brightly colored finishes.	**Properties:** Antacid and digestive. **Uses:** The Cowrie Speaks sacred stories of the Yoruba in which the Orisa communicate moral, spiritual, and everyday methods to solve conflicts. Other stories about the cowrie teach humility and respect toward your elders. Divination is the art of getting insight into the patterns and movements of meaning in life. We like to play with the word and say that it is a matter of dipping into the Divine.

Name	Latin Name	Definition	Uses/Properties
Essential Oil		The oil extracted from real flowers and herbs. Unfortunately, the term is often used loosely to mean any perfumed oil that imitates a real scent.	**Uses:** To provide fragrance and alleviate physical ailments.
Florida Water		The nineteenth-century formula for a commercially prepared toilet water that blends an array of floral essential oils in a water-alcohol base. The name refers to the fabled Fountain of Youth said to have been located in Florida.	**Uses:** Common in rituals of home protection and spiritual cleaning, to scent bowls of water set out for the spirits of the dead and for other rituals. Also has cosmetic purposes among people of African descent in the United States and the Caribbean.
Fragrance Oil		Man-made blends of essential and synthetic ingredients.	**Uses:** Perfumes mixtures.
Honey	*Canicae*	A deliciously sweet substance made by honeybees from flower nectar. Each flower or plant produces a unique honey which is different in color and flavor.	**Properties:** Antibacterial. **Uses:** Treatment of infected wounds; perfect dressing for any external skin problems; used in cosmetics as an astringent and moisturizer.

Name	Latin Name	Definition	Uses/Properties
Lavender Herb	*Lavandula angustifolia* syn. *L. officinalis*	A Mediterranean mint widely cultivated for its narrow aromatic leaves and spikes of lilac-purple flowers, which are dried and used in sachets.	**Properties:** Antiseptic, analgesic, anti-convulsant, anti-depressant, anti-rheumatic, anti-toxic, anti-spasmodic, anti-inflammatory, emmenagogue, anti-toxic, carminative, deodorant, diuretic, restorative, sedative, insecticide and tonic. **Uses:** Soothes and calms the nerves, relieving tension, depression, panic, hysteria, and nervous exhaustion in general; effective for headaches, migraines, and insomnia; beneficial for problems such as: bronchitis, asthma, colds, laryngitis, halitosis, throat infections, and whooping cough; helps the digestive system deal with colic, nausea, vomiting, and gas; relieves pain when used for rheumatism, arthritis, lumbago, and muscular aches and pains, especially those associated with sport; tones the skin and relieves skin problems: abscesses, acne, oily skin, boils, burns, sunburn, wounds, psoriasis, lice, insect bites, stings. Also an insect repellent.

Name	Latin Name	Definition	Uses/Properties
Marigold	*Tagetes glandulifera*	Herbs with showy yellow, orange, or maroon flower heads. The oil has a sweet, fruity almost citrus-like smell and is yellow to reddish-amber in color. It is medium viscosity and turns thick and even gel-like if exposed to the air for a long time.	**Properties:** Anti-infectious, anti-microbial, antibiotic, anti-spasmodic, anti-parasitic, antiseptic, insecticide, and sedative. **Uses:** Repels insects; and helps with chest infections, coughs and catarrh, dilating the bronchi, facilitating the flow of mucus and dislodging congestion; helps heal wounds and cuts, calluses and bunions.
Mica and Pigment		Colored or transparent mineral silicates crystallizing in monoclinic forms that readily separates into very thin leaves.	**Uses:** Aids in colorization.
Oatmeal	*Avena sativa*	Meal of rolled or ground oats.	**Properties:** Treats nervous debility and exhaustion, particularly when associated with depression. **Uses:** Soothing for dry, irritated, or sore skin.

Name	Latin Name	Definition	Uses/Properties
Patchouli Essential Oil	*Pogostemon Patchouli*	Patchouli oil has a musty-sweet, strong spicy smell and is reddish-brown in color. It is thick in viscosity.	**Properties:** Anti-depressant, anti-inflammatory, antiseptic, aphrodisiac, astringent, carmina-tive, diuretic, febrifuge, fungicide, insecticide, sedative and tonic, tissue regenerator. **Uses:** Relieves fungal and bacterial infec-tion; helps insect bites; insect repellent; fights water retention, cel-lulite, constipation and obesity; cools down inflammation and assists with wound healing, scars and sores; relieves acne, eczema and scalp disorders; helps with the re-growth of skin cells and scar tissue; can assist with stress-related conditions and anxiety; and aids in cases of substance ad-dictions.
Rose Absolute	*Rose centifolia and damascena*	The essential oil of the Damask Rose has a deep, rosy, fresh aroma. The color ranges from clear to a pale yellow or greenish tint. The viscosity is watery to crystalline, when warm or cold re-spectively.	**Properties:** Anti-infectious, anti-depressant, antiseptic, anti-spasmodic, aphrodisiac, astrin-gent, bactericidal, di-uretic, emmenagogue, hepatic, laxative, seda-tive, splenetic and general tonic, aphro-disiac, stimulates of the heart chakra.

Name	Latin Name	Definition	Uses/Properties
Rose Absolute *(continued)*			**Uses:** Helps with depression, grief, nervous tension and stress; helpful for poor circulation and heart palpitations; can assist asthma, coughs and hay fever; beneficial to the digestive system for liver congestion and nausea; regulates menstruation, leucorrhoea, menorrhagia and uterine disorders; excellent skin tonic, aids in broken capillaries, dry skin, eczema, herpes, mature and sensitive skin, and wrinkles. Rose water can be used for conjunctivitis.
Roses	*Rosa*	A prickly shrub with showy flowers having five petals in the wild state—more under cultivation.	**Uses:** Strengthens the heart, refreshes the spirit, mitigates eye pain, induces sleep.

Name	Latin Name	Definition	Uses/Properties
Sage, smudge sticks	*Salvia officinalis*	A mint with grayish green aromatic leaves.	**Properties:** Astringent, antiseptic, and irritant. **Uses:** Treats mouth sores, mouth ulcers, and sore throats; can be used as an astringent, an antiperspirant, a compress on cuts and wounds; can lower diabetic blood sugar; also combats digestive problems and gas.
Sandalwood Essential Oil	*Santalum albumu; Santalaceae*	Sandalwood oil is extracted from East Indian sandalwood. It has a woody, exotic smell, subtle and lingering. The color of the oil is pale yellow to pale gold.	**Properties:** Antiseptic, diuretic, aphrodisiac, astringent, carminative, emollient, expectorant, sedative, and tonic. **Uses:** Helps release tension, depression, nervous exhaustion, chronic illness, and anxiety; aids in the relief of chest infections, sore throats, and dry coughs that accompany bronchitis and lung infections; alleviates cystitis and bladder infections; helpful with sexual problems such as frigidity and impotence; relieves itching and inflammation of the skin; good for scarring, dry eczema, aging and dehydrated skin.

Name	Latin Name	Definition	Uses/Properties
Sea Salt		The Dead Sea salt is composed of potassium and magnesium salts. The slate oil acts by checking inflammations, relieving itching, alleviating pain, regenerating the skin, normalizing cell mitosis, and enhancing the skin's moisture.	**Uses:** Soothes and revitalizes the whole body; helps cure joint pains and skin disorders; relieves pain and suffering caused by arthritis, rheumatism, psoriasis, eczema, stress; nourishes and softens, exfoliates and hydrates the skin; stimulates circulation; enhances cell regeneration; improves skin tone; keeps the skin healthy; refreshes and cures muscular pains and stress.
Shea Butter		A pale solid fat from the seeds of the shea tree used in food, soap, and candles.	**Properties:** Anti-inflammatory. **Uses:** Combats blemishes, itching, sunburn, dry skin, small skin wounds, eczema, skin allergies, and wrinkles.

Name	Latin Name	Definition	Uses/Properties
Sweet Almond Oil	*Prunus amygdalus var. dulcis*	One of the most commonly used carrier oils in aromatherapy massage. Sweet almond oil is obtained from the dried kernels of the almond tree and it is an excellent emollient.	**Properties:** Anti-inflammatory **Uses:** Non-greasy, spreads easily, and great for nourishing the skin. Suitable for all skin types; helps relieve irritation, inflammation, and itching; smooths, softens, and conditions the skin; promotes a clear, young looking complexion; also helps to relieve muscular aches and pains.
Unscented Creams and Lotions			**Uses:** A medium to apply essential and fragrance oils to the skin.
Vanilla Bean	*Vanilla planifolia*	The long encapsulated fruit of a vanilla plant that is an important article of commerce.	**Properties:** Aphrodisiac **Uses:** Soothes nerves, helps against impotence.
Vodka		A colorless liquor made of neutral spirits distilled from a mash (rye or wheat).	**Uses:** Preserves and dilutes fragrance oils.

Name	Latin Name	Definition	Uses/Properties
Wheat Germ Oil	*Triticum vulgare*	The wheat grain consists of three parts—the husk, the germ (heart), and the endosperm—and it is the germ that is used in the manufacture of the oil.	**Uses:** Rich in vitamins E, A, and B. Its antioxidant properties help keep oil base preparations from going rancid. Helps regenerate tissue and promote skin elasticity; promotes smoother, younger looking skin; assists in healing scar tissue and stretch marks; improves circulation; helps to repair sun damage; also helps relieve dermatitis.

Suppliers—addresses, Web sites and numbers

FRONTIER NATURAL PRODUCTS CO-OP
P.O. Box 299
3021 78th St.
Norway, IA 52318
Email: www.frontiercoop.com
Phone: (800) 669-3275

ATLANTIC SPICE
P.O. Box 205
North Truro, MA 02652
Email: www.atlanticspice.com
Phone: (800) 316-7965

RAINBOW MEADOW
P.O. Box 457
Napoleon, MI 49261
Email: www.rainbowmeadow.com
Phone: (800) 207-4047

THE GOOD SCENTS COMPANY
Email: www.thegoodscentscompany.com
Phone: (414) 764-2659

SWEET CAKES
Minnetonka, Minnesota
Email: www.sweetcakes.com
Phone: (952) 945-9900

Cited Sources:

Rose, Jeanne. *Jeanne Rose's Kitchen Cosmetics: Using Herbs, Fruit, & Flowers for Natural Bodycare.* North Atlantic Books. Berkeley, CA, 1990.

Lavabre, Marcel. *Aromatherapy Workbook.* Healing Arts Press. Rochester, VT. 1990.

Tisserand, Maggie. *Aromatherapy for Women: A Practical Guide to Essential Oils for Health and Beauty.* Healing Arts Press. Rochester, VT, 1985.

Tisserand, Robert B. *The Art of Aromatherapy: The Healing and Beautifying Properties of the Essential Oils of Flowers and Herbs.* Healing Arts Press. Rochester, VT, 1977.

INTERNET SOURCES:

http://www.essentialoils.co.za/index.htm
http://www.webster.com/home.htm
http://www.candleman.com/
http://www.luckymojo.com/floridakanangawater.html
http://www.unaniherbalist.com/cahv.htm
http://honey.bio.waikato.ac.nz/
http://www.gardensablaze.com/HerbSageMed.htm
http://www.ccel.org/h/herbert/temple/Rose.html
http://www.listening-in.com/divinate.html
http://www.ifama.com/page7.html

Lisa's Acknowledgments

In a perfect world I would name every single person that has come into my life, befriended me, taught me and, in short, contributed to who I am today, but that list could prove to be longer than this book. So, I offer my love and thanks to the following people:

Francis and Marguerite Warwell, my "Nana and Gramps," and Robert and Hilda Hairston Sr., my grandpa and grandma. My aunts and uncles: Sonny & Judy Warwell, Ruby & Stan Byer, Hugh Warwell, Sylvia & Robert Lynch, Joan & Robert Porter, Ron & Norma Warwell, Judith Rosenbauer, Marilyn Williams, Larry Ramsey, and Virginia Rawlerson. My siblings, both sides—Philip Hairston, Tselane Price, Hilary Price, Aerol Hutson, Autumn Hairston, Meredith Hairston, Phillip Miles Hutson, Christian Hutson, Sean Hutson, Tura Hutson, and Khoret Hutson. My cousins: Michael Warwell, Karen Coston, Donna Green, Dennis Warwell, Aisha Guillermo, Ronnie Warwell, Sharon Warwell-Murden, M. Gina Middleton, Chris Warwell, David Rosenbauer, Rebecca Rosenbauer, Inga Warwell, Scott Warwell, Debra Warwell, and Michael Freeman. Thank you Jeffrey, for the months in the warehouse. The strong women who taught me how to be a boss: Marie Gibson, Debbie Penchina, Betsy Alexander, Robin Seidon, and Cleo. For all of your hard work in the beginning: Aikeem Hunter, Debra Phillip, Jennifer McNeil, Yolanda Johnson, Sarah Felix, David T. Hobday, and Renita Miller. Thank you, Marl, my sister witch, for the magic we worked in our circles around the track. For all of your help and encouragement: Kim & Ira James, Lynne Allison, Elaine Martinelli & the Martinelli clan, the whole *Sesame Street* crew, Ivy Mitchell, Lisa Benjamin, Lisa Clarke, Gary Dourdan, Nathan Busch, Alake Angaza, Ojinga Angaza, Rhonda Cowan, Terri Haskins, and Rebekah Foster.

Muchisimas gracias a Nellie, "Tashia," y Delores por el amor que ustedes tienen por mis niños. Gracias a Manuela por nuestras conversaciones y su corazón. Gracias a Ana por sus abrazos. Samia, te amo todo el tiempo. Mami te amo tambien.

Thank you, Quentin, for making the ladies smile. Thank you to my staff for all of your hard work every day and for always giving the job your best. Thank you to my mother-in-law, Elmira, for stirring her love into the pots and to Johnnie for being the support. Thank you to Jim & Josephine Thomas for helping it all add up correctly. Tuau MenAtchetu-t Maart—dema meri hur hetep. Thank you, Meloney Ramirez, for being the voice on the line and prayer partner when needed. Thank you, Steve Stoute, for giving me a glimpse of the future. I love you, KC, the big sister I never had. Thank you, M. Scott, for always bringing excellence and balance.

Thank you, Kim Fields, for gracing my company with your beauty, sharing your passion with the world, and bringing your light to our lives.

Thank you to the following for the support, love, free press, and unsolicited "shout-outs": Will and Jada Smith, E. Badu, Queen Latifah, Halle Berry, Oprah Winfrey, Harriet Cole, Mikki Taylor, Mia Stokes, Michaela Angela Davis, Anthony Anderson, Usher, Christopher Williams, and Mr. and Mrs. Chris Rock.

Thank you, Melody Guy, for asking Manie to bring you my story and thank you, Manie Baron, for showing me how to tell it.

Hilary's Acknowledgments

I thank our Creator for blessing me abundantly. I am grateful to my amazing parents, Charles and Peggy Beard, and the only grandparents I knew, Florence and George Lanton. We didn't have you long enough, but you loved and had big dreams for us. That, good home training, and a bowl of homemade ice cream, was plenty. Jonathan and Alison, you are the most incredible siblings anyone could hope to have. Thank you for Alex, Kailey, Jadon, and Jennifer. Our extended family brightens my life. Aunt Bonnie and Uncle Ray, you have been surrogate parents and I am forever grateful.

Manie Barron, I'll never know how you knew I was the right writer for this project or why you took a chance on me. I guess that's just what you do, but I am indebted, nonetheless. I am also tremendously grateful that Melody Guy and the team at Random House had vision about this project and were willing to bet on us.

To Claire Lomax and Lydia Woods for your unwavering love and support; Leslie Brown Vincent and Susan Williams McElroy for being such long-lasting friends; Pamela Freeman and JoAnne White for opening my eyes and spirit; my spiritual support sistagirlfriendsages; Kevin Hayden, Tamara Jeffries, Sara Lomax Reese, Linda Villarosa, and the team at NiaOnline for opening the doors to my new career; Mary Krogness, the best educator ever, and Robert Hanson, who brought English class to life at Shaker Heights High School in Cleveland, Ohio; Marita Golden, Nikki Finney, and the team at Hurston/Wright Writer's Week; the Evening Star Writer's Group, Ken Bingham and Amy Rowland, my tremendously gifted writing inner circle in Philadelphia; all the mentors who helped me grow and develop when I worked in the corporate world; and the legion of dear friends whose support has provided the pillars upon which I've built my new life, you are too numerous to list here, but you know who you are, and I am fortunate to have you in my world. And Carrol Tillman-Brown, proprietor of the Point of Destination, thank you for allowing me to use your café as my office when my house was just a little too quiet.

Lisa, we did it! This has been an incredible odyssey—two sistas who had never met (except through the mystical aura of your products), yet trusted our hearts about each other and this project. I can't express how honored I feel to have accompanied you on this leg of your journey down the road less traveled. What courage it takes to make your life an open book to help others grow and heal. I sit at your feet in wonder!

ABOUT THE AUTHORS

LISA PRICE is the creator and founder of Carol's Daughter, Inc., located in Brooklyn, New York, which provides a wide array of homemade body and spirit care products. Crafted and sold by a staff of thirty, the Carol's Daughter line includes products such as Mango Body Butter, Honey Pudding, and Shea Butter Skin Smoothie. Lisa also speaks to college students about being an entrepreneur, trusting that her experience will encourage other entrepreneurial hopefuls. She has taught sold-out seminars in New York City's Open Center on starting a business with little or no money and the importance of following your spirit. She lives with her husband and two sons in Brooklyn.

HILARY BEARD is a writer and editor who lives in Philadelphia. In 1997, she stepped off the corporate fast track to follow her lifelong passion for writing. Currently she is working on two books on values with Venus and Serena Williams. She also writes for *American Legacy Woman, Essence, Health, Odyssey Couleur* and *POZ* magazines, and NiaOnline, a Web site for black women. A Carol's Daughter customer long before she met Lisa, her favorite products are Ginger Mango Fruit Whip and anything fragranced with Ocean. Hilary is an honors graduate of Princeton University and hails from the Shaker Square neighborhood of Cleveland, Ohio.